OKLAHOMA GUN LAW

Armed And Educated

A Complete Guide To Gun Law In Oklahoma

2016-2017 Edition

By Robert R. Robles

Written by Robert R. Robles and published in the United States of America By U.S. Law Shield

ISBN: 978-0-692-75804-5

To order additional books by phone or for wholesale orders call (877) 448-6839.

TABLE OF CONTENTS

PREFACE

As a lawyer with 35 years of representing law-abiding gun owners in cases all over the State of Oklahoma, I see well-intending folks exercising their Second Amendment rights get mixed up in the legal system through not understanding the law. For that reason, I set about creating a one volume resource that provides any gun owner with a base level of knowledge about laws that Oklahoma gun owners need to know.

The law is complicated, it has overlapping titles and sections; it is hard to understand, and in some cases, for the layman it is completely arbitrary to the point of confusion. Laws are written by lawyers for lawyers or are the result of political compromises that generate confusing laws. The courts are ultimately presented the confusing laws and must interpret the myriad laws and balance the competing interests.

After years of legal work in the arena of firearms law, I found an absence of a single resource that explained gun law in a manner that was easy for everyone to understand. Understanding the law goes far beyond just reading statutes or regulations. If I do not know either the process by which the law is being administered or how the courts are interpreting the meaning of the law, then it is impossible for me to understand the full legal story.

That is why I wrote *Oklahoma Gun Law: Armed And Educated*. It is a one volume guide to understand the minimum amount of law every gun owner needs to know in order to stay legal. Whenever appropriate, I tried to present useful analysis and real world applications. My goal was to explain the "law" so willing gun owners could inform and educate themselves. An untold number of attorney hours have gone into producing this resource, always with the goal of education in mind.

My legal experience taught me that anyone, no matter their social status, can become ensnared in the legal system. Many people mistakenly and firmly believe that "it" can't happen to them. Even people that have never been in trouble before can find themselves or their loved ones ensnared in the world of law, lawyers, and law enforcement through ignorance of the law.

I am committed to helping protect our precious Second Amendment rights for all legal gun owners. It is my passion and my mission.

I want people to know the law, because only through eternal vigilance, and an understanding of the law, will the people of the United States and Oklahoma have the tools to protect our cherished right to bear arms. If you own a gun, the laws concerning firearms and their use apply to you. Ignorance of the law is not a valid legal excuse. To be forewarned is to be forearmed. Therefore, if you want to stay legal, know the law!

Sincerely,

Robert R. Robles,
Attorney at Law

CHAPTER ONE

BRIEF LEGAL HISTORY OF THE RIGHT TO BEAR ARMS AND THE LAWS REGULATING FIREARMS

I. Introduction and overview

To fully understand gun rights today in Oklahoma or the United States, one should start first at the beginning: the formation document for our federal government, the United States Constitution. The Constitution was written without any enumerated guaranteed individual rights. The founding fathers thought it obvious and apparent that individuals had rights; therefore, there was no reason to elucidate them in a document that was supposed to control the government. James Madison also thought that by naming certain rights, it would imply that those were the only rights an individual possessed. After much discussion, and a complete change of opinion by Madison, the lack of enumerated rights was remedied in the first Congressional session and the state ratification process. When the dust settled, ten amendments were added to the Constitution; these ten amendments are the Bill of Rights. It is the Second Amendment that concerns firearms specifically, though throughout this book we will reference many others, including the Fourth and Fifth Amendments that both affect your rights to bear arms and the fundamental rights for us all.

II. Do I have a constitutional right as an individual to keep and bear arms?

Yes; the United States Supreme Court has decided that an individual has a constitutional right to keep and bear arms. That right flows from the Second Amendment, which states simply:

> *A well-regulated Militia, being necessary to the security of a free State, the right of the people to keep and bear Arms, shall not be infringed.*

From a plain reading, there are two important parts to this

amendment: first, that a well-regulated militia is necessary to the security of a free state, and second, that there is a right of the people to keep and bear arms. For years, before the issue was decided, anti-gun activists have tried to argue that the Second Amendment only applied to "militias" and not to individuals. Luckily, this argument is not the law. Nevertheless, despite the Supreme Court rulings stating otherwise, this myth seem to persist. What do these parts of the Second Amendment mean? Are they the same, or are they different?

A. What is a "Well-Regulated Militia?"

As we discussed earlier, the first part of the Second Amendment references a "well-regulated militia." What is a well-regulated militia? The U.S. Supreme Court has held what this phrase does and does not mean. In 1939, in the case of *United States v. Miller*, 307 U.S. 174 (1939) (ironically, a ruling that upheld firearms regulation), the Court defined a militia as comprising "all males physically capable of acting in concert for the common defense." Based on how the amendment was drafted, the Court stated, it was clear that the militia pre-dated Article I of the Constitution, because unlike armies and navies, it did not have to be created by Congress. What then is "well-regulated" per the Court? It is exactly what it sounds like: the imposition of discipline and training. So, is this just the National Guard? No.

In the case of *D.C. v. Heller*, 554 U.S. 570 (2008), the Supreme Court stated that the well-regulated militia is not the state's military forces, but a separate entity altogether. The Supreme Court stated that the word "militia" referred to the body of the people, and they—the people—were required to keep a centralized government in check. The Supreme Court considered and rejected the position that the National Guard is the current militia under the Second Amendment.

B. How has the phrase "right to keep and bear arms" been interpreted by the courts?

One of the first cases to directly deal with the Second

Amendment was *United States v. Miller*. In *Miller*, the Supreme Court found that the National Firearms Act ("NFA"), which imposed registration requirements on machine guns, short-barreled weapons, destructive devices, and other similarly unique firearms, did not violate the Second Amendment. The Court used the reasoning that possession of weapons regulated by the NFA did not reasonably relate to the preservation or efficiency of a well-regulated militia, therefore, the NFA was held constitutional.

Court fight where it all began: *United States v. Miller*

United States v. Miller (1939)

The Facts

Defendants, Miller and Layton, transported a double barrel 12-gauge shotgun with a barrel length of less than 18 inches from Oklahoma to Arkansas, and were being prosecuted under the National Firearms Act (which required certain types of firearms to be registered and a tax to be paid). Defendants challenged the NFA as an unconstitutional violation of the Second Amendment.

The Legal Holdings

Upheld the National Firearms Act as Constitutional and not a violation of the Second Amendment.

An interesting quirk of history in the *Miller* case (and not a shining moment for the legal system) is that Miller's attorney never appeared at the arguments before the U.S. Supreme Court because he was court-appointed and had not been paid. There was no written brief and no legal representation at oral arguments by the party arguing that the law was unconstitutional. The Court only heard the government's side. To make matters worse, Miller was shot to death before the decision was rendered.

C. 69 years later, the Supreme Court interpreted the Second Amendment again: D.C. v. Heller

It would be 69 years after *Miller* until the U.S. Supreme Court addressed the Second Amendment directly again, except this time the Court would hear both the government's and the defendant's arguments. Fortunately, freedom and Second Amendment rights prevailed in court that day. The Court held that individuals have a right to keep and bear arms.

District of Columbia v. Heller (2008)

The Facts

Heller had applied for a handgun ownership permit and was denied; without such a permit, D.C. required that all firearms (including rifles and shotguns) be kept unloaded and disassembled, or bound by a trigger lock, even in a person's own home.

The Legal Holdings

1. The Supreme Court found that the Second Amendment protects an individual right of firearms ownership for purposes of self-defense, not connected with any militia or military purposes; it further elaborated that individual self-defense is "the central component" of the Second Amendment. Further, handguns are the primary defensive weapon of choice and are protected by the Second Amendment.
2. A well-regulated militia is not the state's military forces.
3. The Court also discussed what the phrase "bear arms" meant: "wear, bear, or carry... upon the person or in clothing or in a pocket, for the purpose... of being armed and ready for offensive or defensive action in a case of conflict with another person."
4. The D.C. regulation was held to be unconstitutional.
5. The Court concluded that like other rights, the right to bear arms is not completely absolute. Reasonable provisions and restrictions have been upheld.

Keep in mind *D.C. v. Heller* was a split 5-4 decision; only one justice away from a completely different outcome, where the Second Amendment (according to the dissent) had "outlived its usefulness and should be ignored."

D. Can states ignore the Second Amendment? McDonald v. City of Chicago

D.C. v. Heller was fantastic, but there was a slight quirk: the District of Columbia is under the exclusive jurisdiction of Congress and is not part of any state. Therefore, the case shed no light on the question of what states can do when it comes to regulating or banning firearms. How do state constitutions interact with the Second Amendment and can states ban guns outright? *McDonald v. City of Chicago* sought to answer these questions.

McDonald v. City of Chicago (2010)

The Facts

McDonald v. City of Chicago was decided in 2010; Chicago ordinance banned handgun possession (among other gun regulations). McDonald was a 76-year-old retired maintenance engineer who wanted a handgun for self-defense. Chicago required that all handguns had to be registered, but refused all handgun registration after a 1982 citywide handgun ban.

The Legal Holdings

The Supreme Court held that the Second Amendment is fully applicable to the States and that individual self-defense is "the central component" of the Second Amendment. Therefore, the Second Amendment prohibits states from enacting bans on handguns for self-protection in the home.

E. Legal limitations of the right to keep and bear arms

The U.S. Supreme Court has stated: "Of course the right [to keep and bear arms] was not unlimited, just as the First Amendment's right of free speech was not." Courts may have struggled over the years with what the Second Amendment means, but they have been resolute that there is an element of self-defense. The *Heller* Court stated that, "The Second Amendment does not protect the right to carry arms for any sort of confrontation," focusing their decision on self-defense. Further, the *Miller* Court stated that the weapons protected were those "in common use at the time" of the decision. This is supported by historical traditions of prohibiting the carry of "dangerous and unusual weapons" that are commonly used by criminals offensively, as opposed to weapons carried by law-abiding citizens for defensive purposes.

The Second Amendment does not protect against prohibitions on firearm possession by felons and the mentally ill; *Heller* made this point in its decision, and many circuit court cases such as *U.S. v. Everist* follow the same reasoning. The Court of Appeals in *U.S. v. Everist* states that the Second Amendment is subject to, "limited narrowly tailored specific exceptions or restrictions for particular cases that are reasonable; it is clear that felons, infants and those of unsound mind may be prohibited from possessing firearms." *U.S. v. Everist*, 368 F.3d 517, 519 (5th Cir. 2004). Along this same train of thought, the *Heller* Court did not want to eliminate laws that imposed conditions and qualifications on the commercial sales of firearms.

It also does not mean that the Second Amendment includes the right to carry anywhere a person wants. The *Heller* Court stated that their opinion was not meant to allow the carrying of firearms in sensitive places such as schools and certain government buildings.

Practical Legal Tip:

Currently, the two most important court decisions fortifying our gun rights are *Heller* and *McDonald*. But those cases were very, very close to going the other way! Both were decided by a 5-4 majority, meaning that if only one other Supreme Court Justice had decided differently, our individual right to possess and carry firearms could have been severely limited. *–Robert*

III. Major firearms statutes every gun owner needs to know

At the Federal level, there are plenty of laws and regulations that concern firearms, but this section will focus on some of the major legislative actions that all gun owners need to know.

A. Gun Control Act of 1968

The Gun Control Act of 1968 ("GCA") was enacted by Congress to "provide for better control of the interstate traffic of firearms." This law is primarily focused on regulating interstate commerce in firearms by generally prohibiting interstate firearms transfers except among licensed manufacturers, dealers, and importers, however, interstate commerce has been held by the courts to include nearly everything. It also contains classes of individuals to whom firearms should not be sold. For the specifics of who can and can't purchase a firearm, please refer to Chapter 3. Among other things, the GCA created the Federal Firearms License ("FFL") system, imposed importation restrictions on military surplus rifles (adding a "sporting purpose test" and a "points system" for handguns) and marking requirements.

B. The Brady Handgun Violence Prevention Act

The Brady Handgun Violence Prevention Act, commonly referred to as the Brady Law, instituted federal background checks (the National Instant Criminal Background Check System or NICS) for firearm purchasers in the United States. It also prohibited certain persons from purchasing firearms; for more information on who can or can't purchase a firearm, *See* Chapter 3.

C. The Firearm Owners' Protection Act

The Firearm Owners' Protection Act ("FOPA") revised many provisions of the original Gun Control Act, including "reforms" on the inspection of FFLs. This same Act updated the list of individuals prohibited from purchasing firearms that was introduced by the GCA. The FOPA also banned the ownership by civilians of any machine gun that was not registered under the NFA as of May 19, 1986. FOPA created what is called a "safe passage" provision of the law, which allows for traveling across states with a firearm. Finally, FOPA prohibited a registry for non-NFA items that directly linked firearms to their owners.

D. The Public Safety and Recreational Firearms Use Protection Act

The Public Safety and Recreational Firearms Use Protection Act, commonly referred to as the *Federal Assault Weapons Ban*, was a subsection of the Violent Crime Control and Law Enforcement Act of 1994. It banned outright the manufacture and transfer of certain semi-automatic firearms and magazines. This ban grandfathered-in previously legally owned weapons, but no prohibited firearm could be acquired or manufactured after September 13, 1994. With great foresight, the drafters of this law included a so-called "sunset provision," that stated the ban would expire ten years later unless renewed. The ban expired in 2004, and all attempts to renew have been unsuccessful.

E. The National Firearms Act

The National Firearms Act ("NFA") regulates and imposes a statutory excise tax on the manufacture and transfer of certain types of firearms and weapons: machine guns, short-barreled weapons, suppressors, explosive devices, and "any other weapons" (AOWs can range from everyday objects that are actually firearms, such as an umbrella that can fire a round, to other weapons the ATF decides to place in this category). The tax is $200 if you make or transfer an item (other than for the transfer of AOWs); the tax for transferring AOWs is $5. The NFA is also referred to as Title II of the federal firearms laws. For more information on how to navigate the NFA while remaining legal, please *see* Chapter 14.

IV. Do Oklahomans have a right to keep and bear arms under the Oklahoma Constitution?

Yes. The Oklahoma Constitution acknowledges the right to keep and bear arms in Article 2, Section 26. This provision of the Oklahoma Constitution: Article 2, Section 26 reads:

> *The right of a citizen to keep and bear arms in defense of his home, person, or property, or in aid of the civil power, when thereunto legally summoned, shall never be prohibited; but nothing herein contained shall prevent the Legislature from regulating the carrying of weapons.*

The more observant will notice that, as opposed to the Second Amendment of the United States Constitution, this description specifically allows for legislation. The courts in Oklahoma have acknowledged that Section 26 allows the legislature to create laws to prohibit certain types of carrying weapons, and have upheld "unlawful carrying" laws and license requirements. *See Lovett v. State,* 455 P.2d 713 (Okla. Crim. App. 1969).

A. Can Oklahoma prohibit local municipalities from making certain gun laws?

Yes. The Oklahoma Legislature can and does prohibit local municipalities from making certain gun laws by the legal doctrine known as "preemption." A preemption statute is a mechanism by which the Oklahoma legislature sets certain areas off limits to local governments, which helps ensure the uniformity of law across the state, in this case, firearms law.

B. What local governments may not regulate

The Oklahoma preemption statute can be found in Oklahoma Statutes Title 21 Section 1289.24. It states what areas of law municipalities are not allowed to regulate.

> A.1. "The State Legislature hereby occupies and preempts the entire field of legislation in this state touching in any way firearms, knives, components, ammunition, and supplies to the complete exclusion of any order, ordinance, or regulation by any municipality or other political subdivision of this state. Any existing or future orders, ordinances, or regulations in this field, except as provided for in paragraph 2 of this subsection and subsection C of this section, are null and void.
>
> [...]
>
> A.3. As provided in the preemption provisions of this section, the otherwise lawful open carrying of a handgun under the provisions of the Oklahoma Self-Defense Act shall not be punishable by any municipality or other political subdivision of this state as disorderly conduct, disturbing the peace or similar offense against public order.
>
> [...]
>
> B. No municipality or other political subdivision of this state shall adopt any order, ordinance, or regulation concerning in any way the sale, purchase, purchase delay, transfer, ownership, use, keeping, possession, carrying, bearing, transportation, licensing, permit, registration, taxation other than sales and compensating use taxes, or other controls on firearms, knives, components, ammunition, and supplies
>
> [...]
>
> D. When a person's rights pursuant to the protection of the preemption provisions of this section have been violated, the person shall have the right to bring

a civil action against the persons, municipality, and political subdivision jointly and severally for injunctive relief or monetary damages or both."

C. What local governments may regulate

Local municipalities under state law are empowered to and may regulate the following under the Oklahoma Self-Defense Act 1289.24:

"2. A municipality may adopt any ordinance:

a. relating to the discharge of firearms within the jurisdiction of the municipality, and

b. allowing the municipality to issue a traffic citation for transporting a firearm improperly as provided for in Section 1289.13A of this title, provided however, that penalties contained for violation of any ordinance enacted pursuant to the provisions of this subparagraph shall not exceed the penalties established in the Oklahoma Self-Defense Act."

Local governments may regulate the confiscation of property used in violation of the ordinances of the municipality as provided for in Oklahoma Statutes Title 11 Section 28-121. Provided, however, no municipal ordinance relating to transporting a firearm or knife improperly may include a provision for confiscation of property.

This does not apply to a firearm carried to or from an area designated for lawful target practice, hunting, fishing, or historical reenactment events where firearms are commonly used in the activity. 21 O.S. § 1272.

CHAPTER TWO

LEGAL DEFINITIONS AND CLASSIFICATIONS OF FIREARMS: WHAT IS LEGAL?

I. Introduction and overview

Before discussing the law of firearms and all its different facets, it is important first to understand what the law defines as a "firearm." Firearm laws are governed on both the federal and state levels; therefore, throughout this chapter we will explore the interactions federal and state law have on the purchase and possession of firearms.

A. What is a firearm?
Federal definition
Under the federal law, a firearm is defined as "any weapon (including a starter gun) which will or is designed to or may readily be converted to expel a projectile by the action of an explosive." 18 U.S.C. § 921(a)(3). The federal definition of a firearm also includes the frame or receiver of any such weapon, any firearm muffler or silencer, or any "destructive device." This is similar to the Oklahoma definition, but not exactly the same.

Oklahoma definition
The State of Oklahoma had no statutory definition of 'firearm,' but it has the Oklahoma Firearms Act of 1971, which in substance describes a 'firearm' to be an instrument capable of discharging a projectile composed of any material which may be reasonably expected to cause lethal injury and using either gunpowder, gas or any means of rocket propulsion, but not to include flare guns, underwater fishing guns or Blank pistols. *Coleman v. State*, 506 P.2d 558 (Okla. Crim. App. 1972); *see* 21 O.S. § 1289.3. Another case also gives some guidance as to what constitutes a firearm. *Thompson v. State*, 488 P.2d 944 (Okla. Crim. App. 1971) states that a firearm "has been defined by the courts as a weapon from which a shot or projectile is

discharged by force of a chemical explosive such as gunpowder."

Why might it be important to know the different ways the term "firearm" is defined under federal and state law? It is because if a person finds themselves charged with a crime by federal authorities, the federal definition of a firearm will apply. Likewise, if the charge is under a violation of state law, then the Oklahoma definition will apply. Thus, the primary difference in the definitions and their impact on a defendant charged with a crime involving a firearm lies with how a person may be in trouble with the law. As we will see in the next section, the definitions of what does and does not constitute a firearm, although similar in many aspects, contain an array of differences that make violating the law unwittingly easy.

B. Definitions for pistols, rifles, and shotguns

In addition to defining what constitutes a firearm, federal and Oklahoma law further classify and define firearms into categories of pistols, rifles, and shotguns. This section will provide an overview of how federal and state laws classify firearms as well as the physical requirements for a firearm to be legal.

1. What is a pistol?

Ultimately, whether looking at the federal or Oklahoma definition, the term handgun/pistol is defined in a similar manner: it refers to any firearm that is designed to be fired by using only one hand. While it is true that most individuals will use two hands when firing a handgun for safety and accuracy purposes, the emphasis in the legal definition of a handgun rests purely in its design to be held or fired with a single hand.

Federal definition

The United States Code of Federal Regulations defines a handgun as "(a) any firearm which has a short stock and is designed to be held and fired by the use of a single hand; and (b) any combination of parts from which a firearm described in paragraph (a) can be assembled." 27 CFR § 478.11.

Oklahoma definition
A pistol is defined by 21 O.S. § 1289.3: "Pistols" mean any firearm capable of discharging a projectile composed of any material which may reasonably be expected to be able to cause lethal injury, with a barrel or barrels less than sixteen (16) inches in length, and using either gunpowder, gas or any means of rocket propulsion, but not to include flare guns, underwater fishing guns or blank pistols.

The Oklahoma Self-Defense Act builds upon the definition above in Section 1289.3 by adding that a "Pistol" means any derringer, revolver or semiautomatic firearm which "is designed to be held and fired by the use of a single hand." 21 O.S. § 1290.2(A)(3)(c).

2. What is a rifle?
Federal definition
A rifle is "a weapon designed or redesigned, made or remade, and intended to be fired from the shoulder, and designed or redesigned and made or remade to use the energy of the explosive in a fixed metallic cartridge to fire only a single projectile through a rifled bore for each single pull of the trigger." 27 CFR § 478.11. In addition, a legal rifle must have a barrel length of 16 inches or greater, and includes any weapon made from a rifle which is at least 26 inches overall in length.

Oklahoma definition
"Rifle" as defined in Oklahoma means "any firearm capable of discharging a projectile composed of any material which may reasonably be expected to be able to cause lethal injury, with a barrel or barrels more than sixteen (16) inches in length, and using either gunpowder, gas or any means of rocket propulsion, but not to include archery equipment, flare guns or underwater fishing guns. In addition, any rifle capable of firing 'shot' but primarily designed to fire single projectiles will be regarded as a 'rifle'." 21 O.S. § 1289.4.

Minimum lengths

In order for a rifle to not be subject to the National Firearms Act or classified as a short-barreled firearm under Oklahoma law, it must have a barrel of at least 16 inches in length. The ATF procedure for measuring barrel length is accomplished by measuring from the closed bolt (or breech-face) to the furthermost end of the barrel or permanently attached muzzle device. Below is an example of a rifle that does not meet the minimum barrel length requirement after measurement:

The barrel is measured by inserting a dowel rod into the barrel until the rod stops against the bolt or breech-face. The rod is then marked at the furthermost end of the barrel or permanently attached muzzle device, withdrawn from the barrel, and then measured. Any measurement of less than 16 inches will classify the rifle as being short-barreled under Oklahoma and federal law and subject the firearm to the NFA. For short-barreled rifles and other non-compliant firearms, *see* Chapter 14, which discusses the NFA. *Note:* for overall length, rifles with collapsible/folding-stocks are measured from the "extreme ends," unless the stock is "easily detachable," in which case it is measured without the stock.

3. What is a shotgun?

Federal definition

A shotgun is "a weapon designed or redesigned, made or remade, and intended to be fired from the shoulder, and designed or redesigned and made or remade to use the energy of the explosive in a fixed shotgun shell to fire through a smooth bore either a number of ball shot or a single projectile for each single pull of the trigger." 27 CFR § 478.11.

Oklahoma definition
"Shotguns" as defined in Oklahoma means "any firearm capable of discharging a series of projectiles of any material which may reasonably be expected to be able to cause lethal injury, with a barrel or barrels more than eighteen (18) inches in length, and using either gunpowder, gas or any means of rocket propulsion, but not to include any weapon so designed with a barrel less than eighteen (18) inches in length. In addition, any 'shotgun' capable of firing single projectiles but primarily designed to fire multiple projectiles such as 'shot' will be regarded as a 'shotgun'." 21 O.S. § 1289.5.

Like rifles, legal shotguns have requirements for minimum barrel and overall lengths. Shotgun barrels must be at least 18 inches long and must also comply with the same 26-inch overall length requirement.

Minimum lengths
In order for a shotgun to not be subject to the National Firearms Act or classified as a short-barreled firearm under Oklahoma law, it must have a barrel of at least 18 inches in length. The ATF procedure for measuring the barrel length of a shotgun is the same as it is for a rifle. Below is an example of a shotgun that does not meet the minimum barrel length requirement after measurement:

Any measurement of less than 18 inches will classify the shotgun as a short-barreled weapon and illegal under Oklahoma and federal law unless the requirements of the NFA are satisfied. For short-barreled shotguns and other non-compliant firearms, *see* Chapter 14. *Note:* the collapsible/folding-stock rule that applies to rifles applies to shotguns as well.

C. Antique firearms and replica firearms

When is a firearm not legally a "firearm?" It is when the law defines it as not being one, such as with "antique" firearms.

1. Federal definition of "antique firearm"

1898 or prior

The federal definition of firearm under Title 18, Section 921 of the United States Code excludes "antique firearms." Even though an antique firearm still functions ballistically similar to a "modern" firearm, under federal law, antique firearms are regulated differently, if at all. An antique firearm under federal law includes any firearm with a matchlock, flintlock, or percussion cap, or similar type of ignition system manufactured in or before 1898 or any replica of a firearm just described so long as the replica "is not designed or redesigned for using rimfire or conventional centerfire fixed ammunition, or uses rimfire or centerfire ammunition that is no longer manufactured in the United States and is not readily available in ordinary channels of commerce." 18 U.S.C. §§ 921(16)(A) and (B). So, an "antique firearm" is not a "firearm" for purposes of federal regulation; it is an "antique firearm."

Muzzle loading

In addition, federal law does not consider "any muzzle loading rifle, muzzle loading shotgun, or muzzle loading pistol, which is designed to use black powder, or a black powder substitute, and which cannot use fixed ammunition" as a firearm. Be aware, however, that the term "antique firearm" does not include any weapon which incorporates a firearm frame or receiver, any firearm which is converted into a muzzle loading weapon, or any muzzle loading weapon which can be readily converted to fire fixed ammunition by replacing the barrel, bolt, breechlock, or any combination of these parts. 18 U.S.C. § 921(a)(16)(C).

2. Oklahoma definition of "antique firearm"

The Oklahoma definition of a "pistol," "rifle," and "shotgun" include antique firearms by being silent on the subject and not defining nor excluding any firearm that is an antique firearm manufactured before 1899; or a replica of an antique firearm manufactured before 1899. Thus, the general definitions found in Oklahoma law that discuss these firearms apply to muzzle loaders, black powder firearms, antique firearms and replica firearms.

3. Differences in federal and Oklahoma law

Federal and Oklahoma law differ on what is and what is not a firearm. The federal law uses the term "antique firearms," while Oklahoma does not define an antique firearm *per se*. Federal law uses the year of manufacture and includes modern replicas as a test to define an antique firearm, thus the year of manufacture of an otherwise working and deadly firearm will exclude an "antique firearm" from regulation as a firearm by the federal authorities.

The year of manufacture for firearms that are classified as "antiques" is a moot point in Oklahoma because federal law regards antique firearms differently than Oklahoma. Oklahoma does not define nor differentiate between antique firearms and modern firearms. A firearm is defined as a weapon from which a shot or projectile is discharged by force of a chemical explosive such as gunpowder. This is why black powder firearms, antiques, replicas, and muzzleloaders are considered firearms in Oklahoma.

This demonstrates one of the few examples where the federal law is less restrictive than the state law. By these definitions, a person who could not otherwise legally possess a firearm, under federal law, could legally possess a muzzle loading rifle or pistol designed to use black powder that is not a replica of any weapon that was actually previously manufactured before 1899, because federal law does not consider such a weapon to be a firearm due to its mere use of black powder. Oklahoma law does not have an "antique firearm" exclusion. Thus, the possession or use of a black powder firearm would be subject to all other Oklahoma laws governing the use of firearms.

D. What firearms are illegal in Oklahoma?

Under 21 O.S. § 1289.18, certain firearms are prohibited or illegal under Oklahoma law. These firearms include:

- legal handgun loaded with prohibited armor piercing ammunition;
- sawed-off shotguns;
- sawed-off rifles

However, in the case of sawed-off shotguns and rifles, a person may have a defense to prosecution under state law if he or she has complied with the requirements of the National Firearms Act (*See* Chapter 14 for more information on the NFA). *See* 21 O.S. § 1289.18(D).

Under federal law, the same firearms that are prohibited weapons under state law without registration are regulated by the National Firearms Act. These firearms include:

- short-barreled shotguns;
- short-barreled rifles;
- machine guns;
- pistols loaded with armor piercing ammunition;
- weapons or devices capable of being concealed on the person from which a shot can be fired;
- pistols or revolvers having a smooth bore (as opposed to rifled bore) barrel designed to fire a fixed shotgun shell;
- pistols or revolvers with a vertical handgrip;
- destructive devices; and
- weapons classified as "Any Other Weapon," or AOWs.

See 26 U.S.C. § 5845. For more information on these weapons, *See* Chapter 14 discussing the National Firearms Act.

Although these firearms and/or weapons are prohibited by statute, it does not mean a person absolutely cannot possess one. Many of these weapons may be legally possessed with proper documentation under the National Firearms Act. For more information on these prohibited weapons and the NFA, *see* Chapter 14. Some of the items listed under Section 1272 may be possessed for hunting or recreational purposes. A legal pistol may become a prohibited weapon when loaded with armor piercing prohibited ammunition. *See* 21 O.S. § 1290.6.

E. How big of a gun can a person possess?

Federal law dictates that any firearm which has any barrel with a bore of more than one-half inch in diameter is a "destructive device" and is subject to the National Firearms Act. Possession of any such firearm without the proper paperwork associated with NFA firearms is illegal. Note, however, that some shotguns are regulated differently. For more information on destructive devices and the NFA, *see* Chapter 14. Additionally, it is important to remember that § 1290.6 prohibits anyone from carrying a handgun, either concealed or unconcealed, when loaded with ammunition larger than .45 caliber. So if your handgun you are carrying is loaded with ammunition between .45 and .50 caliber, even though you are compliant with federal law, it is a crime in Oklahoma!

II. Ammunition and the law

No discussion concerning firearms laws would be complete without examining laws concerning the ammunition that goes into a firearm. Just like firearms, the law regulates the possession, sale, and even composition of "legal" ammunition. This section addresses the essential aspects of the law concerning ammunition and what gun owners need to know, both under federal and Oklahoma law.

A. How does the law define ammunition?

Under federal law, the term ammunition is defined under 18 U.S.C. § 921(a)(17)(A) and means "ammunition or cartridge cases, primers, bullets, or propellant powder designed for use in any firearm." Thus, the federal definition of ammunition includes the finished product and all of the components in making a round of ammunition. However, the federal definition of ammunition does not include (1) any shotgun shot or pellet not designed for use as the single, complete projectile load for one shotgun hull or casing, nor (2) any unloaded, non-metallic shotgun hull or casing not having a primer. *See* 27 CFR § 478.11. In other words, individual ammunition components are legally defined as ammunition themselves, even if they are simply parts, except that shotgun ammunition components, if not completely assembled, are not ammunition.

Under Oklahoma law, there is no statutory definition for mere "ammunition." Oklahoma law only provides a definition for armor-piercing ammunition (which we will discuss later in this chapter) and a definition for the way firearms are discharged: a projectile composed of any material [expelled though] a barrel using either gunpowder, gas or any means of rocket propulsion. See 21 O.S. § 1289.3.

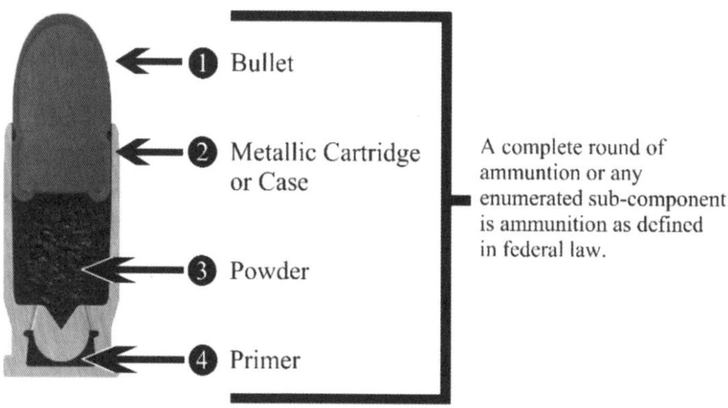

B. Is there a difference in ammunition that is used in different types of firearms?
Yes. Ammunition can be divided into two classifications: ammunition for handguns and ammunition for long guns. Long gun ammunition can be further divided into ammunition for rifles and ammunition for shotguns.

Handgun ammunition means ammunition that is meant to be fired from a handgun, and it comes in many different calibers. Rifle ammunition is meant to be fired from a rifle and is similar to handgun ammunition in that it comes in many different calibers. Shotgun ammunition, on the other hand, comes in self-contained cartridges loaded with some form of shot or a shotgun slug which is designed to be fired from a shotgun.

C. What ammunition is illegal?
Armor-piercing ammunition is the only ammunition which has explicit prohibitions under both federal and Oklahoma law. The federal definition of armor-piercing ammunition is found in 18 U.S.C. § 921(a)(17)(B) and means "[1] a projectile or projectile core which may be used in a handgun and which is constructed entirely (excluding the presence of traces of other substances) from one or a combination of tungsten alloys, steel, iron, brass, bronze, beryllium copper, or depleted uranium; or [2] a full jacketed projectile larger than .22 caliber designed and intended for use in a handgun and whose jacket has a weight of more than 25 percent of the total weight of the projectile."

Federal law
Under federal law, while there is no blanket prohibition on the mere possession of armor-piercing ammunition, it is prohibited under four conditions:

1. *Prohibition one: it is illegal to make or import armor-piercing ammunition.* Under 18 U.S.C. § 922(a)(7) it is unlawful for any person to manufacture or import armor-piercing ammunition unless (1) the manufacture of such ammunition is for the use of the United States, any department or agency of the United States, any state, or any department, agency, or political

subdivision of a state; (2) the manufacture of such ammunition is for the purpose of exportation; or (3) the manufacture or importation of such ammunition is for the purpose of testing or experimentation and has been authorized by the United States Attorney General.

2. *Prohibition two: it is illegal for manufacturers and importers to sell or deliver armor-piercing ammunition.* Federal law states that it is unlawful for any manufacturer or importer to sell or deliver armor-piercing ammunition unless such sale or delivery is (1) for the use of the United States, any department or agency of the United States, any state, or any department, agency, or political subdivision of a state; (2) for the purpose of exportation; or (3) for the purpose of testing or experimentation and has been authorized by the United States Attorney General. *See* 18 U.S.C. § 922(a)(8).

3. *Prohibition three: an FFL or other license-holder cannot sell or deliver armor-piercing ammunition without the proper documentation.* Under 18 U.S.C. § 922(b)(5), it is unlawful for any licensed importer, licensed manufacturer, licensed dealer, or licensed collector to sell or deliver armor-piercing ammunition to any person unless the licensee notes in his records, as required under 18 U.S.C. § 923, the name, age, and place of residence of such person if the person is an individual, or the identity and principal and local places of business of such person if the person is a corporation or other business entity.

4. *Prohibition four: it is illegal to possess armor-piercing ammunition if a person is involved in a crime of violence or a drug-trafficking crime.* Pursuant to 18 U.S.C. § 924(c)(5), it is unlawful for "any person who, during and in relation to any crime of violence or drug trafficking crime (including a crime of violence or drug trafficking crime that provides for an enhanced punishment if committed by the use of a deadly or dangerous weapon or device) for which the person may be prosecuted in a court of the United States, use or carries armor piercing ammunition." Individuals who use or carry armor-piercing

ammunition in the commission of a crime of violence or during a drug-trafficking crime are subject to heightened sentencing standards should they be found guilty.

As you can see, while possession of armor-piercing ammunition itself is not illegal, obtaining armor-piercing ammunition without violating one of the foregoing prohibitions is almost impossible.

Oklahoma law

21 O.S. § 1289.19 defines the equivalent of armor-piercing ammunition, also known as a "Restricted bullet." The definition states that a restricted bullet means “a round or elongated missile with a core of less than sixty percent (60%) lead and having a fluorocarbon coating, which is designed to travel at a high velocity and is capable of penetrating body armor.”

21 O.S. § 1289.21 makes the possession, use or attempted use of restricted bullets against another person a felony punishable by a sentence of two to ten years in the penitentiary. Further, 21 O.S. § 1289.20 states that, “it shall be unlawful to manufacture, cause to be manufactured, import, advertise for sale or sell within this state any restricted bullet.” A violation of this section is a felony and punished by a fine of $500-$10,000 and/or imprisonment for up to ten years in the penitentiary.

A couple of notable exceptions to this law are available, however. First, under Oklahoma law, 21 O.S. §1289.22, there is an exemption for possessing or using a restricted bullet for law enforcement agencies if such bullet is used for testing, training, or demonstration. Second, there is an exception to the prohibition on the manufacture, importation, sale, or advertisement for sale of restricted bullets, if such activity was for the purpose of public safety or national security. *See* 21 O.S. §1289.20.

By definition, it should be noted that not all ammunition that *can* pierce armor is actually armor-piercing. Both the federal and Oklahoma definitions contain specific requirements for a particular round of ammunition's composition in order to make it armor-piercing. Federal law requires that the ammunition be comprised of certain alloys while Oklahoma law specifies that the ammunition is less than sixty percent lead and has a fluorocarbon coating. For instance, 5.7 millimeter ammunition for an FN57 handgun or a PS90 rifle, while capable of piercing armor based on its size and velocity, is not ammunition that is armor-piercing as defined under the law because such ammunition, sold commercially, does not have the applicable composition, and is primarily for sporting purposes according to the ATF.

PS90

Practical Legal Tip:

Even with firearms, having the right tool for the job is important. Practically speaking, you should choose the firearm and ammo that you feel most comfortable using. At the end of the day, why you started shooting is always more important than what you chose to shoot with. *–Robert*

D. Does modifying traditional ammunition make it illegal?

No, outside of armor-piercing ammunition, there is no handgun or long gun ammunition that is prohibited under federal or Oklahoma law, with the exception of the caliber size issues discussed earlier. In fact, there are many examples of hollow-point rounds which are modified in a way to become more lethal such as the R.I.P. ammunition, Black Talons, *etc.*, which star outward upon impact in order to do more internal damage. Such ammunition, though it looks different from traditional ammunition rounds, is perfectly legal.

Factory and Expanded Hollow Point Rounds

E. Is it legal to use ammunition that works in both handguns and rifles?

Yes, except for armor-piercing ammunition that is used principally in handguns as defined in federal law. This is because the federal definitions of armor-piercing ammunition contemplate handguns only. Under federal law, armor-piercing ammunition for a rifle is perfectly legal, though it may complicate matters at trial in trying to demonstrate to the jury any differentiation. Beyond armor-piercing ammunition, it is legal to use ammunition that is available in common calibers and that functions in both handguns and rifles.

Oklahoma does not make this distinction between armor-piercing ammunition in pistols and rifles, and therefore under Oklahoma law, the prohibition on armor-piercing ammunition exists regardless of the firearm for which the ammunition is intended.

With a solid understanding of what is and is not a firearm and ammunition, as well as what firearms and ammunition a person may legally possess without the necessity of obtaining additional documentation, we are now ready to move to the next chapter discussing the purchase and possession of firearms.

CHAPTER THREE

PURCHASING, TRANSFERRING, AND POSSESSING FIREARMS

I. Laws of purchasing and possessing: the basics

The laws of purchasing, selling, gifting, or otherwise transferring a firearm are distinct and different from the laws of possessing a firearm. Each of these sets of laws for "purchasing" or "possessing" has a federal and a state component both of which must be satisfied in order to start on the right side of the law.

On the federal level, the Bureau of Alcohol, Tobacco, Firearms and Explosives ("ATF") is charged with regulating firearms including sales, purchases, and transfers through Federal Firearms Licensees ("FFLs" or "dealers"), however, a multitude of federal agencies can be involved in any given firearms law investigation or police function most currently falling under a branch of the U.S. Department of Justice. Oklahoma has no direct state-level counterpart to the ATF.

A. What is an FFL?

A Federal Firearms License is a license required by federal law for those persons or entities who are engaged in the business of buying and selling firearms. A federal firearms licensee is often called an "FFL" or "dealer." When an individual purchases, sells, or transfers a firearm through a dealer, the FFL and the individual must both comply with specific federal law requirements, paperwork, and procedures concerning the buying, selling, or transferring of those firearms. These requirements will be addressed throughout this chapter.

B. Who must obtain an FFL?

Federal law requires a federal firearms license if a person is engaged in business as a firearms dealer, manufacturer, or importer. For the purposes of our discussion in this chapter, a person is engaged in the business when the person "devotes time, attention, and labor to dealing in firearms as a regular course of trade or business with the principal objective of livelihood and profit through the repetitive purchase and resale of firearms, but such term shall not include a person who makes occasional sales, exchanges, or purchases of firearms for the enhancement of a personal collection or for a hobby, or who sells all or part of his personal collection of firearms." 18 U.S.C. § 921(a)(21)(C).

C. What is a private sale?

A private sale is just what it sounds like: a sale, purchase, or transfer of a firearm by parties who are not licensed dealers. A private sale is perfectly legal for both handguns and long guns in Oklahoma, as long as all other legal requirements are met. We will discuss the ins-and-outs of private sales in greater detail in this chapter under Section IV.

D. What is the legal age to purchase and possess a firearm?

Federal law controls all FFL firearms transactions and requires that a person be 21 years of age or older before they may purchase a handgun or 18 for the purchase of a long gun. However, under Oklahoma law, a handgun or long gun may be purchased in a private sale by a person who is age 18. 21 O.S. § 1273 makes it a crime for any person within this state to sell or give to any child (meaning person under 18) any pistol, revolver, shotgun or rifle. Note the exceptions to follow.

Required Age to Purchase Firearms	Federal Law: From Dealer	Oklahoma Law: Private Sale
Handgun	21	18
Long gun	18	18

Under federal law, a person must be at least 18 years of age in order to possess a handgun or ammunition for a handgun. *See* 18 U.S.C. § 922(x)(2). Unlike the law on purchasing a long gun, there is no federal age requirement for the possession of a rifle or shotgun. Oklahoma law directly specifies that persons under 18 are prohibited from possessing a firearm, and that persons under 18 must be supervised and that certain other conditions must be met in order for a juvenile to possess a firearm. *See* 21 O.S. § 1273. Provided, this section shall not authorize the possession of such weapons by any person who is subject to the provisions of Section 1283 of this title. (Convicted juvenile delinquent or convicted felon). Any child violating the provisions of Section 1273 shall be subject to adjudication as a delinquent.

E. Can I buy a firearm if I have permission from my parents?
Before the age of 18, the answer is no. However, minors may own firearms that are given to them by their parents, relatives, or legal guardians. However, they may not generally possess firearms unsupervised until they are 18 years of age. For the federal law regarding juveniles and handguns, *see* 18 U.S.C. § 922(x). Note, an individual must be 21 years old to purchase a handgun from an FFL.

F. Criminal liability for allowing a minor access to firearms
In Oklahoma, 21 O.S. § 1273(B) says that a parent or guardian shall be guilty of a crime if he or she intentionally, knowingly, or recklessly permits a child (younger than 18) to possess any of the arms or weapons designated in § 1272, if such parent is aware of a substantial risk that the child will use the weapon to commit a criminal offense.

Upon a first conviction the offending party shall be guilty of a misdemeanor and the party offending shall be punished by a fine of not less than One Hundred Dollars ($100) nor more than Two Hundred Fifty Dollars ($250), or by imprisonment in the county jail for a period not to exceed thirty (30) days or both such fine and imprisonment. On the second and every subsequent violation, the party offending shall, upon conviction, be punished by a fine of not less than Two Hundred Fifty Dollars ($250) nor more than Five Hundred Dollars ($500), or by imprisonment in the county jail for a period not less than thirty (30) days nor more than three (3) months, or by both such fine and imprisonment. Additionally, a person who violates Section 1273 shall be liable for civil damages for any injury or death to any person and for any damage to property.

G. When may children legally possess firearms?

Oklahoma law allows for the legal possession of firearms under specific exceptions included in the law. These exceptions or "affirmative defenses" include the following:

1. Exception for hunting or sporting purposes

The first affirmative defense to prosecution is found in Section 1273, which says: "The provisions of this section shall not prohibit a parent of a child or legal guardian of a child, or a person acting with the permission of the parent of the child or legal guardian of the child, from giving the child a firearm for participation in hunting animals or fowl, hunter safety classes, education and training in the safe use and handling of firearms, target shooting, skeet, trap or other sporting events or competitions, except as provided in subsection B of this section." Subsection B states, "It shall be unlawful for any parent or guardian to intentionally, knowingly, or recklessly permit his or her child to possess any of the arms or weapons designated in Section 1272 of this title, including any firearm, if such parent is aware of a substantial risk that the child will use the weapon to commit a criminal offense or if the child has either been adjudicated a delinquent or has been convicted as an adult for any criminal offense that contains as an element the threat or use of physical force against the person of another."

2. Self-defense

Second, possession may be lawful if the child's access and possible use of the firearm was "committed in the lawful defense of such person or of another, when the person using force reasonably believes such force is necessary to prevent death or great bodily harm to himself or herself or another or to terminate or prevent the commission of a forcible felony."

21 O.S. § 733(2). For obvious reasons, if a child uses a firearm in self-defense, or in defense of another person or property, there is a general public policy interest in not prosecuting those persons.

Example:

> *One night, armed intruders break into Timmy's home and hold Timmy's parents at gunpoint while burglarizing the home. Timmy, who is 14, covertly sees what is transpiring from the top of the stairs and knowing that his father keeps a loaded handgun in his nightstand, retrieves the weapon. Timmy then shoots the burglar threatening his parents.*

Two questions arise in this scenario: first, is Timmy legally justified in shooting the armed burglar? As we will see later in Chapters 4, 5, and 7, yes, he is. Timmy is justified in defending a third person and property with deadly force under the circumstances. Second, is Timmy's father in trouble legally for leaving his firearm accessible to Timmy? No, he is not in trouble. Timmy's access to the firearm was the result of his necessity in defending his parents who were staring down the barrel of a burglar's gun! This accessibility to a firearm is contemplated under Oklahoma Statutes in the form of the affirmative defense—"lawful defense," and "justifiable homicide."

H. Special duty of firearms dealers involving minors

Federal law requires that FFLs who deliver handguns to non-licensees display at their licensed premises (including temporary business locations at gun shows) a sign that customers can readily see. These signs are provided by the ATF and contain the following language:

(1) The misuse of handguns is a leading contributor to juvenile violence and fatalities.

(2) Safely storing and securing firearms away from children will help prevent the unlawful

possession of handguns by juveniles, stop accidents, and save lives.

(3) Federal law prohibits, except in certain limited circumstances, anyone under 18 years of age from knowingly possessing a handgun, or any person from transferring a handgun to a person under 18.

(4) A knowing violation of the prohibition against selling, delivering, or otherwise transferring a handgun to a person under the age of 18 is, under certain circumstances, punishable by up to 10 years in prison.

In addition to the displayed sign, federal law requires FFLs to provide non-licensee customers with a written notification containing the same four points as listed above as well as sections 922(x) and 924(a)(6) of Title 18, Chapter 44 of the United States Code. This written notification is available as a pamphlet published by the ATF entitled "Youth Handgun Safety Act Notice" and is sometimes referred to as ATF information 5300.2. Alternatively, this written notification may be delivered to customers on another type of written notification, such as a manufacturer's brochure accompanying the handgun or a sales receipt or invoice applied to the handgun package. Any written notification delivered to a customer other than the one provided by the ATF must include the language described here, and must be "legible, clear, and conspicuous, and the required language shall appear in type size no smaller than 10-point type." 27 CFR § 478.103(c).

II. Federal law disqualifications for purchasing and possessing firearms

Federal law lists categories of persons disqualified from legally purchasing and possessing a firearm. This list comprises disqualifications that come from several different pieces of federal legislation including the Gun Control Act of 1968, the Brady Handgun Violence Protection Act, and the Violence Against Women Act. If a person buys or attempts to buy a firearm from an FFL, they must not be disqualified under any of the laws. Before an FFL may sell or otherwise transfer a firearm, the purchaser must fill out an ATF Form 4473. This form has questions concerning each of the criteria that disqualify a person to purchase a firearm under federal law. These disqualifications include:

(1) if the person is not the actual purchaser of the firearm—also known as a "straw man purchaser;"
(2) if the person is under indictment or information in any court for a felony or any other crime for which the judge could imprison the person for more than one year;
(3) if the person has ever been convicted in any court for a felony or other crime for which the judge could imprison the person for more than one year;
(4) if the person is a fugitive from justice;
(5) if the person is an unlawful user of, or addicted to, marijuana, or any depressant, stimulant, narcotic drug, or controlled substance;
(6) if the person has ever been adjudicated as mentally defective or has been committed to a mental institution;
(7) if the person has been dishonorably discharged from the Armed Forces;
(8) if the person is subject to an active protective order restraining the person from harassing, stalking, or threatening the person's child, or an intimate partner or child of such partner;
(9) if the person has been convicted in any court for a misdemeanor crime of domestic violence;
(10) if the person has ever renounced their United States citizenship;
(11) if the person is an alien illegally in the United States; and
(12) if the person is admitted under a non-immigrant visa and does not qualify for an exception.

The purchaser must legally affirm that they are not subject to any of the criteria listed above before they may purchase a firearm. If a prospective purchaser answers any question on the form in a manner that indicates they are legally disqualified, it is illegal for the FFL to sell that person the firearm, and it is illegal for the purchaser to complete the transaction or possess the firearm.

A. Understanding who is disqualified

1. Can I buy a firearm for another person?

No. This would be a "straw man" purchase. In order to legally purchase a firearm from a dealer, you must be the "actual purchaser or transferee." If you are not the actual purchaser or transferee, it is illegal for you to complete the transfer or sale under federal law. Purchases for third persons are often called "straw man" purchases and are illegal. If you are not the actual purchaser, beware!

In fact, the ATF has a campaign called "Don't Lie for the Other Guy" that is targeted at (as they term it on their website) detection and deterrence of "straw man" purchases. The ATF website lists numerous examples of prosecutions for "straw man" purchases and a United States Supreme Court case examined and upheld federal law on this matter. *Abramski v. United States*, 134 S.Ct. 2259 (2014).

So who is the "actual" buyer or transferee so as not to be a "straw man?" The ATF states that you are the actual "transferee/buyer if you are purchasing the firearm for yourself or otherwise acquiring the firearm for yourself (*e.g.*, redeeming the firearm from pawn/retrieving it from consignment, firearm raffle winner)." The ATF goes on to state "you are also the actual transferee/buyer if you are legitimately purchasing the firearm as a gift for a third party."

Example:

Mr. Smith asks Mr. Jones to purchase a firearm for Mr. Smith. Mr. Smith gives Mr. Jones the money for the firearm. Mr. Jones then buys the firearm with Mr. Smith's money and gives Mr. Smith the firearm.

Mr. Jones is not the "actual buyer" (he is legally a "straw man") of the firearm and if Mr. Jones indicates that he is the "actual buyer" of the firearm on ATF Form 4473, he has committed a federal crime. The Supreme Court ruling in *Abramski*, however, did not make "gifts" of firearms illegal.

When completing ATF Form 4473, if a person checks "yes" to the box asking if the person is the "actual purchaser," then that person cannot have engaged in a separate transaction to sell or transfer the firearm privately. Please note: the Supreme Court's ruling held that a person cannot legally purchase a firearm on behalf of another even if the person receiving the firearm would not otherwise be prohibited from making the purchase themselves. So don't buy a firearm for another person no matter how good a friend or relative they are—it is a crime!

FREQUENTLY ASKED QUESTION FROM ATF WEBSITE

Q: May I buy a firearm from an FFL as a "gift" for another person?

A: Yes.

Editor's note: Instead of the previous example where Mr. Smith paid Mr. Jones to purchase a firearm for him, if Mr. Jones decides to buy a firearm with his own money and then give the firearm to Mr. Smith as a present, then Mr. Jones is the actual buyer/transferee of the firearm. Since Mr. Jones is the actual buyer, there exists no sham or "straw man," and the purchase is legal.

Q: May a parent or guardian purchase a firearm as a gift for a juvenile?

A: Yes, however, possession of handguns by juveniles is generally unlawful under federal law. Juveniles may only receive and possess handguns with the written permission of a parent or guardian for limited purposes, *e.g.*, employment, ranching, farming, target practice, or hunting.

See www.atf.gov.

2. A person cannot purchase a firearm if they have been convicted or are under "indictment or information" for a felony or certain misdemeanors

If a person has been convicted of a felony or other crime for which a judge may sentence, or could have sentenced the person to more than one year imprisonment, that person may not legally purchase a firearm (unless the crime was a state misdemeanor punishable by imprisonment of two years or less). *See* 18 U.S.C. § 921(a)(20)(B). Likewise, if a person is under "indictment" or "information" for a felony, or any other crime for which a judge may sentence the person to more than one year imprisonment, that person is disqualified from purchasing a firearm. An "indictment" or "information" is a formal accusation of a crime punishable by imprisonment for a term exceeding one year. It is important to point out that the actual sentence received is not the determining factor for disqualification, rather, it is the possible maximum sentence. A person may have only been sentenced to 30 days imprisonment, but if the crime for which they were charged allowed a maximum penalty of five years, then that person is disqualified. *See Schrader v. Holder*, 831 F.Supp.2d 304 (D.D.C. 2011, *aff'd*, 704 F.3d 980 (D.C. Cir. 2013)).

3. What does it mean to be a "fugitive from justice" so as to be disqualified from purchasing a firearm?

A "fugitive from justice" is a person who, after having committed a crime, flees from the jurisdiction of the court where the crime was committed. A fugitive from justice may also be a person who goes into hiding to avoid facing charges for the crime of which he or she is accused. Such individuals are not eligible to purchase or possess firearms.

4. Unlawful users of or persons addicted to drugs are disqualified from purchasing firearms

Federal law is very broad in that it disqualifies persons from the purchase of firearms if they are either users of or addicted to marijuana or any depressant, stimulant, narcotic drug, or any controlled substance. Under federal law, an "addict" is defined as a person who "habitually uses any narcotic so as to endanger the public morals, health, safety, or welfare, or who is so far addicted to the use of narcotic drugs as to have lost the power of self-control with reference to his addiction." 21 U.S.C. § 802(1). However, in using the terms "users of," no such frequency or dependence seems contemplated in the words, nor did Congress give further guidance. Illegal users and addicts are prohibited from purchasing firearms from any person under federal law, and are likewise prohibited from possessing firearms. *See* 18 U.S.C. §§ 922(d) and (g).

5. A person can't legally buy or possess firearms if they are "mentally defective"

What does "mentally defective" mean? A person is considered to have been adjudicated as "mentally defective" if there has been a "determination by a court, board, commission, or other lawful authority that a person, as a result of marked subnormal intelligence, or mental illness, incompetency, condition, or disease: is a danger to himself or others, or lacks the mental capacity to contract or manage his own affairs." The term "mentally defective" includes "a finding of insanity by a court in a criminal case, and those persons found incompetent to stand trial or found not guilty by reason of insanity or lack of mental responsibility." 27 CFR § 478.11.

"Mentally defective" also includes a person who has been committed to a mental institution by a court, board, commission, or other lawful authority, or a commitment to a mental institution involuntarily. The term includes commitment for mental defectiveness or mental illness, and also includes commitment for other reasons, such as drug use. However, it does not include a person in a mental institution for observation or a voluntary admission to a mental institution. Individuals who have been adjudicated as mentally defective are also prohibited from possessing firearms under federal law. *See* 18 U.S.C. § 922(g)(4).

6. A person subject to a restraining order may not purchase or possess a firearm

Under 18 U.S.C. § 922(g)(8), firearms may not be sold to or received by a person subject to a court order that: (a) was issued after a hearing which the person received actual notice of and had an opportunity to participate in; (b) restrains the person from harassing, stalking, or threatening an intimate partner or child of such intimate partner or person, or engaging in other conduct that would place an intimate partner in reasonable fear of bodily injury to the partner or child; and (c) includes a finding that such person represents a credible threat to the physical safety of such intimate partner or child; or by its terms explicitly prohibits the use, attempted use, or threatened use of physical force against such intimate partner or child that a person would reasonably be expected to cause bodily injury. An "intimate partner" of a person is the spouse or former spouse of the person, the parent of a child of the person, or an individual who cohabitates with the person.

7. Domestic violence issues and disqualifications

A person who has ever been convicted of the crime of domestic violence may not purchase or possess firearms under federal law. These restrictions were passed in what is known as the *Violence Against Women Act* in 1994 and amended in 1996. This is an often misunderstood law, and, in fact, the ATF has numerous "Frequently Asked Questions" concerning this disqualification on its website: www.atf.gov. The ATF does a good job of explaining the scope of this subject in their FAQs. Due to the complexity of this issue, the ATF examples are included here:

FREQUENTLY ASKED QUESTION FROM ATF WEBSITE

Q: What is a "misdemeanor crime of domestic violence?"

A: A "misdemeanor crime of domestic violence" means an offense that:

1. is a misdemeanor under federal or State law;
2. has, as an element, the use or attempted use of physical force, or the threatened use of a deadly weapon; and
3. was committed by a current or former spouse, parent, or guardian of the victim, by a person with whom the victim shares a child in common, by a person who is cohabiting with or has cohabited with the victim as a spouse, parent, or guardian, or by a person similarly situated to a spouse, parent, or guardian of the victim.

However, a person is not considered to have been convicted of a misdemeanor crime of domestic violence unless:

1. the person was represented by counsel in the case, or knowingly and intelligently waived the right of counsel in the case; and
2. in the case of a prosecution for which a person was entitled to a jury trial in the jurisdiction in which the case was tried, either-
   1. the case was tried by a jury, or
   2. the person knowingly and intelligently waived the right to have the case tried by a jury, by guilty plea or otherwise.

In addition, a conviction would not be disabling if it has been expunged or set aside, or is an offense for which the person has been pardoned or has had civil rights restored (if the law of the jurisdiction in which the proceedings were held provides for the loss of civil rights upon conviction for such an offense) unless the pardon, expunction, or restoration of civil rights expressly provides that the person may not ship, transport, possess, or receive firearms, and the person is not otherwise prohibited by the law of the jurisdiction in which the proceedings were held from receiving or possessing firearms. 18 U.S.C. 921 (a)(33), 27 CFR 478.11.

Editor's note: A significant number of people make the mistake of overlooking or forgetting about a court issue or family law judicial proceeding. However, if you meet the above criteria, you are federally disqualified from possessing a firearm. The fact that it may have happened a long time ago, or that you did not understand the ramifications, is legally irrelevant.

Q: What is the effective date of this disability?

A: The law was effective September 30, 1996. However, the prohibition applies to persons convicted of such misdemeanors at any time, even if the conviction occurred prior to the law's effective date.

Editor's note: For those wondering why this is not an unconstitutional *ex-post facto* law, multiple federal appeals courts have ruled against that argument and the Supreme Court has consistently declined to review any of those cases, effectively accepting the ruling of the courts of appeals and upholding the law.

Q: X was convicted of misdemeanor assault on October 10, 1996, for beating his wife. Assault has as an element the use of physical force, but is not specifically a domestic violence offense. May X lawfully possess firearms or ammunition?

A: No. X may not legally possess firearms or ammunition. 18 U.S.C. 922(g)(9), 27 CFR 478.32(a)(9).

Editor's note: In this situation because X's conviction for assault was against a person in the statute's protected class, the conviction would be, for purposes of firearms purchasing disqualification, a domestic violence conviction.

Q: X was convicted of a misdemeanor crime of domestic violence on September 20, 1996, 10 days before the

effective date of the statute. He possesses a firearm on October 10, 2004. Does X lawfully possess the firearm?

A: No. If a person was convicted of a misdemeanor crime of domestic violence at any time, he or she may not lawfully possess firearms or ammunition on or after September 30, 1996. 18 U.S.C. 922(g)(9), 27 CFR 478.32(a)(9).

Q: In determining whether a conviction in a State court is a "conviction" of a misdemeanor crime of domestic violence, does Federal or State law apply?

A: State law applies. Therefore, if the State does not consider the person convicted, the person would not have the Federal disability. 18 U.S.C. 921(a)(33), 27 CFR 478.11.

Q: Is a person who received "probation before judgment" or some other type of deferred adjudication subject to the disability?

A: What is a conviction is determined by the law of the jurisdiction in which the proceedings were held. If the State law where the proceedings were held does not consider probation before judgment or deferred adjudication to be a conviction, the person would not be subject to the disability. 18 U.S.C. 921(a)(33), 27 CFR 478.11.

Q: What State and local offenses are "misdemeanors" for purposes of 18 U.S.C. 922(d)(9) and (g)(9)?

A: The definition of misdemeanor crime of domestic violence in the GCA (the Gun Control Act of 1968) includes any offense classified as a "misdemeanor" under Federal or State law. In States that do not classify offenses as misdemeanors, the definition includes any State or local offense punishable by imprisonment for a term of 1 year or less or punishable by a fine. For example, if State A has an offense classified as a "domestic violence misdemeanor" that is punishable by up to 5 years imprisonment, it would be a misdemeanor crime of domestic violence. If State B does not characterize offenses as misdemeanors, but has a domestic violence offense that is punishable by no more than 1 year imprisonment, this offense would be a misdemeanor crime of domestic violence. 18 U.S.C.

921(a)(33), 27 CFR 478.11.

Q: Are local criminal ordinances "misdemeanors under State law" for purposes of sections 922(d)(9) and (g)(9)?

A: Yes, assuming a violation of the ordinance meets the definition of "misdemeanor crime of domestic violence" in all other respects.

Q: In order for an offense to qualify as a "misdemeanor crime of domestic violence," does it have to have as an element the relationship part of the definition (e.g., committed by a spouse, parent, or guardian)?

A: No. The "as an element" language in the definition of "misdemeanor crime of domestic violence" only applies to the use of force provision of the statute and not the relationship provision. However, to be disabling, the offense must have been committed by one of the defined parties. **18 U.S.C. 921(a)(33), 27 CFR 478.11**.

Editor's note: This basically means that if illegal force was used against another person, regardless of the language in the underlying statute, if the illegal force was used against a member of the protected class under the statute, federal law will deem this as satisfying the requirements and disqualify the individual from purchasing and possessing firearms.

Q: What should an individual do if he or she has been convicted of a misdemeanor crime of domestic violence?

A: Individuals subject to this disability should immediately dispose of their firearms and ammunition. ATF recommends that such persons transfer their firearms and ammunition to a third party who may lawfully receive and possess them, such as their attorney, a local police agency, or a Federal firearms dealer. The continued possession of firearms and ammunition by persons under this disability is a violation of law and may subject the possessor to criminal penalties. In addition, such firearms and ammunition are subject to seizure and forfeiture. 18 U.S.C. 922(g)(9) and 924(d)(1), 27 CFR 478.152.

Q: Does the disability apply to law enforcement officers?

A: Yes. The Gun Control Act was amended so that employees of government agencies convicted of misdemeanor crimes of domestic violence would not be exempt from disabilities with respect to their receipt or possession of firearms or ammunition. Thus, law enforcement officers and other government officials who have been convicted of a disqualifying misdemeanor may not lawfully possess or receive firearms or ammunition for any purpose, including performance of their official duties. The disability applies to firearms and ammunition issued by government agencies, purchased by government employees for use in performing their official duties, and personal firearms and ammunition possessed by such employees. 18 U.S.C. 922(g)(9) and 925(a)(1), 27 CFR 478.32(a)(9) and 478.141.

Q: Is an individual who has been pardoned, or whose conviction was expunged or set aside, or whose civil rights have been restored, considered convicted of a misdemeanor crime of domestic violence?

A: No, as long as the pardon, expungement, or restoration does not expressly provide that the person may not ship, transport, possess, or receive firearms.

See www.atf.gov.

Practical Legal Tip:

If you or a loved one are going through court proceedings involving family issues and a restraining or protective order is entered in your case, it can suspend your ability to purchase or possess firearms. Language in the court order prohibiting any acts of family violence whether or not family violence actually occurred, make it so the person whom the other impacts is legally barred from the purchase or possession of any firearm. Believe it or not, the Family Courts have the ability to suspend your Second Amendment rights. *-Robert*

8. Illegal aliens or aliens admitted under a non-immigrant visa
Persons who are illegally in the United States may not legally purchase, possess, or transport firearms. Generally, non-immigrant aliens are also prohibited from legally purchasing, possessing, or transporting firearms.

Exceptions for nonimmigrant aliens
However, a nonimmigrant alien who has been admitted under a non-immigrant visa is not prohibited from purchasing, receiving, or possessing a firearm if the person falls within one of the following exceptions:

(1) if the person was admitted to the United States for lawful hunting or sporting purposes or is in possession of a hunting license or permit lawfully issued in the United States;
(2) if the person is an official representative of a foreign government who is accredited to the United States Government or the Government's mission to an

international organization having its headquarters in the United States;

(3) if the person is an official representative of a foreign government who is en route to or from another county to which that alien is accredited;

(4) if the person is an official of a foreign government or a distinguished foreign visitor who has been so designated by the Department of State;

(5) if the person is a foreign law enforcement officer of a friendly foreign government entering the United States on official law enforcement business;

(6) if the person has received a waiver from the prohibition from the Attorney General of the United States.

See 18 U.S.C. § 922(y).

III. Oklahoma law disqualifications: who cannot buy a firearm under Oklahoma law?

As mentioned earlier, Oklahoma has restrictions on the sale, transfer, and possession of firearms that are separate and distinct from the federal restrictions. If a person runs afoul of the law, they could potentially face prosecution in both state and federal court.

A. Oklahoma law disqualifications for "purchasing" a firearm

The disqualifications for purchasing firearms under Oklahoma law are contained in the Self-Defense Act of the Oklahoma Statutes and apply to all firearms transactions in Oklahoma. Sections 1273, 1289.10, and 1289.12 of Title 21 make it a crime for a person:

(1) to knowingly sell, trade, give, transmit or otherwise cause the transfer of rifles, shotguns or pistols to any convicted felon or an adjudicated delinquent;

(2) to sell or give a firearm to any child (under the age of 18);

(3) to knowingly transmit, transfer, sell, lend or furnish any shotgun, rifle or pistol to any person who is under an adjudication of mental incompetency, or to any person who is mentally deficient or of unsound mind.

If a person falls under any of the categories (*see* full explanations below) listed in the foregoing sections, Oklahoma law makes it illegal for a person to sell, transfer, or give the other person a firearm.

B. Oklahoma law disqualifications for "possessing" firearms

Similar to the disqualifications for purchasing firearms, the Oklahoma Self-Defense Act also includes prohibitions on the possession of firearms. These prohibitions on possession are specifically found in 21 O.S. §§ 1283, 1289.9, 1273, 1278, and include:

(1) persons convicted of a felony, or an adjudicated delinquent;
(2) persons under the influence of alcohol or drugs;
(3) persons under the age of 18;
(4) any person in this state who carries or wears any deadly weapons or dangerous instrument whatsoever with the intent or for the avowed purpose of unlawfully injuring another person;
(5) any person who is under an adjudication of mental incompetency.

Note: even though a person may not be disqualified from possession of a firearm under state law, that person may nevertheless still be disqualified to possess a firearm under federal law.

Example:

Scott was convicted of a domestic abuse misdemeanor for family violence in 1992. He has a Smith & Wesson .357 Magnum in his nightstand for self-defense.

Under Oklahoma law, Scott may be in legal possession of his firearm because his conviction was a misdemeanor and misdemeanors do not disqualify him from possessing or owning a firearm. However, if push-comes-to-shove and the Feds ever care, Scott is in unlawful possession of a firearm under 18

U.S.C. § 922(g)(9) and 27 CFR § 478.32(a)(9), regardless of how legal he might be under state law.

C. Understanding who is disqualified under Oklahoma law

1. How does a seller "know" a person has been convicted as a felon?

Under 21 O.S. § 1289.12, a person is prohibited from knowingly selling a firearm to another person when the seller knows that the buyer is a convicted felon. Let's take a look at a couple of examples to highlight the difficulties a seller can face.

The issue of knowledge as it relates to the law can be a mine-field to navigate. Under the law, whenever a statute prohibits a person from doing any certain thing because they "know" it is tantamount to *actual knowledge*. *See State v. Farthing*, 328 P.3d 1208 (Okla. Crim. App. 2014), where the legislature prohibited convicted felons from possessing all firearms. In fact, 21 O.S. § 96 states that "the term 'knowingly,' when so applied, imports only a knowledge that the facts exist which bring the act or omission within the provisions of this code. It does not require any knowledge of the unlawfulness of such act or omission." A person's knowledge can only be established by the facts of each incident. The Oklahoma Uniform Jury Instructions define "knowingly" for weapons offenses as being personally aware of the facts. *See Jones v. State*, 899 P.2d 635, 651 (Okla. Crim. App. 1995).

Example:

> *Tim arranges to sell a handgun to Bob. When Bob arrives at the pre-arranged meeting location to conduct the transaction, Bob inspects the handgun and, without humor, tells Tim, "Ever since I did that 10-year stretch at Big Mac, nobody will sell me a gun!"*

Can Tim legally sell his handgun to Bob? No. Bob has clearly communicated that he was convicted of a felony and that he could not buy a gun elsewhere.

Example:

Alex arranges to sell a hunting rifle to Jim, a man he met briefly at a gun show a couple of weeks prior. When Jim comes over to buy the rifle, he remarks while examining the firearm, "Boy, it'd sure be great to get on my friend's land sometime and shoot some deer, I just got out of the slammer for drugs, my appeal was good, great lawyer and my conviction was reversed."

In this example, does Alex have actual knowledge that Jim is a convicted felon? No, he only has an idea that Jim was in trouble, but now Jim's conviction was reversed. He does not know if the drug charge was a felony or if there were companion cases, or if Jim is just talking big. With only this information in hand, it would not be illegal for Alex to sell the rifle to Jim. Ultimately, what a seller did or did not know can only be established by looking at the totality of the circumstances and may ultimately be decided by a jury in court.

2. What does Oklahoma law define as a "child" for the purpose of selling a firearm?

A "child" refers to any person who is under 18 years of age. *See* age discussion under Section I(D) of this Chapter. 21 O.S. § 1273.

3. A person may not sell a firearm to a "mentally incompetent person"

A person may not, knowingly, sell a firearm to any person under an adjudication of mental incompetency.

What is an "adjudication of mental incompetency?"

21 O.S. § 1289.10 provides the prohibition of selling a firearm to a person adjudicated to be mentally incompetent. The case of *In re Guardianship of Deere,* 708 P.2d 1123 (Okla. 1985), discusses the rights lost by a person adjudicated to be an

incompetent person. The appellate court states, "One of the historic liberties which is protected by the due process clauses of the Constitution of the United States and the State of Oklahoma is the right to be free from, and to obtain judicial relief for, unjustified intrusions on personal security. Appointment of a guardian results in a massive curtailment of liberty, and it may also engender adverse social consequences. The guardian becomes the custodian of the person, estate and business affairs of the ward; the guardian dictates the ward's residence; the ward's freedom to travel is curtailed; and the ward's legal relationship with other persons is limited. The ward suffers numerous statutory disabilities. He/she loses the right to: remain licensed to practice a profession; marry; refuse medical treatment; possess a driver's license; own or possess firearms; and remain registered to vote."

4. Similarities in federal and Oklahoma law concerning convicted felons possessing firearms
Under federal law, a person convicted of a felony is prohibited from possessing firearms. Oklahoma law has similar restrictions. A convicted felon, absent a governor's pardon, cannot possess a firearm.

5. Will my juvenile record prevent me from purchasing and possessing a firearm?
Generally, if any person, including a juvenile, has been convicted of a crime which carries a punishment of imprisonment for more than one year, then that person will not be permitted to purchase a firearm under either federal or Oklahoma law unless their firearm rights are restored. *See* 18 U.S.C. § 922(g); and *United States v. Walters*, 359 F.3d 340 (4th Cir. 2004).

IV. Understanding "private sales" laws
A. What are the legal restrictions on "private sales" of firearms?
Private individuals may legally buy, sell, gift, or otherwise transfer firearms to another private individual in Oklahoma. However, when doing so, careful attention needs to be paid to

not violate the laws regulating these transactions. So what are the legal restrictions? First, the ATF website has an informative pamphlet entitled "Best Practices: Transfers of Firearms by Private Sellers" located on its website. This pamphlet should be a must-read before entering into a "private sales" transaction involving a firearm. So what are the rules in Oklahoma regarding private sales?

1. Residency requirements

In order for the private sale of a firearm to be legal in Oklahoma, both parties must reside in the same state. This means, for our purposes, that both the buyer and seller of the firearm must be Oklahoma residents. Similarly, under federal law, an unlicensed (non-dealer) may only "transfer" a firearm to another unlicensed person in the same state. This means that if a person is a resident of Oklahoma, federal law prohibits the person from directly (not through a dealer) selling or transferring the firearm to a resident of another state. Federal law makes these transactions illegal from both the buyer/transferee and seller/transferor perspective. It is illegal for a private individual to transport into or receive within his own state a firearm which was purchased in another state from a private seller. *See* 18 U.S.C. § 922(a)(3). Likewise, it is illegal for a private seller to sell or deliver a firearm to an individual whom the private seller knows or has reason to believe is not a resident of the seller's state. *See* 18 U.S.C. § 922(a)(5).

Example:

Bob is visiting his best friend from high school, Jim. Ten years ago after high school was over, Bob moved to Nebraska from Oklahoma. One night, Bob and Jim decide to go to the shooting range during Bob's trip, and Bob borrows one of Jim's handguns. After shooting at the range, impressed with both the feel and action of Jim's handgun, Bob asks Jim if he could buy it from him. Since they've been friends for so many years, Jim says yes, and even offers him a good price for the transaction. Before leaving to go home to Nebraska, Bob pays Jim and packs his new handgun.

Has Jim committed a crime in selling the handgun to Bob? Has Bob committed a crime in purchasing the handgun from Jim? The answer to both questions is yes! Under federal law, Bob is not allowed to privately purchase a handgun in another state and transport it back to his home state. Likewise, Jim is not allowed to sell a firearm legally to a person he knows lives in another state. In this example, both Bob and Jim know that Bob is not an Oklahoma resident—the place where Jim has sold his firearm. Bob has committed the crime of willful receipt of a firearm from out-of-state by an unlicensed person while Jim has committed the federal crime of willful sale of a firearm to an out-of-state resident. *See* 18 U.S.C. § 924(a)(1)(D). The penalties for these crimes include jail time up to 5 years and/or a fine of $250,000!

What if the situation is less obvious? Let's take a look at an example where "reasonable cause to believe" comes into play.

Example:

Frank, an Oklahoma resident, recently posted his Glock 19 for sale on an internet message board in Oklahoma. Frank receives an email from a person named Ted who would like to buy the handgun. Frank and Ted agree, via email, on a purchase price and arrange to meet at a place in Oklahoma one week later to facilitate the transfer. When Ted pulls up in his 1978 Ford LTD Wagon, Frank notices the car's Tennessee license plates. Nevertheless, Frank shrugs and sells Ted the gun anyway without going through any of the formalities of a bill-of-sale, or asking for identification. Two weeks later, Frank finds himself at an FBI field office in Oklahoma City answering questions about a shooting that took place with his (former) Glock 19.

Is Frank in trouble? It is highly likely. Although Frank is not the center of the shooting investigation, Frank is probably the center of an investigation for illegally selling the firearm to an out-of-state resident under federal law.

2. Private sales: don't knowingly sell to the "wrong" people

A private individual may sell a firearm to a private buyer in the same state so long as the seller does not know or have reasonable cause to believe that the person purchasing the firearm is prohibited from possessing or receiving a firearm under federal or state law. *See* 18 U.S.C. § 922(d). Also, *see* discussion in the previous sections on "disqualifications."

Example:

Gordon and Josh are friends and Josh tells Gordon that he has just attempted to buy a gun from a local FFL and that he was denied because he was disqualified for some reason under federal law (something about a conviction or drug use or psychiatric problems—Josh was too mad to remember!). Gordon says, "no problem, I'll just sell you one of mine," and he does.

Gordon has just committed a federal and state crime, because he knew (or at least had reasonable cause to believe) that Josh was prohibited from purchasing a firearm under the law. *See* our earlier discussion concerning disqualifications.

B. How does the law determine a person's residence when buying or selling a firearm?

1. Individuals with one residence

For the purpose of firearms purchases, the person's state of residence is the state in which the person is present and where the individual has an intention of making a home. 27 CFR § 478.11.

2. What if a person maintains a home in two states?

If a person maintains a home in two (or more) states and resides in those states for periods of the year, he or she may, during the period of time the person actually resides in a particular state, purchase a firearm in that state. However, simply owning property in another state does not qualify a person as a resident of that state so as to purchase a firearm in that state. To meet the residency requirements, a person must actually maintain a home in a state which includes an intention to make a particular state a residence. *See* 27 CFR § 478.11. This issue may ultimately be a fact question with evidence of residency being things like a driver's license, insurance records, recurring expenses in the state, as well as other things related to making a particular state a person's residence.

3. Members of the Armed Forces

A member of the Armed Forces on active duty is a resident of the state in which his or her permanent duty station is located. If a member of the Armed Forces maintains a home in one state and the member's permanent duty station is in a nearby state to which he or she commutes each day, then the member has two states of residence and may purchase a firearm in either the state where the duty station is located or the state where the home is maintained. *See* 18 U.S.C. § 921(b). See also ATF FAQs on residency at www.atf.gov.

4. Nonimmigrant aliens

Persons who are legally present in the United States are residents of the state in which they reside and where they intend to make a home. Such persons, provided they meet all other requirements and are not otherwise prohibited from purchasing a firearm are lawfully permitted to purchase a firearm.

C. Suggestion on how to document a private firearms sale

Protect yourself! This is practical advice that should not be ignored. If you engage in the private sale of a firearm, here are some practical tips:

- Ask for identification whether you are the buyer/transferee or seller/transferor to establish residency;
- Get and/or give a "bill of sale" for the transfer and keep a copy—identify the firearm including make, model, and serial number, as well as the date and place of transfer;
- Put the residency information on the "bill of sale" including names, addresses, and phone numbers;
- Do not sell or transfer a firearm or ammunition if you think the person may not be permitted or is prohibited from receiving the firearm.

Why do this? Not only will it help establish residency, but if you unfortunately happen to buy or sell a firearm that was previously used in a crime, or if you sell or transfer a gun that is later used in a crime, you want to be able to establish when you did and did not own or possess the firearm.

Further, as a matter of good course, if you are a seller or transferor in a private sale, you might ask whether there is any reason the buyer/transferee cannot own a firearm. Why? So that if there is an issue later, you can at a minimum say that you had no reason to know the buyer could not legally possess firearms. However, do not overlook behavior that may indicate the buyer is not telling you the truth, because law enforcement will not overlook facts that show you did know, or should have had reasonable cause to believe that the buyer/transferee could not own a firearm at the time of the transfer if a legal issue arises later.

V. Buying, selling, and transferring through an FFL

A. Basic procedures

Persons purchasing firearms through dealers must comply with all legal requirements imposed by federal law. These include both paperwork, and appropriate background checks or screenings to ensure that the purchaser is not prohibited from the purchase or possession of a firearm under federal law.

When purchasing through a dealer, the first thing a prospective buyer will do is select a firearm. Once a selection has been made, the prospective purchaser is required to show proper identification and complete ATF Form 4473. This form requires the applicant, under penalty of law, to provide accurate identifying information, as well as answer certain questions in order to establish whether a person may legally purchase a firearm. The information provided on Form 4473 is then provided to the National Instant Criminal Background Check System (NICS) for processing and approval in order to proceed with the transfer (however, no NICS background may be required if the transferee is legally exempt for reasons such as possessing a state-issued firearms license). Some states issue a firearms dealer license; however, Oklahoma does not require firearms dealers to obtain a state license. An FFL dealer can submit the check to NICS either by telephone or through the online website and only after the FFL completes all of these steps successfully is a purchaser/transferee allowed to take possession of the firearm.

B. What is Form 4473?

ATF Form 4473 is the ATF's form known as a Firearms Transaction Record which must be completed when a person purchases a firearm from an FFL. *See* 27 CFR § 478.124. Form 4473 requires the applicant to provide their name, address, birth date, state of residence, and other information including government issued photo identification. The form also contains information blanks to be filled-in including the NICS background check transaction number, the make, model, and serial number of the firearm to be purchased, and a series of questions that a person must answer. *See* 27 CFR § 478.124(c). This series of questions and the corresponding answers help determine a purchaser's eligibility under federal law to purchase a firearm. Once the form is completed, the prospective purchaser will sign the form and attest that the information provided thereon is truthful and accurate under penalty of federal law. This means that if you lie or make false statements on this form, the Feds can and will prosecute you for a crime!

Likewise, the dealer must also sign Form 4473 and retain it for at least 20 years. The ATF is permitted to inspect, as well as receive a copy of Form 4473 from the dealer both during audits and during the course of a criminal investigation. The 4473 records must be surrendered to the Bureau of Alcohol, Tobacco, Firearms and Explosives in the event the FFL dealer retires or ceases business.

C. How are background checks administered when purchasing a firearm?

1. NICS: National Instant Criminal Background Check System

Background checks by dealers when transferring firearms are completed through the National Instant Criminal Background Check System or NICS, if required, prior to the transfer of a firearm from an FFL dealer to a non-dealer. When the prospective purchaser/transferee's information is given to NICS, the system will check the applicant against at least three different databases containing various types of records. Applicants are checked against the records maintained by the Interstate Identification Index (III) which contains criminal history records, the National Crime Information Center (NCIC) which contains records including warrants and protective orders, as well as the NICS Index which contains records of individuals who are prohibited from purchasing or possessing firearms under either federal or state law. In addition, if the applicant is not a United States Citizen, the application is processed for an Immigration Alien Query (IAQ) through the Department of Homeland Security's Immigration and Customs Enforcement Division.

2. Responses from NICS

NICS responses to background checks come in three basic forms: proceed, delay, or deny. The "proceed" response allows for the transfer to be completed. The "delay" response means that the transfer may not legally proceed. If the dealer receives a response of "delay," NICS has three business days to research the applicant further. If the dealer has not received notice the transfer is denied after three business days, then the transfer may proceed. "Deny" means the transfer does not take place; a transferee's options after a "deny" are discussed below.

3. *What transactions require background checks?*

A background check is required before each and every sale or other transfer of a firearm from an FFL to a non-licensee unless an exception is provided under the law. For every transaction that requires a background check, the purchaser/transferee must also complete ATF Form 4473. This includes:

- The sale or trade of a firearm;
- The return of a consigned firearm;
- The redemption of a pawned firearm;
- The loan or rental of a firearm for use off of an FFL's licensed premises;
- Any other non-exempt transfer of a firearm.

4. *What transactions do not require a background check?*

A background check is not required under the following circumstances:

- The sale or transfer of a firearm where the transferee presents a valid state permit/license that allows the transferee to carry a firearm (for example, a Handgun License) from the state where the FFL is located and the state permit/license is recognized by the ATF as a qualifying alternative to the background check requirement;
- The transfer of a firearm from one FFL to another FFL;
- The return of a repaired firearm to the person from whom it was received;
- The sale of a firearm to a law enforcement agency or a law enforcement officer for official duties if the transaction meets the specific

requirements of 27 CFR § 478.134 including providing a signed certification from a person in authority on agency letterhead stating that the officer will use the firearm in official duties and where a records check reveals the officer does not have any misdemeanor convictions for domestic violence;

- The transfer of a replacement firearm of the same kind and type to the person from whom a firearm was received;
- The transfer of a firearm that is subject to the National Firearms Act if the transfer was pre-approved by the ATF.

Note: an Oklahoma handgun license currently does not qualify as an alternative to the NICS background check requirement. A complete permit chart for all states is available on the ATF's website at www.atf.gov.

Practical Legal Tip:

Thinking about buying a gun on behalf of your buddy? Not a good idea! One of the purposes of ATF Form 4473 is to conduct a background check on individuals who want to purchase firearms in order to make sure they are legally allowed to do so. Acting as a "straw man" by purchasing it for your buddy circumvents this process and is a crime. *–Robert*

5. If a person buys multiple handguns, a dealer must report that person to the ATF

Under federal law, FFLs are required to report to the ATF any sale or transfer of two or more pistols, revolvers, or any combination of pistols and revolvers totaling two or more to an unlicensed (non-FFL) individual that takes place at one time or during any five consecutive business days. This report is made to the ATF on Form 3310.4 and is completed in triplicate with the original copy sent to the ATF, one sent to the designated State police or local law enforcement agency in the jurisdiction where the sale took place, and one retained by the dealer and held for no less than five years.

6. FFLs must report persons who purchase more than one rifle in southwest border states

In Texas, Arizona, New Mexico, and California, dealers are required to report the sale or other transfer of more than one semiautomatic rifle capable of accepting a detachable magazine and with a caliber greater than .22 (including .223 caliber/5.56 millimeter) to an unlicensed person at one time or during any five consecutive business days. *See* 18 U.S.C. § 923(g)(3)(A). This report is made via ATF Form 3310.12 and must be reported no later than the close of business on the day the multiple sale or other disposition took place. This requirement includes (but is not limited to) purchases of popular semiautomatic rifles such as AR-15s, AK-47s, Ruger Mini-14s, and Tavor bullpup rifles.

VI. What if I'm denied the right to purchase a firearm?

A. If I am denied the right to purchase, how do I appeal?

Persons who believe they have been erroneously denied or delayed a firearm transfer based on a match to a record returned by the NICS may request an appeal of their "deny" or "delay" decision. All appeal inquiries must be submitted to the NICS Section's Appeal Service Team (AST) in writing, either online or via mail on the FBI's website at www.fbi.gov. An appellant must provide their complete name, complete mailing address, and NICS Transaction Number. For persons appealing a delayed transaction, a fingerprint card is required and must be submitted with the appeal, although the fingerprint card is recommended on appeals for denied applications. This may seem counter-intuitive, but it is required per the FBI's website.

B. What if I keep getting erroneously delayed or denied when I am attempting to buy a firearm?

Apply for a PIN (personal identification number) that is designed to solve this issue. Some individuals may have a name which is common enough (or happens to be flagged for other reasons) that it causes undue delays or denials in the background check verification process through NICS. For that reason, NICS maintains the Voluntary Appeal File database (VAF) which allows any applicant to apply by submitting an appeal request and then obtain a UPIN or Unique Personal Identification Number. A person who has been cleared through the VAF and receives a UPIN will then be able to use their UPIN when completing Form 4473 in order to help avoid further erroneous denials or extended delays. A person can obtain a UPIN by following the procedures outlined on the FBI's website at www.fbi.gov.

VII. Additional considerations in firearms purchasing and possession laws

A. How can I legally purchase a firearm from someone in another state?

Any individual who wishes to purchase a firearm from a person who lives in another state must complete the transaction through an FFL. Sellers or transferors are legally authorized to facilitate a private transaction or transfer by shipping the firearm to the purchaser's FFL in the recipient/buyer's state, where the FFL will complete the transfer process. It is a federal crime to sell or transfer a firearm between persons who are residents of different states, or where a transfer takes place in a state other than the transferee/transferor's singular state of residence.

B. Can I purchase firearms on the Internet?

Yes. However, all legal requirements for a transfer must be followed. If the buyer and seller are both residents of Oklahoma, then the two may lawfully conduct a private sale so long as all other legal issues are satisfied (*see* our earlier discussion on disqualifications to purchasing and possessing firearms in this chapter). However, if buyer and seller are not residents of the same state, the transaction can only be legally facilitated through the intervention of an FFL.

C. Shipping firearms

1. Can I ship my firearm through the postal service?

Long guns: yes. Handguns: no. However, under federal law, a non-licensed individual may not transfer (and this would include shipping to someone) a firearm to a non-licensed resident (non-FFL) of another state. However, a non-licensed individual may mail a long gun to a resident of his or her own state, and they may also mail a long gun to an FFL of another state. To that end, the USPS recommends that long guns be mailed via registered mail and that the packaging used to mail the long gun be ambiguous so as to not identify the contents. Handguns are not allowed to be mailed. *See* 18 U.S.C. §§ 1715, 922(a)(3), 922(a)(5), and 922(a)(2)(A). Rather, handguns must be shipped using a common or contract carrier (*e.g.*, UPS or FedEx).

2. Shipping handguns and other firearms through a common or contract carrier

Under federal law, a non-licensed individual may ship a firearm (including a handgun) by a common or contract carrier (*i.e.*, UPS or FedEx) to a resident of his or her own state, or to a licensed individual (FFL) in another state. However, it is illegal to ship any firearm to a non-FFL in another state. It is a requirement that the carrier be notified that the shipment contains a firearm, however, carriers are prohibited from requiring any identifying marks on the package which may be used to identify the contents as containing a firearm. *See* 18 U.S.C. §§ 922(a)(2)(A), 922(a)(3), 922(a)(5), 922(e), 27 CFR 478.30 and 478.31.

D. Can I ship my firearm to myself for use in another state?

Yes. In accordance with the law as described in the preceding section, a person may ship a firearm to himself or herself in care of another person in another state where he or she intends to hunt or engage in other lawful activity. The package should be addressed to the owner and persons other than the owner should not open the package and take possession of the firearm.

E. If I am moving out of Oklahoma, may I have movers move my firearms?
Yes, a person who lawfully possesses firearms may transport or ship the firearms interstate when changing the person's state of residence so long as the person complies with the requirements for shipping and transporting firearms as outlined earlier. *See* 18 U.S.C. § 922(e) and 27 CFR § 478.31. However, certain NFA items such as destructive devices, machine guns, short-barreled shotguns or rifles, and so forth, require approval from the ATF before they can be moved interstate. *See* 18 U.S.C. § 922(a)(4) and 27 CFR § 478.28. It is important that the person seeking to move the firearms also check state and local laws where the firearms will be relocated to ensure that the movement of the firearms into the new state does not violate any state law or local ordinance.

F. May I loan my firearm to another person?
There is no prohibition on loaning a firearm to another person, so long as the person receiving the firearm may lawfully possess one.

G. What happens to my firearms when I die?
Depending on the manner in which a person leaves his or her estate behind, firearms may be bequeathed in a customary manner like other personal property. However, firearms held in an estate are still subject to the laws of transfer and possession. This careful consideration needs to be given in estate planning with consideration for firearms law of both the jurisdiction in which the estate is located as well as consideration of who is to receive the firearms.

VIII. Ammunition: the law of purchasing and possession

A. Who is legally prohibited from purchasing ammunition under federal law?

Under federal law, there are six primary situations where a person is prohibited from buying, selling, or possessing ammunition (beyond armor-piercing ammunition which was discussed in Chapter 2).

1. Under 18 U.S.C. § 922(b)(1), it is unlawful for a person to sell long gun ammunition to a person under the age of 18;
2. Under 18 U.S.C. § 922(b)(1), it is unlawful for a person to sell handgun ammunition to a person under the age of 21;
3. Under 18 U.S.C. § 922(x)(2)(B), it is unlawful for a juvenile to possess handgun ammunition;
4. Under 18 U.S.C. § 922(d), it is unlawful to sell ammunition to a person who is prohibited from purchasing firearms;
5. Under 18 U.S.C. § 922(g), it is unlawful for a person who is disqualified from purchasing or possessing firearms to possess firearm ammunition if such ammunition has moved in interstate commerce (which is nearly all ammunition); and
6. Under 18 U.S.C. § 922(h), it is unlawful for a person who is employed by a person who is disqualified from purchasing or possessing ammunition to possess or transport ammunition for the disqualified individual.

For the statutes that involve juveniles, there are a couple of notable exceptions to the law: first, the law against selling handgun ammunition to a juvenile and possession of handgun ammunition by a juvenile does not apply to a temporary transfer of ammunition to a juvenile or to the possession or use of ammunition by a juvenile if the handgun and ammunition are possessed and used by the juvenile in the course of employment, in the course of ranching or farming-related activities at the residence of the juvenile (or on property used for ranching or farming at which the juvenile, with the permission of the property owner or lessee, is performing activities related to the operation of the farm or ranch), target practice, hunting, or a course of instruction in the safe and lawful use of a handgun. The law also does not apply to the temporary transfer to or use of ammunition by a juvenile if the juvenile has been provided with prior written consent by his or her parent or guardian who is not prohibited by federal, state, or local law from possessing firearms. *See* 18 U.S.C. § 922(x)(3).

Additionally, juveniles who (1) are members of the Armed Forces of the United States or the National Guard who possesses or are armed with a handgun in the line of duty, (2) receive ammunition by inheritance, or (3) possess ammunition in the course of self-defense or defense of others are permitted to possess ammunition.

B. When is a person prohibited from purchasing or possessing ammunition under Oklahoma law?

Oklahoma law provides for occasions where the sale/possession of ammunition is prohibited under Title 21:

1. § 1289.19: prohibits/restricts body armor piercing bullets coated with fluorocarbon;
2. § 1289.20: except for the purpose of public safety or national security, it shall be unlawful to manufacture, import, advertise for sale or sell restricted bullets defined in §1289.19;
3. §1289.21: it shall be unlawful for any person to possess, carry upon his person, use or attempt to use against another person any restricted bullet as defined in § 1289.19 of this title;
4. § 1289.6: any concealed or unconcealed handgun when carried in a manner authorized by the provisions of the Oklahoma Self-Defense Act and when loaded with any ammunition which is either a restricted bullet as defined by § 1289.19 of this title or is larger than .45 caliber or is otherwise prohibited by law shall be deemed a prohibited weapon for purposes of the Oklahoma Self-Defense Act.

C. Can a person be disqualified from purchasing ammunition if they are disqualified from purchasing firearms?

Yes, under federal law. Under 18 U.S.C. § 922(g) it is unlawful for a person who is disqualified from purchasing or possessing firearms if the ammunition has moved in interstate commerce. Since nearly all ammunition or ammunition components move through interstate commerce in one form or another, this disqualification includes essentially all ammunition. There is no disqualification under Oklahoma law.

D. Can a person purchase ammunition that is labeled "law enforcement use only"?

Yes. Although some handgun ammunition is sold with a label "law enforcement use," such a label has no legal meaning and is only reflective of a company policy or, viewed more skeptically, as a marketing strategy.

CHAPTER FOUR

WHEN CAN I LEGALLY USE MY GUN: PART I
UNDERSTANDING THE LAW OF JUSTIFICATION
SOME BASIC LEGAL CONCEPTS

I. Ignorance of the law is NO excuse!

Now we start to get into the meat of our discussion: when is it legal to use a gun in self-defense? The purpose of this chapter is to look at the essential, basic legal concepts of the law of when and under what circumstances a person is legally justified in using force or deadly force against other persons or animals. Know when you may legally shoot, because ignorance of the law holds no weight in a courtroom! It is critical for you to know the law so that you are in the best possible situation to preserve your legal rights if you ever need to assert them as a legal defense.

II. Oklahoma gun owners are governed by Title 21 of the Oklahoma Statutes, related statutes, and case law

In Oklahoma, legal justification for the use of non-deadly and deadly force is cited in a number of statutes. Of particular importance to gun owners are the defenses found in a section of Title 21 of the Oklahoma Statutes dealing with justifiable use of deadly force, 21 O.S. § 733 entitled "Justifiable Homicide by any Person" which I cover in detail throughout this book. The full text of relevant statutes of Title 21 are found in the Appendix.

III. To legally use force or deadly force, you must be "justified." What is legal justification?

A. Basic definition of justification: an acceptable legal excuse

The question on everyone's mind is: when is it legal to use force or deadly force against another person? Or, when is it legal to *threaten* to use force or deadly force against another? The answer is: when there is a legal "justification," or defense. A legal justification is a reasonable excuse, acceptable in a court of law for someone's use of non-deadly or deadly force that under different circumstances would be a crime.

Example:

> *Rick is in his neighborhood park playing with his dog when out of nowhere, a pit bull jumps over the fence and charges toward Rick and his dog. Rick draws his handgun and shoots the pit bull.*

The owner of the pit bull heard Rick discharge his firearm in public, a crime under 21 O.S. § 1364, and the owner of the pit bull demanded that Rick be charged with cruelty to animals under 21 O.S. § 1685.

Why will Rick likely be found not guilty of the crimes of discharging a firearm and acts of cruelty to animals? The law is quite clear: *Grizzle v. State*, 707 P.2d 1210, 1212 (Okla. Crim. App. 1985) provides justification/full defense for people threatened by animals:

> "We hold today, therefore, that one is 'privileged to destroy [or injure] an animal for the purpose of defending himself or third persons against harm threatened by the animal, (a) if its actions led him to know or reasonably believe that the animal would inflict such harm and (b) the destruction [or injury] was reasonable in view of the gravity of the harm threatened, and (c) the person reasonably believed the harm could only be prevented by immediate destruction [or injury] of the animal.'" Grizzle, at 1212.

Rick was legally justified in shooting the animal! That is, the law will likely say the excuse for discharging the firearm in public and shooting the animal – protecting himself and his dog – makes Rick's actions reasonable and, therefore, legally justified.

Practical Legal Tip:

A defense to prosecution is not the same as a bar to prosecution. A "bar to prosecution" is where a person can't be prosecuted for engaging in certain conduct, whereas a "defense to prosecution" allows prosecution for the conduct, but offers defendants a justification that must be demonstrated with evidence in court. *–Robert*

B. Basic requirement: you must admit your action

In order to raise the defense of justification in court, a person is required to admit all of the elements of the crime for which they are charged. Then the person must present "sufficient evidence" of justification before the judge will give the jury an instruction that "a person is legally justified to use force if..." The "sufficient evidence" requirement is that the evidence offered must be legally tenable, admissible under the law of evidence, and related to the incident of self-defense at issue. In plain English, a person will not be allowed to say "I didn't do it, but if I did do it, I was justified!" In court the Defendant must admit the underlying elements of the charge.

Example:

> *Jane is walking home one night, when a man jumps out of the bushes and demands her purse. Jane pulls out her handgun and points it at the man, who then runs away. Unfortunately, Jane does not call the police, but the criminal immediately does, reporting a crazy woman threatening him with a gun which caused him to suffer fear and intimidation. Jane ends up charged with pointing a firearm, a violation of 21 O.S. § 1289.16, even though Jane was the victim of an attempted robbery.*

Pointing a firearm to prevent a robbery is a legally justified act in Oklahoma. If Jane's case goes to trial, in order to use self-defense, Jane's attorney must offer this legal justification for Jane committing the alleged crime of "Pointing a Firearm." Pointing a firearm at a person without the purpose of engendering fear in the victim is a misdemeanor under 21 O.S. § 1279; pointing a firearm at a person for the purpose of threatening, or with malice, or for the purpose of injuring that results in the victim expressing fear due to intimidation, will result in a charge of a felony under 21 O.S. § 1289.16. In order to use the legal justification of self-defense, Jane must admit in court that she pulled her handgun and pointed it at the robber in order to prevent the commission of the forcible felony of robbery.

On the other hand, if Jane does not admit to the elements of pointing a firearm, and denies that she pointed the firearm, she will not be allowed to use self-defense under 21 O.S. §§ 1279 or 1289.16 depending on the crime she is charged with. Legal justification is, therefore, literally the law of "Yes, I did it, BUT…!"

Section 733 of Title 21 is the statute authorizing the use of deadly force, by an individual, when confronted with the threat of death or great bodily harm or when preventing a forcible felony. Section 733 states the phrase forcible felony means any felony which involves the use or threat of physical force or violence against any person. Some felonies, like grand theft, will not qualify, but robbery, burglary, rape, aggravated assault and other violent felonies will qualify as forcible felonies.

Practical Legal Tip:

A jury instruction is a statement made by the judge to the jury informing them of the law applicable to the case in general, or some aspect of it. *-Robert*

IV. Categories of force for justification under Title 21

Anytime a person takes physical action against another person, they use force. Title 21 of the Oklahoma Statutes divides the use of force into different levels. Whether or not a use of force was justified under the law often depends on how that force is categorized. These categories, which we will address throughout this book, are: 1) *non-deadly force*, 2) *deadly force*.

A. What if a person uses greater force than the law allows?

If a person uses more force than is "reasonably believed by the jury to be necessary" (*see* section V), that person will not be justified in using excessive force. Therefore, it is important to understand the difference in the levels of force and the circumstances under which the law allows the use of each.

For example, if a person uses deadly force, and the law allows only for the use of non-deadly force, that person will not be justified in the use of the clearly excessive force. If a person uses force when no force is allowed, that use of non-deadly force will not be justified and the court will punish the offender.

Example:

> *Harry Homeowner looks out his window and sees a person standing on his front lawn. Harry yells at the fellow to get off his land. The fellow on the lawn does not respond. Harry rushes out to confront the fellow and demands that he leave Harry's lawn.*

This fellow is now clearly a trespasser! What degree of force may Harry use to remove the trespasser?

The law in 21 O.S. § 643, analyzed and discussed later, will show that Harry is allowed to use reasonable force, short of deadly force, in removing a trespasser. If Harry uses deadly force against the trespasser, he will not be justified and would be guilty of using unreasonable/unlawful force against the trespasser. Ultimately, using the correct degree of force is critical in determining whether a person has committed a crime or a legally justifiable action.

B. What is the legal definition of "non-deadly force"?

Surprisingly, the basic terms "force," as well as "non-deadly force," are not specifically defined in the Oklahoma Statutes. However, "deadly force" *is* defined. Therefore, one may conclude that mere non-deadly force must be something less than deadly force. Even though non-deadly force is not defined, some context can be gained by looking at the instances when non-deadly force can be used.

21 O.S. § 643(3) presents the statutory authorization for use of non-deadly force in self-defense. Although this appears to indicate that a person using force to protect himself is limited to the amount of force "sufficient to prevent" bodily harm, and no more, the Court of Criminal Appeals has interpreted 21 O.S. § 643(3) to permit a person to use as much force as reasonably appears necessary, even though in reality no force is necessary. Thus, there are possible situations where more force than was actually necessary could be used. Use of non-deadly force is justifiable because the harm defended against does not reasonably arouse fear of death or great bodily harm. The amount of non-deadly force permissible under 21 O.S. § 643(3) must be reasonably related to the amount of force defended against. Hence, as the amount of force defended against becomes greater, the amount of force which may justifiably be used in response becomes greater. *See* OUJI-CR 8-48.

Example:

> *Timmy is being harassed and picked on by a bully, when the bully suddenly clenches his first and takes a swing at Timmy. Timmy ducks the swing and punches the bully in the face.*

The bully's action was a use of non-deadly force. Even though he missed Timmy, the bully placed Timmy in fear of harm. Timmy's reaction of striking the bully was likewise a use of non-deadly force, and as will be discussed later, legally justified when Timmy engaged in conduct which caused harm or a fear of harm to the bully.

C. What is "deadly force?"

The Oklahoma Court of Criminal Appeals defined "deadly force" by holding that deadly force is any force intended or likely to cause death or great bodily harm. *See Gransden v. State,* 158 P. 157 (Okla. Crim. App. 1916).

1. Deadly force does not have to cause death!

On the surface, the legal definition of deadly force seems simple. Force intended or likely to cause death or great bodily harm; however, the meaning of what is and is not deadly force can be legally tricky. A particular action does not necessarily have to result in death to be legally defined as deadly force—it just needs to be *intended or likely* to cause death or great bodily harm. *Note*: great bodily harm is defined as "serious and severe bodily injury. Such injury must be of a greater degree than a mere battery." *See* OUJI-CR 8-12.

> Example:
>
> *Jim is being robbed and beaten by a group of thugs when he manages to draw his handgun and fire it at the biggest, baddest bandit. His shot misses but breaks the group up, causing the robbers to flee.*

In our example, even though the bullet did not kill or even strike the bandits, Jim used deadly force because his conduct fit the legal definition of "intended to cause death or great bodily harm." Thus, death is not a necessary result from the use of deadly force! Almost any object can be used as a weapon in a particular circumstance. Therefore, in this section of the law, the focus is on the object's intended use and not just on the object itself. A cell phone or a bottle may be used as a club, and harmless piece of rope may be fashioned into a noose.

2. "Intended or likely" as a component of deadly force

Deadly force, by its legal definition, occurs when a person takes an action that is *intended* or *likely* to cause death or great bodily harm. This intention to cause great bodily harm or death is called a person's mental state. A prosecutor must prove beyond a reasonable doubt that a Defendant possessed a *mens rea*, or an intentional, particular mental state applicable to a crime, in order to meet the state's burden of proof and convict someone of a crime.

Often a person's intent is easily understood from the circumstances. For example, if a person is the would-be victim of a robbery, and the person resists by pulling his or her gun and firing at the robber, the law will likely find the victim used justifiable deadly force, because the victim of the crime resisted and reasonably used force that the victim intended to cause death or great bodily harm.

The weapon used is not always dispositive evidence of someone's intent to use deadly force. Hammers, toasters, pipes, baseball bats, and almost any other object can "likely cause" great bodily harm or death under a particular circumstance. The case legally turns, then, on how and why the person uses force.

3. "Pointing" as deadly force

A person may only point a firearm if they are entitled to use deadly force under the circumstances. Under 21 O.S. § 1289.16, willfully or without lawful cause pointing a firearm...with the intent to discharge, with malice, or for any purpose of injuring is considered a felony. This would seem to mean that *any* time you point a firearm, it's a felony! Luckily, the law provides that a person may point a firearm under circumstances where they would be entitled to use deadly force, such as "in defense of any person, one's home or property."

D. When is the use of deadly force justified?

Justifiable Homicide by Other Persons: 21 O.S. § 733
Homicide is also justifiable when committed by any person in any of the following cases: when resisting any attempt to murder such person, or to commit any felony upon him, or upon or in any dwelling house in which such person is; when committed in the lawful defense of such person or of another, when the person using force reasonably believes such force is necessary to prevent death or great bodily harm to himself or herself or another or to terminate or prevent the commission of a forcible felony; or when necessarily committed in attempting, by lawful ways and means, to apprehend any person for any felony committed; or in lawfully suppressing any riot; or in lawfully keeping the peace.

Section 733 of Title 21 Oklahoma Statutes says that the use of deadly force is justified when reasonably necessary to protect a person from death or great bodily harm. Thus, if a person threatens deadly force by the pointing of a firearm, it is a use of deadly force which is justified only when it is reasonable to believe such force is necessary to prevent death or great bodily harm.

Example:

> *Billy is walking to his car after work when three individuals with baseball bats confront him in the parking lot and surround him in an aggressive manner. Fearing that they are about to attack him with the bats, Billy draws his gun and clearly demands that they leave him alone, at which point they all flee from the scene.*

Has Billy legally used deadly force by pointing his gun? Yes, according to the analysis in sub-section 3 of section C earlier. Billy's threat and the use of deadly force, by pointing the gun was based upon meeting force with force, including deadly force. The use of deadly force by Billy was excused or justified by the reasonable belief that he needed to protect himself from death or great bodily harm from the strangers threatening him with the baseball bats.

The Oklahoma Court of Criminal Appeals has clarified the term "forcible felony." The language "a forcible felony" is limited to those that involve imminent danger of death or great bodily harm to the other person. 21 O.S. § 733. *See also Mammano v. State*, 333 P.2d 602 (Okla. Crim. App. 1958).

E. Dangers inherent in the use of warning shots

Warning shots get a lot of good folks in legal trouble! Warning shots are commonly portrayed in movies and television as a good idea—and people like to mimic what they see in movies and on TV! Leaving aside all practical issues of whether under a particular set of circumstances a warning shot is a good idea (and experience has taught us that very rarely are they a good idea), what does Oklahoma law say about warning shots?

1. Are warning shots a use of deadly force?

First, the term "warning shot" does not appear in the Oklahoma Statutes. Without clear guidance from statutory law, courts are left to determine if the action of firing a warning shot is to be considered under the use of deadly force standard.

Although the firing of a warning shot is not *per se* legally forbidden, you should be aware that if you fire a warning shot, it is highly likely that your conduct will be judged as using deadly force. This means that a person may only be allowed the legal argument of justification if a warning shot is fired in situations in which deadly force is justified under the law. There are few appellate court cases demonstrating how Oklahoma courts have addressed the issue of warning shots. Every gun owner should be aware that one likely argument a prosecutor may put forth against a defendant at trial is that the simple discharge of a firearm is an action that is capable of causing death or great bodily harm. Such an argument, when successful, will shift the analysis of warning shots into the use of deadly force arena. If the use of force situation is limited to non-deadly force then a warning shot will likely not be justified.

Why is it important whether the law classifies a warning shot as a use of non-deadly force or a use of deadly force, even if no one is injured? Let's take a look at an example.

Example:

Harry Homeowner looks outside during broad daylight and sees a trespasser on his property. Not knowing what the trespasser is doing, Harry grabs his firearm to investigate. Harry confronts the trespasser and demands that he leave the property, but the trespasser ignores Harry. Being both scared and agitated, Harry fires a "warning shot" to get the trespasser's attention and compliance.

Does Harry's discharging his gun fit the definition of the use of deadly force? Likely, yes. Harry very likely may be guilty of a crime and not have a justification available as a defense, because he used a higher degree of force than the law allows. 21 O.S. § 643(3) limits the use of force when a person attempts to protect their real or personal property to non-deadly force. Non-deadly force may be used to protect against a trespass to real or personal property as long as it is limited to the force required to prevent the offense.

"The law affords ample redress for trespasses committed on a man's land, but does not sanction the taking of life to prevent it. The owner may, no doubt, oppose force with force to protect his property from injury or destruction, but not to the extent of taking life, or in excess of the necessity of the case. When he carries resistance to excess and uses more force than is reasonably necessary, he becomes a wrongdoer." *Hendrick v. State*, 73 P.2d 184, 190 (Okla. 1937).

2. Warning shots: "But, I never meant to hurt anyone!"
Going back to our example, assume Harry will say he fired the warning shot, but that he never aimed at or even meant to hit anyone. In fact, assume Harry will say he only shot into the dirt to get the trespasser to leave. How will the law view Harry's "warning shot?"

First, Harry Homeowner was confronted in this example with a mere trespasser and under Oklahoma law as we have seen, a person may legally use force, but not deadly force to remove a trespasser. Therefore, if the "warning shot" that was fired by Harry is legally classified as deadly force under the law, Harry will not be legally justified, and instead, a jury may decide he is guilty of a crime such as shooting with intent to kill if a stray bullet fragment or ricochet hits or touches the trespasser or an innocent bystander. So, the classification between non-deadly force and deadly force is the difference between guilt and innocence in this example.

Now, let us change the example a bit to see how things may get even more complicated.

Example:

> *Harry Homeowner confronts the same trespasser (Tom) as before and fires a warning shot. This time, however, the shot startled Tom out of his zoned state of self-meditation and wandering in which he likes to contemplate the universe. Tom was so deep in his personal world, he didn't realize he had accidentally wandered onto Harry's property. In fact, Tom the trespasser was so deep in meditative strolling and enjoying the Oklahoma air that he didn't even hear Harry's verbal demands, but, the sound of Harry's 30.06 hunting rifle got Tom's full attention! As a result, Tom does exactly what his 25 years of police training have taught him—he draws and fires at Harry,*

> *believing that Harry's shot had meant to end his days of strolling and meditation!*

Where do we start the legal analysis? First, Harry Homeowner is in what Oklahoma legal circles often call a "big mess!" Harry has very likely used unlawful deadly force against a mere trespasser. After Harry's shot, does this turn our absent-minded wandering Tom into a victim who reasonably believes his life is threatened? Does this fact then allow Tom the trespasser some legal justification to return fire, *etc.*?

Continuing the issue, if our wandering Tom Trespasser then returns fire at Harry, is Harry then legally justified in using deadly force to defend himself? Or, because Tom is an accidental trespasser, is Tom required to retreat first before he takes any action? Keep in mind that Harry knows nothing about Tom's meditation or walks—he is just confronted with a trespasser who did not respond to verbal requests, but has now responded to Harry's "warning shot" with muzzle flashes from a pistol. Ultimately, you can see how messy this type of scenario can become, which all started with a well-intentioned "warning shot."

After the dust clears (assuming perfect knowledge), Harry likely used a higher degree of force than the law allows. But who decides if a "warning shot" is just a warning and not a shot at someone that simply missed? Who decides if a response to a situation is reasonable? In the vast majority of cases in Oklahoma, a jury ultimately decides. There are no bright lines on warning shots so be advised that a warning shot is viewed as a use of deadly force whether or not you subjectively intended it to be deadly force, and therefore, should never be used without careful consideration.

V. What does it mean to "reasonably believe force is necessary?"

In Oklahoma, the legal standard for a justified use of deadly force is generally expressed as a person must "reasonably" believe that the use of deadly force was necessary to protect against death or great bodily harm. 21 O.S. § 733.

But what does "reasonable" mean? The answer to this question is how the legal process decides guilt or justification for the use of deadly force. For all gun owners, these concepts are critical.

A. How does the law determine "reasonableness?"

In determining what is reasonable, the law often uses a concept known as the "reasonable person" standard to evaluate a person's conduct. It uses a hypothetical "reasonable person." Who is a reasonable person, and how does he or she act? Ultimately, a reasonable person is whatever a jury says a reasonable person would do under the same or similar circumstances.

The legal analysis behind the reasonable person goes like this: if a person used non-deadly or deadly force, they must act as a reasonable person would have acted under the same or similar circumstances in order to be legally justified! However, if a person fails to act as a reasonable person, their conduct will fall below the acceptable legal standard and will not be justified. The reasonable person standard is the law's attempt to make the concept of reasonableness an objective and measurable test.

Under this standard, the law does not focus on whether you *subjectively* (personally) believed force was reasonable, but whether a "reasonable person" would have considered it reasonable, an objective standard. If the legal system (and ultimately, again, this could be a jury) determines that a reasonable person would have believed that force was necessary to prevent great bodily harm, then you will be found legally justified in using force.

Keep in mind, however, that judges, juries, and prosecutors are simply human beings, and people can have vastly different ideas of how a reasonable person should act under any given circumstances. This is particularly true if asked to decide whether force or deadly force was necessary or not.

Practical Legal Tip:

Throughout this book, we refer to juries making the ultimate determination of fact. There are, however, some limited occasions where a judge makes the determinations. For example, if all parties waive their right to a jury, the Court may conduct what is called a "bench trial." *-Robert*

B. Legal presumptions: stop legal second-guessing

Under certain circumstances, a person's belief in the necessity of force or deadly force will be presumed "reasonable" under 21 O.S. § 1289.25. This legal presumption can be a very powerful legal tool to stop legal second-guessing or "Monday morning quarterbacking" of the amount of force or timing of when the force was used. A jury will be told that if a given set of circumstances exists (*e.g.,* a person is the victim of a home invasion or carjacking), the law will presume "reasonable" a person's belief in the necessity of using any force or deadly force, and that use of force or deadly force would, therefore, be legally justified.

Example:

> *Harry Homeowner is asleep in his house when he hears a noise in his kitchen. Harry enters his kitchen with his .45 drawn and confronts a burglar. Harry fires his weapon and the burglar will burgle no more!*

In this situation, was Harry's use of deadly force in firing his gun necessary, or, more precisely, was Harry's belief that deadly force was necessary reasonable? Did Harry, legally, have to take additional actions before firing in order to have acted reasonably? In Harry's current situation, the law will give Harry a powerful legal presumption that his belief that the use of deadly force was necessary was "reasonable." In Harry's example, 21 O.S. § 1289.25 will provide him with the presumption of "reasonable fear of imminent peril of death or great bodily harm ... when using defensive force that is intended or likely to cause death or great bodily harm to another" because he is a victim of a home invasion in his occupied dwelling or residence. In Oklahoma this presumption will prevent any second-guessing by prosecutors that deadly force was not necessary. This has a practical effect of preventing arguments that a person should have used less force, no force, or retreated first. The legal presumption of "reasonable fear of imminent peril of death or great bodily harm" is a powerful tool in the defense tool box for anyone facing a criminal charge and claiming legal justification.

C. No presumption of reasonableness: prosecutors are allowed to second-guess

As we discussed above, under certain circumstances, the law will presume the reasonableness of a person's belief that force or deadly force is necessary. However, if a person uses non-deadly force or deadly force under circumstances that do not qualify for this presumption, the issue of whether a belief of the necessity to use force or deadly force was or was not reasonable is left to the jury, and prosecutors are allowed to second-guess the reasonableness of the timing and/or degree of force used by a defendant.

Accordingly, when a defendant does not qualify for a legal presumption, a prosecutor has the opportunity to argue that a person's use of force or deadly force was not necessary or reasonable. This allows for arguments in court like "should have de-escalated," "should have used less force," and so forth. In many circumstances (such as situations involving defense of personal property), no legal presumption of reasonable belief is afforded for uses of force or deadly force at all! In all other cases, a jury will decide the issue of the reasonableness of a person's belief and, ultimately, whether or not a person is guilty of a crime.

Practical Legal Tip:

Note: a presumption is not an absolute ticket to victory. A prosecutor may attempt to overcome the presumption with other evidence that shows you did not act in self-defense. *-Robert*

VI: The burden of proof in criminal cases

In criminal cases, the state attorneys or prosecutors have the burden of proof. This means that it is the State's responsibility to present enough evidence to prove the defendant committed a crime. This burden of proof that the prosecutor bears is a standard called "beyond a reasonable doubt." It is the highest level of proof used in the American justice system. The State's job at trial in attempting to prove the defendant's guilt must eliminate any reasonable doubt that the defendant's conduct was justified.

We are now ready to look at under what circumstances Oklahoma law allows a person to use deadly force to protect themselves and others in the next chapter.

Practical Legal Tip:

A word about juries. Juries are not "picked" in Oklahoma. Rather, they are the first twelve people that are not "struck" from the pool of folks called a jury pool. Most of the time, in my opinion, juries get it "right," but after years of practice, some juries' decisions leave you scratching your head... That is why these legal presumptions can be critical. *-Robert*

CHAPTER FIVE

WHEN CAN I LEGALLY USE MY GUN: PART II SELF-DEFENSE AND DEFENSE OF OTHERS UNDERSTANDING WHEN FORCE AND DEADLY FORCE CAN BE LEGALLY USED AGAINST ANOTHER PERSON

I. Introduction and overview

The question of "when can a person legally use deadly force against another person" is of critical importance if you are a legal Oklahoma firearms owner. Although a firearm is nothing more than a tool, it is a tool that by its very nature has the ability to deliver deadly force. Thus, all responsible firearms owners should understand when they are justified in using force and deadly force under the law. Failure to understand the law gets lots of good folks in serious trouble!

> The primary Oklahoma statutes dealing with self-defense and defense of other people are contained in three sections of the Oklahoma Statutes:
> 21 O.S. § 643: Lawful use of force upon another
> 21 O.S. § 733: Justifiable homicide by other persons
> 21 O.S. § 1289.25: Physical or deadly force against intruder

The law of justified self-defense is split between justification for the use of non-deadly force in section 643, justification for the use of deadly force in section 733 and deadly force against an intruder in section 1289.25. Only section 1289.25 contains a legal presumption of reasonableness available under certain circumstances and is considered an extremely powerful tool of persuasion when arguing to the jury whether a use of deadly force was legally justified. The language found in section 1289.25 contains Oklahoma's version of the "Castle Doctrine" and "Stand Your Ground" laws. The Castle Doctrine, as a specific term, is not mentioned in the statute, however, section 1289.25 specifically mentions "Stand Your Ground" in subsection D. Section 733 was amended in 2014, to expand the meaning of the term "third persons" as any member of the public instead of limiting "third persons" to immediate family, servants, masters or mistresses (female version of master). Previously, neighbors, people at the mall, cousins, grandparents, fraternity members, club members and all other third parties were not included.

In Chapter Four, several legal concepts, such as reasonableness and the categorization of force and deadly force were discussed. Those concepts have practical applications in this chapter. In this chapter, we will expand upon these topics to include when a person may be justified in using non-deadly force or deadly force in self-defense, as well as those circumstances when the law specifically prohibits the use of force or deadly force.

II. Self-defense with non-deadly force or deadly force

A. General self-defense justification: no presumption of reasonableness

The primary self-defense statutes in Oklahoma are sections 643, 733, and 1289.25 found in Title 21 of the Annotated Oklahoma Statutes. 21 O.S. § 643(3) lays out the legal requirements for the justified use of force, but not deadly force, for self-defense. This section establishes that a person is legally justified in using force against another "when [it is] committed either by the person about to be injured, or by any other person in such person's aid or defense, in preventing or attempting to prevent an offense against such person, or any trespass or other unlawful interference with real or personal property in such person's lawful possession; provided the force or violence used is not more than sufficient to prevent such offense."

Section 733 establishes the general standard for the justifiable use of deadly force against an aggressor. The statute clearly instructs how a victim of a forcible felony may protect himself/herself or another person from the aggressor's use of deadly force or force perceived in the victim's mind as leading to great bodily harm. When the person uses deadly force for self-defense of himself/herself or on behalf of another person, the use of deadly force will be judged/scrutinized under the reasonable person standard. The question, for the jury will be, "was the use of deadly force reasonable under the circumstances?" 21 O.S. § 733(2) says homicide is justifiable, "When committed in the lawful defense of such person or of another, when the person using force reasonably believes such force is necessary to prevent death or great bodily harm to himself or herself or another or to terminate or prevent the commission of a forcible felony." As discussed in the previous chapter, what a person believes about the presence of deadly force, the necessity to respond with force/deadly force, and whether that belief is reasonable is the difference between justification for homicide, acquittal (not guilty), and no justification for homicide, conviction (guilty).

Who decides whether a Defendant's belief is or is not reasonable? Who decides whether force or deadly force is necessary? Who decides if the degree of force used by someone was reasonable under a particular set of circumstances? The answer to all of these questions is the jury.

Therefore, if a person finds himself or herself facing criminal charges and is claiming self-defense under the general self-defense provisions of sections 643 or 733, the jury will decide if that person's belief was or was not reasonable regarding the Defendant's perceived necessity of using non-deadly force or deadly force.

As can be imagined, this leaves a lot of room for juries to interpret whether the actions of the Defendant, in using non-deadly force or deadly force, were reasonable under the circumstances from the Defendant's point of view. The use of force by the Defendant leaves the door open for legal second-guessing by the prosecutor as to when and how much force was used, including arguments that there was no threat of death or great bodily harm or that the perceived threat of death or great bodily harm was unreasonable. In short the prosecutor will argue that the use of force or deadly force was not "necessary." If the prosecutor convinces a jury that the Defendant used force or deadly force when it was not "reasonable," the Defendant will be found guilty of using unlawful force or deadly force. However, under certain circumstances, section 1289.25 allows a person a powerful additional protection in the form of a legal presumption of reasonableness in their belief that the use of non-deadly or deadly force was immediately necessary. Beyond that, it is possible that section 1289.25 could provide immunity from prosecution!

B. Immunity from prosecution under 21 O.S. § 1289.25(F)

Immunity from Criminal Prosecution and Civil Action:
Oklahoma Statutes Title 21 § 1289.25(F)

A person who uses force, as permitted pursuant to the provisions of subsections B and D of this section, is justified in using such force and is immune from criminal prosecution and civil action for the use of such force.

21 O.S. § 1289.25 contains several circumstances when the law gives far more protection than is available under sections 643 and 733. Subsection (F), referred to by the media and prosecution when deriding the law as "Make My Day," states that a person who uses non-deadly or deadly force as permitted under the "castle doctrine" or "stand your ground" subsections is justified in using such force and is immune from criminal prosecution and civil action for the use of such force.

In June of 2015, there was an Oklahoma Court of Criminal Appeals case that finally addressed some of the fundamental issues surrounding how this immunity functions on a procedural, as well as substantive level. However, it is a bit of an odd case in that the court chose not to publish the opinion, which raises questions as to when and where the opinion may be binding. On top of that, the court specifically stated, "these procedures shall govern future cases." This blatant contradiction of ideas leaves many of us scratching our heads, but for the purpose of discussion, here is what the court says about immunity and how it is to be used:

- A defendant must assert entitlement to Stand Your Ground immunity before trial, or the immunity is waived.
- Arrest and prosecution of the accused is allowed upon a showing of probable cause to believe that the use of force was unlawful.
- A pretrial order granting statutory immunity under the Stand Your Ground law is appealable by the state solely as a reserved question of law. This means the accused walks free.
- The proper procedure is for the accused to file a motion to dismiss and request for an evidentiary hearing at the district court arraignment (and at the hearing the defendant need only show, by a preponderance of the evidence, that the use of force warrants immunity).
- A defendant may seek pretrial appellate review of denial of immunity (via writ of prohibition). *State v. Julio Juarez Ramos & Isidro Juarez Ramos*, Nos. S-2013-509 & S-2013-510 (Okla. Crim. App., June 9, 2015) (unpublished).

C. The "Castle Doctrine" and "Stand Your Ground" laws in 21 O.S. § 1289.25

1. The "Castle Doctrine"

The term "Castle Doctrine" does not appear in the Oklahoma Statutes, however, the legal concept comes from the philosophy that every person is a King or Queen of his or her "castle." As such, no king or queen is required to retreat before using force or deadly force against an intruder into their castle. In Oklahoma, the "Castle Doctrine" type law is implemented under section 1289.25 and takes the form of a powerful presumption of reasonableness. This legal presumption, if and when available to the Defendant, is a potentially powerful legal argument that limits prosecutors in court from second-guessing the amount of force used by the accused in defending himself or herself. For example, the prosecutor might argue: The accused should have used non-deadly force, should have resorted to dispute resolution methods, and so forth. If a Defendant meets the conditions enabling him or her to be afforded the protection of the presumption, found in the Castle Doctrine, the law will deem "reasonable" that the Defendant held a fear of imminent peril of death or great bodily harm to himself, herself, or another. The Oklahoma "Castle Doctrine" extends to a person's dwelling, residence, occupied vehicle, and place of business.

As we discussed earlier, the general rule is that a person is legally justified in using force or deadly force:

> *When and to the degree a person reasonably believes that force or deadly force is necessary to protect against the unlawful use of force or deadly force.*

The person who uses defensive force knew or had reason to know that an unlawful and forcible entry or unlawful and forcible act was occurring or had occurred.

If you are a victim of unlawful force or deadly force when you are in your dwelling, residence, occupied vehicle, or place of business, the law will provide you protection beyond the general rule of using deadly force to respond to deadly force. In these specific "Castle Doctrine" geographic locations, the law will allow you the presumption of having a reasonable fear of imminent peril of death or great bodily harm to yourself or another when using defensive force that is intended or likely to cause death or great bodily harm to another person.

This presumption applies when:

a. A person has unlawfully and with force entered, or was

attempting to enter your: dwelling, residence, occupied vehicle, or place of business;
b. A person has unlawfully and with force removed, or is attempting to remove you or another from your: dwelling, residence, occupied vehicle, or place of business.

This presumption does not apply when:
a. The person against whom the defensive force is used has the right to be in or is a lawful resident of the dwelling, residence, or vehicle and there is not a protective order from domestic violence in effect;
b. The person or persons sought to be removed are children or grandchildren, or are otherwise in the lawful custody of the person against whom force is used; or
c. The person who uses defensive force is engaged in an unlawful activity or is using the dwelling (etc.) to further an unlawful activity.

As can be seen, this covers conditions when someone is entering or attempting to enter your "castle" as well as situations when you or someone else is being unlawfully removed from your "castle." A "Castle Doctrine" presumption of "reasonableness" is a powerful legal tool for any person who is accused of a crime and claiming justification. The presumption is further enhanced by having no duty to retreat (*see No Duty to Retreat* later in this chapter).

What is a dwelling/residence under the "Castle Doctrine?"
Oklahoma law, in defining "Castle Doctrine" rights, does not use the term apartment, hotel room, house, or property; it uses the terms "dwelling, residence, occupied vehicle, or place of business." The presumption under section 1289.25 is specific, limited, and does not cover an entire piece of real property—just the place of business, dwelling, residence, or vehicle. The terms "residence," "dwelling" and "vehicle" are defined by 21 O.S. § 1289.25 as:

1. "Dwelling" means a building or conveyance of any kind, including any attached porch, whether the building or

conveyance is temporary or permanent, mobile or immobile, which has a roof over it, including a tent, and is designed to be occupied by people;

2. "Residence" means a dwelling in which a person resides either temporarily or permanently or is visiting as an invited guest; and
3. "Vehicle" means a conveyance of any kind, whether or not motorized, which is designed to transport people or property.

This means that structures which are detached from the building where you sleep at night, are not considered to be your residence or dwelling. For example, Oklahoma law does not consider your detached garage, shed, and/or barn as part of your residence or dwelling. Therefore, any justified use of force or deadly force would not qualify for a presumption of reasonable fear of imminent peril of death under this particular part of the law. However, if your garage, front porch, or back porch is connected to the structure containing your sleeping quarters (as exists in many suburban communities), it is considered part of your dwelling or residence as defined by the Oklahoma Statutes.

What is a vehicle under the "Castle Doctrine?"

Oklahoma "Castle Doctrine" legal presumptions and protections are applicable to occupied vehicles. You may use deadly force against a person who is attempting to "carjack" you. "Carjack" means to unlawfully and with force enter your vehicle while you are in it, or unlawfully and with force remove you from your vehicle. When presenting an argument of self-defense, this crime is covered under the "Castle Doctrine." What does Oklahoma define as a vehicle?

Under Oklahoma Law, a vehicle is defined as: a conveyance of any kind, whether or not motorized, which is designed to transport people or property.

This is a very broad definition and appears to include anything that carries people or property from one place to another, including cars, trucks, boats, airplanes, golf carts, bicycles, and so forth.

Practical Legal Tip:

Numerous jurisdictions like Oklahoma have "no duty to retreat" laws that do not require fleeing before the legal use of deadly force. However, several states impose a duty on a person to retreat if reasonably available as a prerequisite to using deadly force. So when traveling, make sure you know the law of the state you are visiting. *-Robert*

2. In Oklahoma, "Stand Your Ground" means no duty to retreat! "Stand Your Ground" is a common term for laws that provide that a person has no legal duty to retreat before using force or deadly force against a person who is a threat.

The provision establishing no duty to retreat, stand your ground, is located in the self-defense statute, Title 21 section 1289.25(D). This provision limits a prosecutor from arguing in court that a person's use of non-deadly or deadly force was unreasonable because prior to its use the person had the opportunity to retreat.

In order to receive the "Stand Your Ground," protection under this statute, first, a person must satisfy all the conditions in the Oklahoma Statute:

1. Not engaged in unlawful activity;
2. Attacked in any place where he or she has a right to be;
3. Reasonable belief it is necessary to do so to prevent death or great bodily harm to himself or herself or another or to prevent the commission of a forcible felony.

All three of these conditions must be satisfied in order for the

"Stand Your Ground" provisions to apply. Further, if a person does not qualify under the "Stand Your Ground" provisions, it does not mean that the person's use of force or deadly force was not legally justified. It simply means that a jury will evaluate whether the person's belief was "reasonable" or that the use of force or deadly force was necessary under sections 643 or 733. If a person cannot satisfy all three requirements, the prosecutor will be free to argue that because the accused could have but did not retreat, the Defendant's belief that the use of force or deadly force was necessary was unreasonable.

Example:

> *One day, looking for a shortcut through the neighborhood, Tom hops a fence (a trespass) and is walking across open property to reach the street on the other side of the property. Tom is confronted by the property owner and tries to explain that he meant no harm and was just taking a shortcut. However, the property owner becomes irate and cocks his gun, aims it at Tom, and says "I'm going to kill you!"*

Under this example, Tom is a trespasser. Tom is disqualified from claiming protection under the Stand Your Ground Law. As such, any jury instruction on standing his ground and meeting force with force, up to and including the necessity of using non-deadly or deadly force will not be given to Tom, even though the property owner made his intention to kill Tom very clear. It has been held by the Oklahoma Court of Criminal Appeals that a person who is a trespasser can utilize the defense of self-defense but only if the trespasser has availed himself of every reasonable means of retreat. If a trespasser has tried every reasonable means of retreat, or if no reasonable means of retreat exist, the trespasser may use force to defend himself against imminent danger of death, great bodily harm, or bodily harm. Of course, the trespasser may respond only with the amount of force which is reasonably necessary to prevent the imminent harm reasonably believed to exist. Use of excessive force destroys the defense of self-defense for the trespasser, just as it does for all other persons claiming self-defense. *See Thompson v. State*, 462 P.2d 299 (Okla. Crim. App. 1969); *Womack v. State*, 253 P. 1027 (1927). The definition of trespasser is a subject with many variations. There are many cases in which self-defense has been claimed either by a trespasser or against a trespasser. *See Turpen v. State*, 204 P.2d 298 (1949); *Hovis v. State*, 176 P.2d 833 (1947); *Grindstaff v. State*, 165 P.2d 846 (1946).

Thus, a prosecutor will argue that before Tom's use of force or deadly force was necessary, Tom should have retreated. It does not mean Tom may not be ultimately legally justified in defending himself, it just makes the case of the prosecutor stronger and makes it more difficult for the Defendant to convince a jury of his justification.

D. Oklahoma presumption for victims of certain violent crimes in specific locations

In Oklahoma, the presumption of a reasonable fear of imminent peril of death or great bodily harm by an attacker when deadly force is used only applies in the following specific locations: the home, automobile, tent, temporary place of lodging, place of business, and other geographic locations listed in section 1289.25. Unfortunately, there is NO automatic legal presumption of imminent peril of death for people confronted with certain classifications of violent crime, like kidnapping, robbery, assault, rape, and others if they happen outside of these specific areas. However, subsection (D), the "stand your ground" subsection, allows a Defendant to use non-deadly and deadly force to prevent death or great bodily harm to himself or herself or another or to prevent the commission of a forcible felony. The aforementioned violent crimes against the person are classified as forcible felonies. A good faith argument could be made for the inclusion of a presumption of reasonableness when a Defendant repels the commission or attempt of these forcible felonies: kidnapping, rape, robbery, and murder when the forcible felonies occur in castle doctrine locations.

E. The following is a short list of forcible felonies and violent crimes covered by §§ 643, 733, and 1289.25

1. Kidnapping

If a person is a victim or a would-be victim of a kidnapping, a forcible and violent felony under Oklahoma law, then the law will allow the victim (if he or she were charged) to argue that it was his or her belief that the use of non-deadly force, or deadly force was necessary to defend against an attacker. Therefore, force or deadly force used by the victim to repel the kidnapping may be argued as self-defense as a necessity; meaning that the Defendant had no other choice but to use force or deadly force, and if the jury agrees, the actions of the Defendant will be legally justified.

What is kidnapping? Generally, kidnapping occurs anytime a person abducts another person and uses violence or force to seize, confine, abduct, or carry away another person.

Kidnapping   **Oklahoma Statutes Title 21 § 741**
Any person who, without lawful authority, seizes, confines, inveigles, decoys, kidnaps, abducts, or carries away another, with intent, either: 1. To cause such other person to be confined or imprisoned in this state against the will of the other person; or   2. To cause such other person to be sent out of this state against the will of the other person; or   3. To cause such person to be sold as a slave, or in any way held to service against the will of such person, shall be guilty of a felony.

As stated above, the crime of kidnapping is a forcible felony and can actually occur in several different circumstances, some without much violent force.

Example 1:

Jane is out jogging one evening, when a white van pulls up next to her, and a masked man with a gun jumps out, trying to grab her and drag her into his van. Jane pulls out her pepper spray, sprays the man in the face, and he runs away.

Example 2:

Jane is out jogging one evening, when a white van pulls up next to her, and a masked man with a gun jumps out, trying to grab her and drag her into his van. Jane pulls out her Glock 42 and fires two shots, killing her attacker.

In the first example, was Jane legally justified in her use of force against the man? What about her use of deadly force in example two? The answer to both *should* be yes. The law of Oklahoma does not provide for an automatic finding or presumption justifying her belief in the immediate necessity of using force or deadly force when the attempted kidnapping occurred outside of the geographic limitations stated in § 1289.25(B). The jury will have to decide whether Jane's actions were "reasonable."

Jane's use of non-deadly force (pepper spray) was necessary to repel a kidnapper, however, under section 643 the force used must be sufficient to repel the act but not be an excessive use of force. The man in the white van was attempting to commit the forcible felony of kidnapping! Likewise, in the second example, self-defense under section 733, Jane's belief that deadly force was necessary will be a question for the jury and the issues of imminent peril of death or great bodily harm will be put to the jury for reasons related to Jane's perception of the kidnapping, and should result in the conclusion that Jane's use of deadly force was justified.

In these hypothetical scenarios, the masked man with the gun was trying to abduct Jane. According to section 1289.25(F), if she is found to have reasonably believed it was necessary to use force or deadly force to prevent death or great bodily harm to herself or another or to prevent the commission of a forcible felony, she will be justified in using such force and be immune from criminal prosecution. These are two clear examples. We will discuss later how the law is applied in more ambiguous cases.

2. Attempted murder

It is the basic law of self-preservation that if someone is trying to kill you, you may defend yourself with non-deadly or deadly force. Thus, it is not surprising that sections 643 and 733 of the Oklahoma Statutes combine to allow for the use of non-deadly or deadly force to prevent someone from murdering you. As with the other listed violent crimes, a person who defends himself or herself against an attempted murder is justified in using non-deadly or deadly force in self-defense against the attacker.

Murder in the First Degree:
Oklahoma Statutes Title 21 § 701.7

A. A person commits murder in the first degree when that person unlawfully and with malice aforethought causes the death of another human being. Malice is that deliberate intention unlawfully to take away the life of a human being, which is manifested by external circumstances capable of proof.

B. A person also commits the crime of murder in the first degree, regardless of malice, when that person or any other person takes the life of a human being during, or if the death of a human being results from, the commission or attempted commission of murder of another person, shooting or discharge of a firearm or crossbow with intent to kill, intentional discharge of a firearm or other deadly weapon into any dwelling or building as provided in section 1289.17(A) of this title, forcible rape, robbery with a dangerous weapon, kidnapping, escape from lawful custody, eluding an officer, first degree burglary, first degree arson, unlawful distributing or dispensing of controlled dangerous substances or synthetic controlled substances, trafficking in illegal drugs, or manufacturing or attempting to manufacture a controlled dangerous substance.

How would the law under Title 21 sections 643, 733 and 1289.25 be applied after a self-defense shooting?

Example:

One busy day at his job, David is working quietly at his desk when he hears an angry voice yell out, "I hate this company, and I'm going to kill every one of you!" About that time, David spots a machete in a deranged-looking stranger's hand. The stranger turns toward David with an evil look. David draws a gun from his desk drawer. As the man continues toward

> *David with the machete raised, David fires two shots at the attacker, killing him.*

In this situation, the law allows David to use non-deadly or deadly force when and to the degree he reasonably believes it is necessary to defend himself. Here, David skipped non-deadly force and immediately used deadly force. Was this reasonable? Should David have first used non-deadly force? Should he have used a method of dispute resolution? If he could have retreated out of a back door, was his use of deadly force really necessary? Did the attacker unlawfully and forcefully enter the business? If David does not qualify for the legal presumption under section 1289.25, then, what happens to David? These are the types of questions and issues that will be presented to the jury for their deliberation.

However, in this example, because David is about to be murdered, at his place of business, the "Castle Doctrine" applies and the law will deem "reasonable" his belief that deadly force was immediately necessary to protect his life from imminent peril of death or great bodily harm! This is a powerful legal presumption and limits prosecutorial arguments regarding the lack of reasonableness of when the deadly force should be used or the degree of force used, because the use of deadly force is legally presumed reasonable, under section 1289.25(B). How do we know David acted in self-defense? In this example, the attacker makes it easy, because he cleared up any ambiguity of his intentions when he declared "I am going to kill every one of you" while wielding a machete, an instrument of deadly force. Thus, under Oklahoma law, David, as a would-be victim of murder, is entitled to a legal presumption that he held a reasonable belief that it was immediately necessary to use deadly force against the attacker to prevent his own murder. Therefore, David was legally justified in using deadly force.

If, for some reason, David was ever charged with a crime for killing the would-be murderer, and David puts forth "sufficient evidence" in trial that he was about to be the victim of murder, the jury would then get to decide whether David acted in self-defense under sections 733 and 1289.25. For a discussion of the legal concept of "sufficient evidence," *see* Section F. The jury will be told that if David reasonably believed he was about to be murdered, the law will presume that deadly force was immediately necessary because of the reasonable fear of imminent peril of death. The prosecution would then have the burden of establishing beyond a reasonable doubt that David did not act in self-defense (*i.e.*, David did not know or have reason to believe he was about to be murdered). If the jury finds that the prosecution did not meet this burden of proof, the jury will decide his use of deadly force was legally justified.

But, how does the self-defense statute work when the example is not so clear?

Example:

> *Police respond to a two-car collision in a parking lot. When the police arrive, they discover that the collision has sparked a violent road-rage incident. At the scene, one man is dead on the ground with a tire iron beside him. The remaining driver—the shooter—Michael, a 45 year-old man with no previous criminal record, fired two shots and is now a suspect in a murder investigation. Michael claims that the other driver became irate after the collision, threatened him, and aggressively came toward him with the tire iron raised in his hand. However, the position of the physical evidence makes it so that determination of who was the true victim in this incident is unclear. In fact, one investigator thinks Michael is lying. There are no other witnesses.*

If Michael ultimately faces criminal charges for murder and claims self-defense at his trial, how does the determination of presumption and, ultimately, legal justification under sections

643, 733 and 1289.25(D) work in practice?

In order to receive the protection of self-defense, Michael has the initial burden of producing "sufficient evidence" in court to support the defense that he "knew or had reason to believe" that he was about to be the victim of murder (*e.g.*, the man screamed threats at him and was about to strike him with the tire iron, and Michael was in fear of his life, so he shot the man). If Michael puts forth "sufficient evidence" that the aggressor was about to murder him, the law requires the prosecution to then prove beyond a reasonable doubt that the accused (in this case, Michael) did not act in self-defense.

In order for the court to consider whether the Defendant is claiming self-defense and before the Court will authorize an instruction of self-defense, the defendant must comply with 22 O.S. § 745, trial procedure, which puts the burden of coming forward with evidence of mitigation, justification, or excuse on the defendant. If the defendant does not come forward with evidence of self-defense as justification, the issue of self-defense is not raised, unless the evidence of the State has raised the issue. *Meadows v. State*, 487 P.2d 359 (Okla. Crim. App. 1971).

In Oklahoma, the trial court/judge will decide if sufficient evidence was either raised by the prosecution's witnesses or the defense witnesses to support a jury instruction of self-defense. Once there has been sufficient evidence to raise self-defense as an issue, the State has the burden of proof to overcome the defense beyond a reasonable doubt.

It is a decision for the jury as to whether the State has met the burden of proof of guilt. The prosecution will have an opportunity to put forth evidence that Michael was not about to be the victim of murder based on the physical evidence found at the scene as well as the investigating officer's testimony.

In the fact situation recited above, it is not clear whether

Michael was inside of the car when he was approached by the irate aggressor with the tire iron. If he was inside of the car when threatened by the aggressor with the tire iron, section 1289.25(B), the "Castle Doctrine," will provide a legal presumption that Michael was in fear of imminent death or great bodily harm from an attack by the aggressor and justify the use of deadly force. However, there may be forensic evidence to counter the presumption; *i.e.,* evidence that the body was found an unthreatening distance from the occupied car with bullet holes in the back could overcome the presumption of fear of imminent danger of death or great bodily harm to Michael.

If the jury believes Michael acted in self-defense to an attempted murder or, more precisely, that the prosecution did not prove beyond a reasonable doubt that Michael did not act in self-defense, the jury will vote to acquit Michael and find him not guilty of the charge of murder.

3. Rape

Like murder, if a person is the victim of rape, Oklahoma law allows for the legally justified use of non-deadly force or deadly force to stop the rape. These two self-defense statutes will also provide any victim of these crimes who resists with force or deadly force, the defense of self-defense based upon "reasonableness" related to his or her belief in the necessity of non-deadly or deadly force against the attacker. How does the law define rape?

Examples of Rape

Rape: ***Rape by Instrumentation:*** **Oklahoma Statutes Title 21 § 1111**
A. Rape is an act of sexual intercourse involving vaginal or anal penetration accomplished with a male or female who is not the spouse of the perpetrator and who may be of the same or the opposite sex as the perpetrator under any of the following circumstances: 1. Where the victim is under sixteen (16) years of age; 2. Where the victim is incapable through mental illness or any other unsoundness of mind, whether temporary or permanent, of giving legal consent; 3. Where force or violence is used or threatened, accompanied by apparent power of execution to the victim or to another person; 4. Where the victim is intoxicated by a narcotic or anesthetic agent, administered by or with the privity of the accused as a means of forcing the victim to submit; 5. Where the victim is at the time unconscious of the nature of the act and this fact is known to the accused; 6. Where the victim submits to sexual intercourse under the belief that the person committing the act is a spouse, and this belief is induced by artifice, pretense, or concealment practiced by the accused or by the accused in collusion with the spouse with intent to induce that belief. In all cases of collusion between the accused and the spouse to accomplish such act, both the spouse and the accused, upon conviction, shall be deemed guilty of rape; 7. Where the victim is under the legal custody or supervision of a state agency, a federal agency, a county, a municipality or a political subdivision and engages in sexual intercourse with a state, federal, county, municipal or political subdivision employee or an employee of a contractor of the state, the federal government, a county, a municipality or a

political subdivision that exercises authority over the victim; or

8. Where the victim is at least sixteen (16) years of age and is less than twenty (20) years of age and is a student, or under the legal custody or supervision of any public or private elementary or secondary school, junior high or high school, or public vocational school, and engages in sexual intercourse with a person who is eighteen (18) years of age or older and is an employee of the same school system.

9. Rape is an act of sexual intercourse accomplished with a male or female who is the spouse of the perpetrator if force or violence is used or threatened, accompanied by apparent power of execution to the victim or to another person.

Rape by Instrumentation:
Oklahoma Statutes Title 21 § 1111.1

Rape by instrumentation is an act within or without the bonds of matrimony in which any inanimate object or any part of the human body, not amounting to sexual intercourse is used in the carnal knowledge of another person without his or her consent and penetration of the anus or vagina occurs to that person. Provided, further, that at least one of the circumstances specified in Section 1111 of this title has been met; further, where the victim is at least sixteen (16) years of age and is less than twenty (20) years of age and is a student, or under the legal custody or supervision of any public or private elementary or secondary school, junior high or high school, or public vocational school, and engages in conduct prohibited by this section of law with a person who is eighteen (18) years of age or older and is an employee of the same school system, or where the victim is under the legal custody or supervision of a state or federal agency, county, municipal or a political subdivision and engages in conduct prohibited by this section of law with a federal, state, county, municipal or political subdivision employee or an employee of a contractor of the state, the federal government, a county, a municipality or a political subdivision that exercises authority over the victim, consent shall not be an element of the crime.

Rape in the first degree and second degree: Oklahoma Statutes Title 21 §1114

A. Rape in the first degree shall include:

1. Rape committed by a person over eighteen (18) years of age upon a person under fourteen (14) years of age; or
2. Rape committed upon a person incapable through mental illness or any unsoundness of mind of giving legal consent regardless of the age of the person committing the crime; or
3. Rape accomplished where the victim is intoxicated by a narcotic or anesthetic agent, administered by or with the privaty of the accused as a means of forcing the victim to submit; or
4. Rape accomplished where the victim is at the time unconscious of the nature of the act and this fact is known to the accused; or
5. Rape accomplished with any person by means of force, violence, or threats of force or violence accompanied by apparent power of execution regardless of the age of the person committing the crime; or
6. Rape by instrumentation resulting in bodily harm is rape by instrumentation in the first degree regardless of the age of the person committing the crime; or
7. Rape by instrumentation committed upon a person under fourteen (14) years of age.

B. In all other cases, rape or rape by instrumentation is rape in the second degree.

Forcible Sodomy:
Oklahoma Statutes Title 21 O.S. § 888

B. The crime of forcible sodomy shall include:
1. Sodomy committed by a person over eighteen (18) years of age upon a person under sixteen (16) years of age; or
2. Sodomy committed upon a person incapable through mental illness or any unsoundness of mind of giving legal consent regardless of the age of the person committing the crime; or
3. Sodomy accomplished with any person by means of force, violence, or threats of force or violence accompanied by apparent power of execution regardless of the age of the victim or the person committing the crime; or
4. Sodomy committed by a state, county, municipal or political subdivision employee or a contractor or an employee of a contractor of the state, a county, a municipality or political subdivision of this state upon a person who is under the legal custody, supervision or authority of a state agency, a county, a municipality or a political subdivision of this state; or
5. Sodomy committed upon a person who is at least sixteen (16) years of age but less than twenty (20) years of age and is a student of any public or private secondary school, junior high or high school, or public vocational school, with a person who is eighteen (18) years of age or older and is employed by the same school system.

4. First degree robbery and second degree robbery

Like the other forcible felonies discussed above, if a person is a victim or would-be victim of a robbery, Oklahoma law allows the victim to protect himself or herself against the robber with legally justified non-deadly or deadly force. Further, like the other crimes listed above, the issue of reasonableness related to the use of non-deadly or deadly force in a self-defense situation remains a question to be settled by the jury. How does Oklahoma law define robbery?

Robbery:
Oklahoma Statutes Title 21 § 791

Robbery is a wrongful taking of personal property in the possession of another, from his person or immediate presence, and against his will, accomplished by means of force or fear.

Robbery is separated into First and Second Degree Robbery based upon the amount of violence perpetrated upon the victim by the robber.

Robbery First and Second Degree:
Oklahoma Statutes Title 21 § 797

A. Robbery in the first degree is when, in the course of committing the theft, the defendant:
1. Inflicts serious bodily injury upon the person;
2. Threatens a person with immediate serious bodily injury;
3. Intentionally puts a person in fear of immediate serious bodily injury; or
4. Commits or threatens to commit a felony upon the person.
B. When robbery is accomplished in any other manner, different than 1-4 above, it is robbery in the second degree.

Example:

Tina is on her way home from work. She stops by a local convenience store for some bread and milk. As she enters the store, a masked man suddenly approaches her with a knife, grabs her by the arm, and demands her money. Tina, scared and shaken, remembers her training, opens her purse and pulls a .357 revolver and fires, killing the masked robber.

In this example, Tina's life was threatened by a knife. The threat to her life and demand for her money met the definition of a first degree robbery. Tina's life was endangered; section 733 and 1289.25 allowed for Tina to use deadly force in response to this danger as well as to repel a forcible felony. The facts as stated, provided justification for Tina's use of deadly force in response to deadly force used by the robber (the knife). Tina's use of deadly force when faced by an armed robber was reasonable. Tina had no choice but to use deadly force. Had she run, the robber may have stabbed her in the back, had she pleaded with the robber for mercy, he could have cut her down anyway. Thus, her defending herself with deadly force was both justified and necessary.

What if the example is less clear?

> Example:
>
> *Hank, a sixty-six year old disabled man, works downtown. He has to park four blocks from his company's office building and has to walk through some rough parts of town in order to get to his car. A man suddenly appears in front of him and says, "Hey man—give me some money!" Hank, feeling very frightened and intimidated, walks on with the now louder and more aggressive panhandler demanding, "Hey! Man! I said give me some money!" Hank now becomes extremely concerned for his safety. About that time, Hank makes a wrong turn into an alley where he is cornered. He again hears, "HEY! MAN! I SAID GIVE ME SOME MONEY!" When Hank turns around, he sees the same man, now very aggressive, with something in his hand.*

Is the panhandler just being annoying, or is Hank about to be the victim of a first or second degree robbery? This is the ultimate issue Hank may face if Hank decides to use non-deadly or deadly force against the alleged aggressor. How will the law evaluate a use of deadly force under sections 1289.25 and 733?

This is an example with a lot of gray area. The man never verbally threatened Hank, nor did he ever physically touch him. All the man said was "give me some money;" he didn't even demand *all* of Hank's money—just some. Do robbers ever demand just some money? If Hank is in genuine fear of a first degree robbery, does he have a duty to retreat? What about the fact that Hank was cornered in an alley? If Hank takes out his legally concealed carry pistol and fires it to defend himself, what happens? Was Hank really about to be robbed, or is he a paranoid trigger-happy fellow as the prosecutor may try to portray him? Beyond that, who decides what the facts really were? This goes to show that there are lots of questions and gray areas.

If Hank finds himself charged with unlawfully using non-deadly or deadly force against his alleged attacker, he can assert a legal justification based on self-defense. Again, the law will allow Hank to use non-deadly or deadly force for self-defense when and to the degree he reasonably believes it is necessary to stop unlawful force against him. In this example, before a jury will be allowed to decide if Hank acted in self-defense, Hank must present "sufficient evidence" at trial that he reasonably believed he was about to be robbed (*see* our discussion of what constitutes "sufficient evidence" in the next section).

Hank may attempt to satisfy the "sufficient evidence" requirement by testifying that he was in fear for his safety and had seen the panhandler acting violently on the same street many times in the past. Hank may also say the man raised a weapon in his hand and was moving aggressively toward him, and that the assailant out-weighed Hank by 75 pounds and was about a foot taller. Hank will absolutely testify he felt he was being robbed. If Hank puts forth "sufficient evidence" in court that he was the victim of an attempted forcible felony, the jury will decide if Hank is credible and if his belief would have been held by a reasonable person in the same situation. After the court sees "sufficient evidence" supporting self-defense, the burden shifts to the prosecution; then the law requires the prosecution to prove beyond a reasonable doubt that Hank did not act in self-defense. However, if Hank fails to put forth "sufficient evidence" that he acted in self-defense, he will not be entitled to a self-defense jury instruction and the jury will not get to decide the issue. *See West v. State,* 798 P.2d 1083, 1085 (Okla. Crim. App. 1990).

F. What is "sufficient evidence?"

So, how much evidence does a person have to offer in a trial to constitute "sufficient evidence" in order to be entitled to a jury charge regarding self-defense? The Oklahoma Court of Criminal Appeals, in the case of *West v. State*, 798 P.2d 1083, 1085 (Okla. Crim. App. 1990) stated:

> "It is well established that a defendant is entitled to any instructions on his theory of defense, provided such theory is tenable as a matter of law, or the court finds support in the evidence. *Green v. State*, 611 P.2d 262, 266 (Okl. Cr. 1980); *Gann v. State*, 397 P.2d 686, 690 (Okl. Cr. 1964). If there is no evidence in the record to support an instruction, it should not be given. *Coulter v. State*, 721 P.2d 818, 819 (Okl. Cr. 1986). Self-defense is an affirmative defense that must be raised by the defendant unless the State's case shows that the homicide was justifiable. When the record reveals no evidence of self-defense, the trial court is not bound to instruct the jury on that defense. *Holloway v. State*, 712 P.2d 68, 69 (Okl. Cr. 1986)."

This means that in court, a defendant must offer admissible evidence that raises the issue of self-defense, and he is entitled to receive a jury instruction regarding self-defense under sections 643 and 733. The requirement is that the evidence offered must be legally tenable, admissible under the law of evidence and related to the incident of self-defense at issue.

Sometimes, the Defendant is desperate for a defense of

any sort. There may be little or no evidence in the record supporting self-defense. There may be little or no "sufficient evidence" submitted in court to obtain a self-defense jury instruction and the last witness available may be the Defendant. The "sufficient evidence" needed to obtain a self-defense instruction may be satisfied when the evidence offered by the Defendant is as simple as the Defendant's own testimony. The testimony of the Defendant without corroborating testimony of witnesses, without supporting forensic evidence, standing naked and alone, which is quite alone, will be sufficient to raise the self-defense theory. It is important to note that, in determining whether the testimony of a Defendant raises an issue of self-defense, the truth or credibility of the Defendant's testimony is not at issue for the court to decide. Rather, determining the truth or credibility of the Defendant's testimony is the role the jury undertakes in its deliberations. The jury decides the facts and credibility of the witnesses and the judge decides the applicable law.

Practical Legal Tip:

My experience in over 35 years as a trial lawyer is that many people serving on juries tend to ignore the rule of "innocent until proven guilty." Even though every person has a Constitutional right to not testify against themselves, by not doing so, it can cloud a juror's mind so as to make the notion of innocent until proven guilty viewed with skepticism. *-Robert*

Of course, relying on a defendant's testimony to be the sole source of evidence in order to obtain a jury instruction on self-defense can be fraught with peril as well. All defendants have the right to *not* testify at their trial—which can be a sound trial tactic in that it prevents the State from examining the defendant under oath and on the witness stand. Once a defendant takes the witness stand, however, that defendant will be subject to examination by not only his attorney, but will also be cross-examined by the State. A cross examination may ultimately contain evidence which sways a jury away from seriously considering acquittal on self-defense grounds.

G. Self-defense not available to an aggressor

A person who is the aggressor in an altercation is not entitled to the defense of self-defense. *Ruth v. State*, 581 P.2d 919 (Okla. Crim. App. 1978); *Martley v. State*, 519 P.2d 544 (Okla. Crim. App. 1974). A person cannot provoke an altercation as an excuse to inflict bodily injury upon another. *Moutry v. State*, 132 P. 915 (Okla. Crim. App. 1913). A person cannot use self-defense if that person has voluntarily entered into mutual combat. *Jenkins v. State*, 161 P.2d 90 (Okla. Crim. App. 1945).

H. When is the use of non-deadly or deadly force explicitly not legally justified?

Oklahoma case law and statutes outline four specific situations where a person is not justified in using non-deadly or deadly force and one related instance where it is a question of fact as to whether a peace officer is using excessive force. Of course, since being justified in the use of force is an absolute prerequisite to the use of deadly force, any time a person is not justified to use force under the law, that person is also automatically disqualified from being justified to use deadly force under section 733.

1. Force is never legally justified for verbal provocation alone.

If you think back to your childhood, you probably remember the saying: "sticks and stones will break my bones, but words will never hurt me!" Believe it or not, the law agrees wholeheartedly with this concept. Under Oklahoma law, a person is not justified in using force when words are the only provocation to a situation.

Example:

Samantha is walking to her car in the grocery store parking lot when a woman starts screaming at her: "You're a terrible driver, and you park like an idiot!" Samantha runs over to the woman and punches the woman in the face.

In this instance, Samantha is not legally justified in her use of force because the only thing happening was the other woman screaming at her—a mere verbal provocation. The use of force against another is not justified in response to verbal provocation alone. *Ruth v. State*, 581 P.2d 919 (Okla. Crim. App. 1978).

2. Force usually not legally justified to resist arrest

Resisting Arrest: **Oklahoma Statutes Title 21 § 268**
Every person who knowingly resists, by the use of force or violence, any executive officer in the performance of his duty, is guilty of a misdemeanor.

Example:

Justin has been pulled over for speeding and is removed from his vehicle by a uniformed police officer. While sitting on the curb, the officer begins to search Justin's vehicle without his consent and without probable cause. Feeling violated, Justin gets up and pulls the officer out of his car and throws the officer to the ground.

Even though the officer's behavior is unusual for a mere

speeding violation, and even though it appears Justin is being subjected to an illegal search and seizure, his legally justifiable recourse is to pursue the matter through the court system—not to use force against the officer!

Unfortunately, there are instances where police officers arrest people without legal authority and exceed the authority they are allowed under the law. Sometimes there are many factors leading to that excessive use of authority, but officers have to follow the law, too! For that reason, the Court of Criminal Appeals fashioned a remedy: If a peace officer lacks authority to arrest a person without an arrest warrant and attempts to do so, the officer is a trespasser, and the person sought to be arrested may reasonably resist. *Davis v. State*, 12 P.2d 555 (Okla. Crim. App. 1932). *See also Sandersfield v. State*, 568 P.2d 313 (Okla. Crim. App. 1977).

A person may only use reasonable force in resisting an unlawful arrest. In *Davis, supra*, the Court of Criminal Appeals stated: "The right to resist an unlawful arrest is limited and varies with the circumstances. If the official character of the officer is known to the person sought to be arrested, or if the officer informs him of his official character and his reason for the arrest, and the person sought to be arrested has no reason to apprehend any treatment other than detention, he is not justified in the use of a deadly weapon in resisting the arrest." *Davis*, at 418.

There are exceptions in the case law crafted to protect a person in those rare scenarios where an officer lacks the authority to arrest. Having said that, pay very close attention to how narrow and specific this is in its application—a person must meet some very specific requirements before he or she is afforded any legal protection.

The Court of Criminal Appeals has elaborated upon the risk of resisting arrest which was found to be unlawful. In *Ajeani v. State*, 610 P.2d 820 (Okla. Crim. App. 1980), the defendant was arrested and charged with breach of the peace and public intoxication. The defendant resisted the officer in the officer's efforts to make the arrest. As a result, the defendant was also charged with resisting an officer and assault and battery upon a police officer. The defendant was acquitted of the public-intoxication and breach of the peace charges. He was convicted of resisting an officer and for assault and battery upon a police officer. On appeal, the defendant claimed that since he had been acquitted of the charges forming the basis for his arrest, no public offense had in fact been committed in the officer's presence and his arrest was unlawful. As a result, he claimed that he was lawfully resisting an unlawful arrest. Judge Bussey, in writing for a divided court, stated: "We hold that an arrest for a misdemeanor, without a warrant, where the arresting officer has probable cause, based on information coming to his senses or his personal observation at the time, to believe that a misdemeanor or other public offense is being committed in his presence by the arrestee, is not, unlawful, even though arrestee is subsequently found innocent of the charges." *Id.* at 822.

In spite of the questionable decision, it appears that, if the officer's mistake is honest and reasonable, the arrest is lawful. The court did state, however, that mere suspicion or subterfuge would not justify a warrantless misdemeanor arrest and that information supplied by a third person would not suffice.

Any time a person uses force against a law enforcement officer, he or she should be aware that the cards are stacked against him or her from the beginning! Ultimately, the lack of available evidence may make it so exceptionally difficult to claim this statute's protections legitimately that it loses its value except in rare instances.

Practical Legal Tip:

The right to remain silent is a fundamental Constitutional right which is why it is so disturbing that in 2010, the US Supreme Court held that you have to say the magic words of "I invoke my right to remain silent and to counsel" in order to trigger it. Seemingly, by the Court's standard, if you don't say the magic words, police could interrogate you until the end of time. - *Robert*

3. Consent to force

The law regarding mutual combat serves the purpose of preventing individuals who arrange to fight each other from avoiding criminal responsibility for their actions by claiming self-defense.

Example:

> *Andy and Dwight are having an argument about whose favorite football team will win the championship. In the heat of the argument, Andy calls Dwight a derogatory name and Dwight asks if Andy wants to take it outside. Andy agrees, and they both begin fighting in the parking lot. Shortly after they begin fighting, the police show up and arrest them for disorderly conduct, simple assault and battery.*

Mutual combat, force, is not justified, if the actors consented to the exact force used or attempted by the other. *Phelps v. State*, 64 P.2d 240 (Okla. App. Civ. 1938). The law is clear: if a person agrees to the force used against him or her by another person, that person cannot later claim that he or she fought back in self-defense! *See Weatherholt v. State*, 131 P. 185 (Okla. Crim.

App. 1913). This law also applies to individuals who agree to participate in unlicensed "fight clubs." That now explains why "the first rule of fight club is you do not talk about fight club!"

4. Provocation not justified

The general rule is the use of force against another is not justified if the actor provoked the other's use or attempted the use of unlawful force. Oklahoma's highest criminal court, the Court of Criminal Appeals, defined what it means for an aggressor to provoke an attack.

The Court of Criminal Appeals held that a person who provokes an attack loses the legal right of self-defense (so certainly any legal presumption would be lost as well).

Neither may a person provoke an altercation as an excuse to inflict bodily injury upon another, *Moutrey v. State*, 132 P. 915 (Okla. Crim. App. 1913); nor may a person use self-defense if that person has voluntarily entered into mutual combat. *Jenkins v. State*, 161 P.2d 90 (Okla. Crim. App. 1945); *Koozer v. State*, 123 P. 554 (Okla. Crim. App. 1912).

The Oklahoma Court of Criminal Appeals has not considered when a person has "provoked" another person under sections 643, 733 and 1289.25. However, the legal doctrine of provocation is well established in Oklahoma jurisprudence and is best summed up in a 1912 case, *Turnbul v. State*, 128 P. 743 (Okla. Crim. App. 1912).

> This is always essential when there is proof in the record tending to show that the overt act relied upon by the state to establish the contention that the accused **provoked** the difficulty was an act which he had a right to do. Counsel for the state do not contend that the accused in this case did not have a right to ask the deceased to refrain from the use of the language complained of, and to remonstrate with him in the manner the proof tends to

> show he did. The court should have told the jury just how far the accused could go before he would forfeit his right of self-defense and be held the aggressor or liable as unwarrantedly **provoking** the difficulty under the law.
>
> It is said by Wharton in his work on Homicide, sec. 320 (3d Ed.):
>
> "The rule that to justify homicide as committed in self-defense the slayer must not have been the original aggressor, and must not have been at fault in bringing on the difficulty, applies in cases where there was no felonious intent on his part at the time he entered into or **provoked** the difficulty as well as where such intention existed. And if the slayer **provoked** the combat, or produced the occasion for it, in order to have a pretext for killing his adversary or doing him great bodily harm, the killing would be murder no matter to what extremity he may be reduced."

Under current Oklahoma jurisprudence, if a person has provoked an attack, self-defense is not available as a defense to any resulting criminal charge from the provocation.

5. Self-Defense Reestablished by Aggressor Who Withdraws from Initial Altercation

Sometimes, an initial aggressor will flee or withdraw from an initial altercation due to many circumstances, such as a bully observing that his chosen victim may not be an easy mark. The initial victim or mark may turn the tables on the aggressor and pursue him, thus becoming the aggressor. This discussion will focus on what happens when the victim, turns into the aggressor and pursues the initial aggressor.

What the Court of Criminal Appeals is saying is that a person cannot "lure" or "bait" another person into a violent confrontation and then hide behind the law by claiming that their (the aggressor's) conduct should be presumed reasonable because the other fellow, who ran away, took the first swing! In Oklahoma, the courts are concerned with determining the identity of the aggressor. That is to say that the court must determine the identity of the aggressor in order to strip the aggressor of claims to self-defense. The one who swung first may wind up getting the worst of the fight, so the identity of the true aggressor is very important to the court for purposes of allowing self-defense to be argued at trial.

What is the result if a Defendant withdraws from a difficulty caused by provocation and there is a claim of self-defense? For example: a person who started a fight soon realizes they bit off more than they can chew. Under the law, that person can abandon the fight and retreat. If, after a person abandons or attempts to abandon the encounter, and the person who was provoked pursues and uses unlawful force against the original provocateur, the provocateur may then be legally justified to fight back and assert self-defense.

Abandonment of provocation may allow justification:
Townley v. State, 355 P.2d 420 (Okla. Crim. App. 1959)

The use of force against another is not justified if the actor provoked the other's use or attempted use of unlawful force, unless the actor abandons the encounter, or clearly communicates to the other his intent to do so reasonably believing he cannot safely abandon the encounter, and the other nevertheless continues or attempts to use unlawful force against the actor.

Example:

Dave is at a bar when he notices another man checking-out his girlfriend. Dave tells the other man, "take a hike or you'll regret it" and slightly shoves the admirer. The other man responds by punching Dave in the face. Dave, who didn't

> *really want a confrontation, holds both his hands up in surrender and says, "I don't want any more trouble!" However, the other man pulls out a knife and lunges at Dave.*

In this scenario, Dave is legally justified to fight back: he attempted to abandon the incident and made his intention known to the other person. When the other man continued to attack, Dave is now legally justified to defend himself, even though he made the initial provocation.

III. Do I have a legal responsibility to defend another person?

Under Oklahoma law, the ordinary person has *no duty to come to the defense of another*, so long as that lay person was not the cause of the situation or occurrence. This is true even if a crime is in progress (but note: this lack of a legal duty does not include police officers and other professionals who may have affirmative legal duties to assist). But, if a person is present at a riot and is asked by the police to help arrest any rioter, the person has the duty to assist the officer under penalty of law, 21 O.S. § 1318. If you see a third person, a victim of what you believe to be the unlawful use of force or deadly force, you have no legal duty to aid that person—it is your decision. This is equally true if you are legally carrying a gun pursuant to a handgun license. But what if you decide to help the third person?

A. When does Oklahoma law allow for the justifiable use of force or deadly force to protect someone else?

In the previous sections, we addressed the law of legal justification for the use of non-deadly force or deadly force in self-defense. We now turn to when the law allows the justified use of non-deadly force or deadly force to protect another person or persons.

21 O.S. §§ 643, 733(2), and 1289.25 allow a person to protect a third person from the unlawful use of force or deadly force by another in the same circumstances in which a person could justifiably use force or deadly force to protect themselves. In

general, if you place yourself in the "shoes" of the third person, and the law would allow the third person to use non-deadly or deadly force to protect themselves, then you are legally justified to use the same level of force to protect a third person.

Therefore, the same legal justifications and presumptions related to the reasonable fear of death and/or great bodily injury and the general standard of "reasonableness" for self-defense are also available for the defense of third persons.

If a person (rescuer) decides to aid a third person, the law of justifiable use of force will allow the rescuer to defend a third person to the extent the rescuer may defend himself or herself. As long as the rescuer defending another person reasonably believes that the third person would be justified in using non-deadly or deadly force to protect himself or herself, the person defending may step in and use non-deadly or deadly force on that person's behalf. In 2014, the Oklahoma Legislature expanded the justification for using non-deadly and deadly force to defend third persons. Prior to November 1, 2014, there was a short list of persons who were defined under section 733(2) qualifying as third persons. As of November 1, 2014, the law in Oklahoma was changed and the definition of person was expanded from: husband, wife, parent, child, master, mistress, or servant. Now the law includes everyone defined as a person. This means that you may come to the aid of a third party without any special relationship with the victim.

An important case that began to move Oklahoma law in the direction of being able to protect all third parties was *OWM v. State*. In that case, the soon to be dead assailant weighed 300 pounds and was on top of and choking the rescuer's brother. The rescuer shot the assailant three times who then crawled away and died. Under the facts and the law, brothers were not in the class of people previously listed under § 733, who could come to the aid of a family member for purposes of self-defense. Brothers could not assert the defense of coming to the aid of a family member. Family members were limited to husband, wife, son, daughter, master, mistress, servant as persons who could come to the aid of each other and claim self-defense. However, the Criminal Court of Appeals ruled, under a general statute, 21 O.S. §§ 31-33, that the trial judge should have instructed the jurors as to the use of reasonable force to prevent the offense of choking the brother to death, thus overruling the conviction. *See OWM v. State,* 946 P.2d 257 (Okla. Crim. App. 1997).

If a person decides to defend a third person, prudence dictates that the person defending must be sure they know what is truly happening in a situation before using force or deadly force. If the person's belief in the necessity of the use of force or deadly force turns out to be unreasonable, the use of force or deadly force will not be legally justified no matter how well intentioned the rescuer may be.

B. What if the situation is not as I thought it appeared to be?
A third person and a "Good Samaritan" may not potentially see things as they really are. When a person elects to use non-deadly or deadly force to defend a third person, it can all go terribly wrong.

Example:

> *Peter, a licensed handgun owner, decides to get some lunch, so he pulls into a local burger joint to eat. He parks and exits his vehicle whereupon he witnesses a man walking out of the restaurant and across the parking lot. Suddenly, another man comes running up and points a gun in the first man's face. Peter, not wanting to become a victim of a robbery, drops to one knee while drawing his handgun. Still seeing the gun pointed at the first man, Peter decides to protect the would-be victim of robbery and fires his gun striking the robber.*

If there was in fact an armed robbery taking place, Peter's use of deadly force is likely justified, because Peter would be legally justified in using deadly force to stop the First Degree robbery. Thus, the law will deem Peter's belief that the use of deadly force was necessary and reasonable. But what if there was no armed robbery?

In fact, what would happen if in the instant after Peter fires his gun, the man Peter sought to protect immediately turns to help the wounded suspected robber yelling "murderer!" at Peter while screaming in fear and grief, "why did you shoot my friend?" It turns out that there was no robbery, just a couple of fellows pranking each other, and the gun Peter saw was a toy. How does the law deal with this scenario?

In such a situation, Peter's perspective and knowledge is very different from the person he sought to defend. The man clearly knew there was no robbery in progress since he recognized that his friend was pulling a prank. In this situation, if Peter's observation would lead a reasonable person to believe that an robbery was in progress, then Peter will be legally justified. However, if a jury finds that his belief was unreasonable, Peter will not be legally justified and likely guilty of a crime.

C. Do I have a duty to report a crime?

Oklahoma statutes do not prescribe a duty for a member of the public to report a crime. However, false reports are prohibited.

False Reports of Crime
21 O.S. § 589(A)

It shall be unlawful to willfully, knowingly and without probable cause make a false report to any person of any crime or circumstances indicating the possibility of crime having been committed, including the unlawful taking of personal property, which report causes or encourages the exercise of police action or investigation. Any person convicted of violating the provisions of this subsection shall be guilty of a misdemeanor punishable by imprisonment in the county jail for not more than ninety (90) days or by a fine of not more than Five Hundred Dollars ($500), or by both such fine and imprisonment.

It is not against the law for a member of the general public to fail to report a crime. However, the report must be accurate and true, or the weight of the law may fall upon the transgressor.

CHAPTER SIX

WHEN CAN I LEGALLY USE MY GUN: PART III
UNDERSTANDING WHEN DEADLY FORCE CAN BE USED AGAINST ANIMALS

I. Using deadly force against animals

When it comes to the law on the use of deadly force to defend oneself, others, or property from animal attacks, Oklahoma has a collection of different rules found in the statutes as well as case law.

A. No general self-defense against animals statute

Oklahoma has no general self-defense or defense of others statute that deals with animals. There exist statutes that authorize conduct against dogs and cats and statutes for protection of domestic animals, and livestock, but there is no statutory justification for protecting people against animal attacks. For example, if someone was charged with cruelty to animals under the Oklahoma statute provided below, there is no available statute that provides a legal justification if their actions were taken in self-defense. Luckily, the Oklahoma courts have fashioned a doctrine of self-defense against animal attacks from the case of *Grizzle v. State*, 707 P.2d 1210 (Okla. Crim. App. 1985).

Cruelty to Animals:
Oklahoma Statutes Title 21 § 1685

Any person who shall willfully or maliciously torture, destroy or kill, or cruelly beat or injure, maim or mutilate any animal in subjugation or captivity, whether wild or tame, and whether belonging to the person or to another… shall be guilty of a felony.

Cruelty to Animals - Defense:
Jury Instruction OUJI-CR 7-3

A person is justified in destroying/injuring an animal if:
First, he/she acted to defend himself/herself/(another person)/(his/her home/property) against harm threat-ened by the animal;
Second, the animal's actions led him/her to reasonably believe that it would inflict the harm;
Third, the destruction/injury was reasonable in view of the seriousness of the harm threatened;
Fourth, he/she reasonably believed that the harm could only be prevented by immediate destruction/injury of the animal; and
Fifth, the kind and amount of force used was reasonably proportionate to the kind and amount of danger presented by the animal.
It is the burden of the State to prove beyond a reasonable doubt that the defendant was not justified in destroying/injuring an animal. If you find that the State has failed to sustain that burden, then the defendant must be found not guilty.
The above instruction was derived from *Grizzle v. State*, 707 P.2d 1210, 1213 (Okla. Crim. App. 1985).

B. The Grizzle case: protection against an animal attack

Mr. Everett Chronister went to the lake and took his 11-month-old German Shepherd for a picnic with his family and allowed the dog to run loose. Mr. Tommy Grizzle Sr., and son, got into a fight with Chronister, and while the men rolled around on the ground, Chronister's dog began to bite young Grizzle's leg, then Grizzle Sr. shot Chronister's dog 4 times, killing it. Grizzle Sr. testified that the dog attacked him and his son. Chronister testified that he was threatened with the gun, while Grizzle Sr. allowed his son to beat Chronister. Grizzle Sr. was convicted of two crimes; animal cruelty and pointing a firearm. On appeal, he was exonerated on the charge of cruelty to animals, but the conviction for pointing a firearm was upheld. The appellate court analyzed the case and decided, "The kind of and amount of force, however, should be reasonably proportionate to the kind and amount of danger presented by the animal's attack. Appellant's theory of defense is based upon this rule. In essence, he asserts that if one is reasonably defending himself or another from the attack of an animal, the injury to the animal is not so cruel and malicious as to be within the scope of 21 O.S. 1981 § 1685 (the crime of animal cruelty). Appellant contends that the shooting of this dog was not unreasonable under the circumstance." *Grizzle*, 707 P.2d at 1212. The Court of Criminal Appeals agreed with Grizzle on the self-defense issue as to the cruelty to animals charge but upheld the pointing of the firearm charge.

If it was not for the *Grizzle* case, there would be no law allowing a person to request a jury instruction of self-defense against a normal animal except for a general self-defense concept called "justification by necessity."

C. The doctrine of justification by necessity

As we previously discussed, there is a common law defense of self-defense against an attack by an animal described in the *Grizzle* case. However, to be thorough, it is appropriate to discuss all applicable theories of self-defense, including justification by necessity.

As will be discussed below, sometimes, due to the facts of an individual case, the only claim for legal justification a person can make in court is one of justification by necessity. The common law recognizes a very broad justification/defense to potential criminal liability called "necessity."

Oklahoma recognizes the defense of necessity, and the Court of Criminal Appeals discussed it in the case of *Jones v. City of Tulsa*, 857 P.2d 814 (Okla. Crim. App. 1993). The general rule cited by the appellate court was: "In general, the defense of necessity is allowed when a defendant is faced with the burden of committing a lesser harm to prevent the occurrence of a different and somewhat greater harm. The harm being prevented needs to be *significant* and *immediate*. Here, appellants contend this criteria was met because the trespass was carried out to avoid the termination of human life [a greater harm]."

In the years before the *Grizzle* case, "justification by necessity" was the only defense a defendant who was charged with animal cruelty could muster. *See Laner v. State,* 381 P.2d 905 (Okla. Crim. App. 1963), where Mr. Laner asserted the defense of necessity, but was convicted for cruelty to animals when he, from a distance, shot several trained hunting dogs while they were chasing deer on a neighbor's property. The trial court and the appellate court found his actions to be so cruel and malicious as to defeat the defense of necessity, thus, the harm prevented (hunting dogs chasing deer) was not significant and immediate as to Mr. Laner.

The typical statutory laws you would expect to find regarding self-defense against an animal attacking a person don't exist under Oklahoma law. However, the common law, as explained in the *Grizzle* case, provides the needed defense. The law of necessity still exists in the common law, and is available if needed. The *Grizzle* case, when applied to a fact situation involving self-defense against an animal attack simplifies the defense against a charge of animal cruelty and thus removes any dependence on the defense of justification by necessity. What this means is that one is legally justified for using deadly force against an attacking animal, as explained in the *Grizzle* case. Justification by necessity is therefore a defense to be used as a last resort.

So, how does this all work in an example limited to the application of justification by necessity instead of using the *Grizzle* case as a defense?

Example:

> *Jim is walking in his neighborhood, when out of nowhere, three large pit bulls spot him and immediately begin running toward him barking with sharp fangs showing. Jim barely has time to draw and fire his .40 caliber Glock at the lead dog just before it lunges at him. Having dispatched one dog, the other two dogs flee.*

If, for some reason, Jim finds himself charged with any form of crime for his shooting of the dog that is not animal cruelty (this could be anything from reckless handling of a firearm to discharge of a firearm in public, *etc.*), Jim will not be able to rely on a specific statute for self-defense because none exists. Rather, Jim, for this example, must rely on the legal doctrine of justification by necessity as described above.

Jim would argue that preventing a person (in this case, himself) from being mauled or killed by a dog when walking in his neighborhood outweighs the law against either discharging a firearm in the city limits, or a charge of cruelty to animals. However, a prosecutor would be free to question all aspects of Jim's conduct and second-guess Jim's actions in court. In this case, it will be for the finder of fact, judge or jury, to decide if Jim was immediately in the zone of severe personal injury or if Jim was physically remote from actual danger.

Practical Legal Tip:

Beware! Using deadly force against a dog or cat that is only digging into your flowerbed or getting into your garbage will rarely be justified even under the doctrine of necessity. *-Robert*

D. Protecting livestock

> **Animals chasing or injuring livestock – Right to kill: Oklahoma Statutes Title 4 § 41(A)**
>
> It shall be lawful for a person to kill any animal of the family canidae or the family felidae found chasing livestock off the premises of the owner of the animal if the person is the owner or occupant of the property on which the animal is chasing the livestock or if the person is authorized to kill such an animal by the owner or occupant of such property.

With regard to charges of cruelty to a member of the dog or cat family, a specific statutory defense for killing or injuring an animal is on the books in Oklahoma if a person discovers the dog or cat on his or her property and it is in the act of injuring that person's livestock. Members of the "canidae" or "felidae" family include both domestic and wild dogs and cats including; wolves, coyotes, bobcats, lynx, cougars and any mixed variations. If you catch such an animal chasing, killing or destroying your livestock, you will be authorized by law in using force or deadly force against it.

Livestock is defined at 4 O.S. § 41(I)(1),(2), and includes: cattle, bison, hogs, sheep, goats, equines, domesticated rabbits, chickens, poultry and exotic livestock. Exotic livestock includes bovidae, cervidae, and birds of the ratite group. This defense does not include dogs or cats as livestock animals. *See* 4 O.S. § 85.1.

It is notable that this section is specifically limited to dog and cat attacks on domestic animals, not people. Additionally, please note that for purposes of Title 4, a dog on cat attack or a dog on dog attack is not covered because the statute excludes dogs and cats as domestic livestock animals, *see* 4 O.S. § 85.1.

E. Destructive wild animal pests

It's not uncommon to be troubled by furbearing pests on your property, such as wild hogs, beavers, otters, minks, squirrels, badgers, skunks, raccoons, muskrats, opossums, foxes, and other noisome pests.

Many of these animals destroy property, crops, and so forth in their attempt to build their dens, nests, or find food. But, does the Oklahoma Wildlife Code provide you with recourse in the event you and your property are troubled by one of these animals?

Unlike Title 4 O.S. § 41, which makes it lawful to kill marauding dogs and cats, Title 29 of the Oklahoma Statutes, the Wildlife Conservation Code, is a statutory scheme to promote hunting and fishing in Oklahoma. However, the conservation code provides for severe penalties related to taking game out of season, poaching, and using spotlights and unlicensed traps. Game wardens tend to view the taking of fur-bearing animals by an unlicensed person to be in the nature of unlicensed hunting/illegally killing rather than to be in the nature of self-defense or defense of property. *See* 29 O.S. § 4-112, hunting license requirement.

29 O.S. § 2-118 of the Oklahoma Wildlife Conservation Code defines a "taking" of a fur-bearing animal to include killing that animal. There are hunting seasons for most fur bearing animals that control the hunting/taking of these animals. It is best to consult the Wildlife Conservation Code for applicable hunting seasons, bag limits and methods for trapping, removal, or relocation of fur-bearing pests.

Fortunately, the Oklahoma Wildlife Department provides that nothing in their regulations prevents the killing of furbearers actually found destroying livestock or poultry. In addition, nothing in their regulation prevents the running or chasing of coyote, bobcat, fox or raccoon with dogs for sport only, except on those public lands where such activity is prohibited. There is nothing in the Oklahoma Statutes that specifically authorizes the killing of furbearers found destroying property so we would advise using your best judgment when faced with this situation.

F. Federal law defenses

Federal law, in a comprehensive fashion, has actually had the foresight to specifically provide that a person may kill an animal protected by federal law in defense of human life, such as the regulations concerning the "Mexican wolf" (Canis lupus baileyi) in 50 CFR § 17.84(k)(7)(i), or the Grizzly bear in 50 CFR § 17.40(b)(1)(i)(B). Unlike the Oklahoma statutes, this makes the Federal law clear and comprehensible. Therefore, if you are carrying a firearm in a National Park (*See* Chapters 9 and 10), and you find yourself face to face with a grizzly bear, you will have a legal defense for protecting yourself.

CHAPTER SEVEN

WHEN CAN I LEGALLY USE MY GUN: PART IV UNDERSTANDING WHEN DEADLY FORCE CAN BE USED TO PROTECT PROPERTY

I. Overview of the law to protect property

Oklahoma law allows a person to protect, with non-deadly force, their lawfully possessed property from another's unlawful interference or trespass. Further, Oklahoma law, under certain circumstances, will allow a person to use deadly force to protect occupied property. The Oklahoma statutes dealing with legally justified non-deadly or deadly force to defend property are as follows:

21 O.S § 643: Force against another and unlawful, when—Self Defense—Defense of property

21 O.S § 733: Justifiable homicide by any person

21 O.S. § 1289.25: Physical or deadly force against intruder

Protection of property will be analyzed under the same "reasonable person" standard discussed in Chapters 4 and 5. In addition to the above sections, Oklahoma common law does not promote, but rather punishes the use of traps, spring guns, or dangerous/deadly devices to protect property under the law of negligence. In *Julian v. Sinclair Oil & Gas,* 32 P.2d 31 (Okla. 1934), a negligence case, the court stated: "Where there is something done by the owner which is in the nature of a... wanton injury, he will be liable to an action for negligence even by a trespasser, as if an owner of premises with great recklessness shot a trespasser, or if the owner set spring guns upon his premises and injure a trespasser. "The case of *Ladow v. Oklahoma Gas & Elec. Co.*, 119 P.2d 250 (Okla. 1911), discusses and criticizes negligent or intentional setting of traps, "Such, too, is the humanity of the law, that one may not justifiably, or even excusably, place a dangerous pitfall, a wolf-trap, or a spring-gun, purposely to catch and injure even willful trespassers poaching upon his grounds."

II. When is someone legally justified to use "non-deadly force" but not "deadly force" to protect their own property?

A. Prevent trespass or unlawful interference with property

The law answers this question based upon the justified use of non-deadly force to protect property contained in section 643. Subsection 643(3) provides that a person is justified in using force to prevent or attempt to prevent another person's unlawful trespass or interference with their property, *e.g.*, stealing property, vandalizing property, *etc.*

Defense of Property:
Oklahoma Statutes Title 21 § 643(3)

To use or to attempt to offer to use force or violence upon or toward the person of another is not unlawful in the following cases:
(3) When committed either by the person about to be injured, or by any other person in such person's aid or defense, in preventing or attempting to prevent an offense against such person, or any trespass or other unlawful interference with real or personal property in such person's lawful possession...

B. What if you catch someone in the act?

In plain terms, if someone is unlawfully taking your personal property, you are justified in using sufficient force to stop them. 21 O.S § 643, authorizes a person to prevent an illegal attempt, by force, to take or interfere with your property in his or her lawful possession. Of course, just like instances of self-defense, you must also meet the standard of *reasonable belief in the necessity of the use of force*. The force used must be limited to "sufficient" under the circumstances to prevent the offense. The catch is that there is a fine but blurry line between sufficient force and excessive force used to prevent the offense.

Sufficient Force to Protect Your Property:
Oklahoma Uniform Jury Instructions CR 8-16

The amount of force used may not exceed that amount of force a reasonable person, in the circumstances and from the viewpoint of the defendant, would have used to prevent the trespass or unlawful interference.

C. Legal presumption of reasonableness when defending property

Oklahoma law provides no legal presumptions of reasonableness for uses of force to protect property when it comes to preventing or terminating a trespass or interference with property. Thus, the jury will be the ultimate arbiter of the reasonableness of conduct, as well as whether the force used was limited to force "sufficient" to prevent the offense.

The analysis so far leads us to the question: if force may legally be used to prevent or terminate a trespass or interference with property, what constitutes a trespass or interference with property?

1. What is trespassing?

The commonly understood meaning of trespass is "an unlawful act committed against the person or property of another, especially wrong entry of another's property" *Black's Law Dictionary, 10th edition. Black's Law Dictionary* also defines criminal trespass as: "a trespass on property that is clearly marked against trespass by signs or fences." This commonly understood definition of trespass and criminal trespass is different than the offense of criminal trespass found in 21 O.S. § 1835.

Oklahoma Criminal Trespass
21 O.S. § 1835

Whoever shall willfully or maliciously enter the garden, yard, pasture or field of another after being expressly forbidden to do so or without permission by the owner or lawful occupant thereof when such property is posted shall be deemed guilty of trespass and upon conviction thereof shall be fined in any sum not to exceed Two Hundred Fifty Dollars ($250); provided, that this provision shall not apply to registered land surveyors and registered professional engineers for the purpose of land surveying in the performance of their professional services; and, provided further, that anyone who willfully or maliciously enters any such garden, yard, pasture or field, and therein commits or attempts to commit waste, theft, or damage shall be deemed guilty of a misdemeanor and upon conviction thereof shall be fined in any sum not less than Fifty Dollars ($50) nor more than Five Hundred Dollars ($500), or by confinement in the county jail for not less than thirty (30) days nor more than six (6) months, or both such fine and imprisonment. For purposes of this section, "posted" means exhibiting signs to read as follows: "PROPERTY RESTRICTED"; "POSTED - KEEP OUT"; "KEEP OUT"; "NO TRESPASSING"; or similar signs which are displayed. Property that is fenced or not fenced must have such signs placed conspicuously and at all places where entry to the property is normally expected.

In other words, unlike the common definition of trespass where a person becomes a trespasser whether they realized it or not (unwittingly walking across the King's hunting grounds, for instance), under Oklahoma statutes, prior to committing a criminal offense a person must have knowledge that they are in a place they do not belong or are not welcome, and the landowner must take specific steps, according to law, to communicate that knowledge. In addition, the crime of criminal trespass is strictly limited to when a person is found in or on a piece of real property without permission—the offense does not cover situations involving personal property.

2. Trespass, for legal justification, is not just "Criminal Trespass"
How is "trespasser" defined in section 643 for purposes of defending property? Because the plain language of section 643 refers only to terminating "the other's trespass" and does not reference a "criminal trespass," it is clear that the statute intends to follow a broader definition of trespass than just the offense of criminal trespass found in section 21 O.S. § 1835. In other words, a person may be potentially justified in using force against a person found trespassing on their land—even if that person has not committed the crime of criminal trespass; but only so long as the use of force is accompanied with a reasonable belief that it is necessary to terminate the trespass. However, in the event an unwitting trespasser has no intention of remaining on or damaging the property, under the standard of "sufficiency" found in section 643, the use of force would not be necessary. Without a specific definition of what "trespass" means as found in section 643, a jury will ultimately decide whether or not a person had a reasonable belief that it was necessary to use force to terminate another person's trespass on the land and that the force used was merely sufficient force required to resist or prevent the offense.

3. What is unlawful interference with property?
You have a legal right to prevent "interference with property," but what does this mean? It can be a theft, destruction, vandalism, or anything else that diminishes a person's right to their property. Whether particular conduct rises to "interference with property" is an issue that a jury decides.

4. Is there a statutory minimum value of property before force may be legally used to protect it?
No. There exists no statutory minimum value for property before force may be used to protect it. 21 O.S. § 643 does not specify that property a person seeks to protect must be of a

minimum dollar value in order for a person to protect it.

Having said that, what the Oklahoma statutes generally specify is that a person must have a reasonable belief that the use of force is necessary to protect property before a person would be justified in using non-deadly force.

Realistically, even though a bad guy may be in the process of taking or injuring property in another's lawful possession, some property may be of such little value that the use of force to prevent the taking or injuring would not be deemed reasonable by the reasonable person (people on a jury).

> Example:
>
> *One day at work, Fred walks into Ricky's office and takes a half-eaten bag of chips off of Ricky's desk and walks away. Ricky, upset at having his favorite chips pilfered from his desk, jumps up, chases Fred down, shoves him to the ground, and starts beating on Fred to prevent the taking of his chips. On his way to chase Fred, Ricky also passes the office kitchen where identical bags of chips are available for community consumption.*

Was Ricky's use of force against Fred legally justified? Probably not. It may be a very hard sell to a jury that a person was beat up over a half-eaten bag of potato chips. However, some members of a jury may value a potato chip very differently. What if a thief is stealing irreplaceable family photos? There's no monetary value on the photos—only personal sentiment. Again, the law is silent on the subject of any monetary value of property to be defended.

> The point to be made here is that some items simply may not have enough value (financial, sentimental, or otherwise) to provide a person with a legal excuse to exercise sufficient force necessary to prevent the taking of the item. In this example, not only do the chips have little

monetary value, but there are others readily available for replacement from the kitchen. It would be hard to imagine a jury finding a person to be justified in using any force, for such a petit larceny! Remember, your conduct will always be evaluated under a reasonable person standard and that there are no legal presumptions available for defending property under section 643.

Practical Legal Tip:

There are plenty of clever signs and bumper stickers out there advocating the use of a firearm. "Keep honking, I'm reloading," and "Trespassers Will Be Shot" are seen often on the bumpers of Oklahoma cars and the fence posts of Oklahoma homeowners. But these signs, despite the chuckle they may elicit from a passerby, are not a good idea. Even if meant only to prompt a laugh, if you are forced to use your firearm to defend yourself and end up in court, you can bet that the prosecutor will attempt to bring these signs up to the jury for consideration. Remember, a prosecutor will use every avenue to paint you in the worst light. Keep the laughs to yourself and take the signs down! *-Robert*

III. When is someone legally justified in using "deadly force" to protect occupied property?

When a person may legally use deadly force (force that is intended or likely to cause death or great bodily harm) to defend his or her property is addressed in sections 733 and 1289.25 of the Oklahoma Statutes.

A. Defense of Habitation

> ***Justifiable Homicide by Other Persons:***
> **21 O.S. § 733**
>
> A. Homicide is also justifiable when committed by any person in any of the following cases:
> 1. When resisting any attempt to murder such person, or to commit any felony upon him, or upon or in any dwelling house in which such person is;
> 2. When committed in the lawful defense of such person or of another, when the person using force reasonably believes such force is necessary to prevent death or great bodily harm to himself or herself or another or to terminate or prevent the commission of a forcible felony; or
> 3. When necessarily committed in attempting, by lawful ways and means, to apprehend any person for any felony committed; or in lawfully suppressing any riot; or in lawfully keeping and preserving the peace.

The black and white language provides that a person is justified in using deadly force when resisting a felony upon or in any dwelling house in which that person is lawfully present. This defense requires that a reasonable person, in the circumstances and from the viewpoint of the defendant, would reasonably have believed that there was an imminent danger that such felony would occur. This defense of a dwelling is distinguished from the restricted right of defense of other property in section 643, which only permits non-deadly force.

The justification in section 733 does appear somewhat limited.

The defendant must have been preventing a felony, and that felony must have been committed upon or in a "dwelling house." The use of the term "dwelling house" would seem to preclude the use of deadly force in a place of business. OUJI-CR 8-14. Additionally, there is no presumption of reasonableness available within section 733. Although section 1289.25 is based on the same concept of defending your "castle," section 1289.25's applicability is slightly different.

B. Oklahoma's Castle Doctrine

Justified Use of Deadly Force to Protect Your Occupied Property:
Oklahoma Statutes Title 21 § 1289.25(A),(B),(D),(E),(F)

A. The Legislature hereby recognizes that the citizens of the State of Oklahoma have a right to expect absolute safety within their own homes or places of business.

B. A person or an owner, manager or employee of a business is presumed to have held a reasonable fear of imminent peril of death or great bodily harm to himself or herself or another when using defensive force that is intended or likely to cause death or great bodily harm to another if:

1. The person against whom the defensive force was used was in the process of unlawfully and forcefully entering or had unlawfully and forcibly entered, a dwelling, residence, occupied vehicle, or a place of business, or if that person had removed or was attempting to remove another against the will of that person from the dwelling, residence, occupied vehicle, or place of business; and
2. The person who uses defensive force knew or had reason to believe that an unlawful and forcible entry or unlawful and forcible act was occurring or had occurred.

C. A person who is not engaged in an unlawful activity and who is attacked in any other place where he or she has a right to be has no duty to retreat and has the right to stand

> his or her ground and meet force with force, including deadly force, if he or she reasonably believes it is necessary to do so to prevent death or great bodily harm to himself or herself or another or to prevent the commission of a forcible felony.
>
> D. A person who unlawfully and by force enters or attempts to enter the dwelling, residence, occupied vehicle of another person, or a place of business is presumed to be doing so with the intent to commit an unlawful act involving force or violence.
>
> E. A person who uses force, as permitted pursuant to the provisions of subsections B and D of this section, is justified in using such force and is immune from criminal prosecution and civil action for the use of such force. As used in this subsection, the term "criminal prosecution" includes charging or prosecuting the defendant.

As discussed in previous chapters, section 1289.25 contains Oklahoma's "Castle Doctrine" and "Stand Your Ground" law. When it comes to the defense of property in section 1289.25(B), essentially there are two requirements:

1. The person against whom the defensive force was used was in the process of unlawfully and forcefully entering or had unlawfully and forcibly entered, a dwelling, residence, occupied vehicle, or a place of business; and
2. The person who uses defensive force knew or had reason to believe that an unlawful and forcible entry or unlawful and forcible act was occurring or had occurred.

This seems similar to the applicability of section 733, however, the protection afforded in this section extends beyond dwelling house to occupied vehicles and places of business. Additionally, the legal justification for deadly force to protect an occupied residence/dwelling/vehicle/place of business under section 1289.25 is accompanied with two legal presumptions:

1. A person is presumed to have held a reasonable fear of imminent peril of death or great bodily harm to himself or herself. § 1289.25(B).
2. A person who unlawfully and by force enters or attempts to enter the occupied dwelling, residence, occupied vehicle of another person, or a place of business is presumed to be doing so with the intent to commit an unlawful act involving force or violence. § 1289.25(E).

These presumptions do not apply if certain facts exist. If the person against whom defensive force was used had a right to be in or is a lawful resident of the dwelling, residence, or vehicle (and there is not a protective order from domestic violence), the presumption is lost. Additionally, the person who used the defensive force cannot be engaged in an unlawful activity or be using the dwelling, residence, vehicle, or place of business to further unlawful activity. § 1289.25(C).

An old version of section 1289.25 provided that the person using defensive force must be an "occupant." The Court of Criminal Appeals clarified that the Oklahoma Legislature intended for the term "occupant" as used in § 1289.25 to include visitors, *i.e.* persons legally inside the dwelling. *State v. Anderson,* 972 P.2d 32 (Okla. Crim. App. 1998).

Since then, the legislature has changed the language to be more expansive than the previous "occupant" and now covers any "person, owner, manager, or employee," which would seem to indicate that as long as the person is lawfully present, they are covered.

Example:

After a long day at work, Gordon pulls into his driveway just in time to see two masked men running out of his front door with his big screen television and his grandfather's expensive watch on one of the men's wrist. Gordon gets out of his car and demands that the men stop

> *where they are, but they ignore him and run away. Gordon pulls his Glock 17 and fires at the running men, killing one and injuring the other.*

Was Gordon justified under § 733 or § 1289.25 to use deadly force? Likely not. There are no cases wherein a court approved the use of deadly force to prevent a felonious trespass or wrongful interference with property, which did not occur in a dwelling house and did not involve self-defense or defense of another.

Practical Legal Tip:

Under section 1289.25, a person is provided with a presumption to use deadly force against an intruder who has committed a felony while the property is occupied. Section 643 requires non-deadly force, no presumption and property is unoccupied. *-Robert*

IV. Can I protect another person's property?

Defense of Another's Property:
Oklahoma Statutes Title 21 § 643(3)

To use or to attempt to offer to use force or violence upon or toward the person of another is not unlawful in the following cases:
3. When committed either by the person about to be injured, or by any other person in such person's aid or defense, in preventing or attempting to prevent an offense against such person, or any trespass or other unlawful interference with real or personal property in such person's lawful possession provided the force or violence used is not

more than sufficient to prevent such offense.

Section 643 specifically permits the use of non-deadly force sufficient to prevent an offense by someone other than the actual possessor of real or personal property, so long as it is done in aid or defense of the person with lawful possession.

Similarly, neither sections 733 nor 1289.25 require that the person using defensive force to defend property be the owner of the property. Section 733 simply refers to a person *in* a dwelling house and 1289.25 uses the same "person" language.

V. How are the crimes associated with defense of property defined under Oklahoma law?

How does Oklahoma law define those felonies relating to property?

1. Arson in the first degree: Any person who willfully and maliciously sets fire to or burns, or by the use of any explosive device, accelerant, ignition device, heat-producing device or substance, destroys in whole or in part, or causes to be burned or destroyed, or aids, counsels or procures the burning or destruction of any building or structure or contents thereof, inhabited or occupied by one or more persons, whether the property of that person or another, or who willfully and maliciously sets fire to or burns, or by the use of any explosive device, accelerant, ignition device, heat-producing device or substance causes a person to be burned, or aids, counsels or procures the burning of a person shall, upon conviction, be guilty of arson in the first degree, which is a felony... 21 O.S. § 1401(A).

2. Burglary in the First Degree: Every person who breaks into and enters the dwelling house of another, in which there is at the time some human being, with intent to commit some crime therein, either:

> a. By forcibly bursting or breaking the wall, or an outer door, window, or shutter of a window of such house or the lock or bolts of such door, or the fastening of such

window or shutter; or

b. By breaking in any other manner, being armed with a dangerous weapon or being assisted or aided by one or more confederates then actually present; or

c. By unlocking an outer door by means of false keys or by picking the lock thereof, or by lifting a latch or opening a window, is guilty of burglary in the first degree. 21 O.S. § 1431.

3. Burglary in the Second Degree: Acts Constituting: Every person who breaks and enters any building or any part of any building, room, booth, tent, railroad car, automobile, truck, trailer, vessel or other structure or erection, in which any property is kept, [or breaks into or forcibly opens, a coin operated or vending machine or device with intent to steal any property therein or to commit any felony,] is guilty of burglary in the second degree. 21 O.S. § 1435.

A note about "Burglary in the Second Degree"

Oklahoma statutes use the word "burglary" in the most general sense of the word. The statute gives no qualifiers or limitations on what type of "burglary" a person would be justified in using deadly force to thwart. This is important because there are two types of burglary that are criminalized in Title 21, Chapter 58 of Oklahoma statutes. It is generally accepted that deadly force is justified to prevent a burglary of a habitation and burglary of a building that is not a habitation, since these are both felonies, they are contained in statutes containing "burglary" in the title, and they are crimes of a more personal nature where the perpetrator intends on committing other felonies or theft. However, there is an unresolved potential legal issue of whether the crime of burglary in the Second Degree, such as "burglary of a motor vehicle" and "burglary of a coin-operated or vending machine" as defined in 21 O.S. § 1435, should be included as felonies where deadly force is justifiably used under 21 O.S. § 733. There exist legal arguments both for the inclusion and exclusion of these two crimes, as applicable felonies; however, until a court of appeals addresses the issue, they remain mere arguments.

4. Robbery: Robbery in the First Degree is when, in the course of committing the theft, the defendant:
a. Inflicts serious bodily injury upon the person;
b. Threatens a person with immediate serious bodily injury;
c. Intentionally puts a person in fear of immediate serious bodily injury; or
d. Commits or threatens to commit a felony upon the person.

When accomplished in any other manner, it is Robbery in the Second Degree. 21 O.S. § 797. Since robbery is a crime against a person, all self-defense issues discussed in Chapter 5 are in play as well.

VI. How can I assist law enforcement?

A. Acting under a police officer's direction

As an attorney, I am regularly asked about whether one can make a citizen's arrest, and how one can best assist law enforcement in dicey situations. Since every legal situation is unique, here we'll just provide a brief summary of the general law, as well as reference some of the statutes governing the use of citizen's arrests and how to assist authorities.

Refusal to Aid Officer in Arrest
21 O.S. § 537

Every person who, after having been lawfully commanded to aid any officer in arresting any person or in retaking any person who has escaped from legal custody, or in executing any legal process, willfully neglects or refuses to aid such officer, is guilty of a misdemeanor.

A citizen may be pressed into service by a police officer to assist in the arrest or re-arrest of an escaping prisoner. To refuse the officer's command makes one subject to criminal prosecution. Section 537 operates as the statute under which law enforcement is able to use a citizen to assist them in applying force against a suspect. In order to enable officers to use all available resources at their disposal (such as an ordinary citizen), the statute authorizes and commands an individual to act at an officer's direction.

B. Pretending to act under legal authority

Anyone engaging in a citizen's arrest must be aware of the danger of the charge of pretending to be a public officer. Anyone who arrests any other person or detains him or her against his will could be guilty of a misdemeanor.

Arresting Person Under Pretense Authority
Oklahoma Statutes Title 21 § 535

Every public officer or person pretending to be a public officer, who under the pretense or color of any process or other legal authority, arrests any person, or detains him against his will, or seizes or levies upon any property, or dispossesses anyone of any lands or tenements without due and legal process, is guilty of a misdemeanor.

21 O.S. § 535 places a constraint on anyone attempting or completing an arrest or detainer against another person against their will. The risk is that the arrest might be perceived as being an arrest under a pretense of authority, without authority, thus ultimately being without due or legal process. It is highly risky, and not recommended, that one act as a public officer without a peace officer ordering one to assist.

When making a citizen's arrest, one must identify oneself as a citizen. The arrestee must not perceive an appearance or color of legal authority. The arresting party must meet the same "reasonable belief" standards we've outlined throughout this chapter before using force. In order to avoid an accusation of pretending to be a public officer, one must identify oneself as an ordinary citizen, and communicate the reason one is making the arrest. Beware, this specific statute does not authorize the use of non-deadly or deadly force, so justification for the use of force will have to be found elsewhere.

C. Magistrate orders one to arrest another person

21 O.S. § 538 requires that a person ordered or lawfully commanded by a magistrate to arrest another person, must obey or face misdemeanor charges for willfully neglecting or refusing to obey. "Every person who, after having been lawfully commanded by any magistrate to arrest another person, willfully neglects or refuses so to do, is guilty of a misdemeanor."

D. Instituting legal action or making arrest in name of non-existent person

21 O.S. § 584 prohibits every person from making or procuring an arrest in the name of a person who does not exist, or has not consented that the arrest be instituted or made. "Every person who maliciously institutes or prosecutes any action or legal proceeding; or makes or procures any arrest, in the name of a person who does not exist, or has not consented that it be instituted or made, is guilty of a misdemeanor."

Practical Legal Tip:

If you use your firearm for defensive purposes, the first number you should call is 911. But keep your call brief: you only need to tell the operator that you have been the victim of a crime, where you are located, and some identifying information. After that, hang up! You are not required to remain on the line and doing so could cause you problems later. Remember, all 911 calls are recorded and operators are trained to gather as much information as possible. No matter how justified you are in your use of a firearm, something you say on a 911 call may become a real headache later at trial. *-Robert*

Example:

> *Sheriff Boss Hogg normally sends a deputy out to arrest suspects of criminal activity in the town of Boomer Sooner. One day Sam Stranger from out-of-town says to men playing pool at Smitty's Bar and Grill, "Sheriff Boss Hogg said for me to bring you in. Put on your hats boys, you're coming with me." Sam Stranger draws a gun to effectuate the arrest. Sheriff Boss Hogg did not order Sam to assist him in arresting the men and the arrest is unauthorized.*

Sam Stranger will be charged with a misdemeanor, violation of § 584, and any other crimes committed involving the use of firearm not related to self-defense.

VII. What crimes can I be charged with when my use of deadly force is not justified?

We've reached the end of our discussion on when you may be justified in using a firearm in defense of your person or property. Now it's time to give a brief summary of where you'll find yourself in legal trouble if you don't meet the elements of justification as we've described throughout this book. The following list describes some of the crimes involving the use of deadly force by the discharge of a firearm and where relevant provisions may be found in Oklahoma law:

Crimes Involving Deadly Force or a Firearm:

1. Murder in the First Degree: 21 O.S. § 701.7
2. Murder in the Second Degree: 21 O.S. § 701.8
3. Manslaughter in the First Degree: 21 O.S. § 711
4. Manslaughter in the Second Degree: 21 O.S. § 716
5. Assault and Battery with a Deadly Weapon: 21 O.S. §§ 645, 646, 652
6. Pointing a Firearm: 21 O.S. § 1279
7. Felony Discharging a Firearm: 21 O.S. § 1289.17A
8. Misdemeanor Discharging Firearm: 21 O.S. § 1364
9. Felony Pointing a Firearm: 21 O.S. § 1289.16
10. Disturbance by Loud or Unusual Noise or Abusive, Violent, Obscene, Profane or Threatening Language: 21 O.S. § 1362

CHAPTER EIGHT

LAW OF CONCEALED CARRY: PART I
THE LICENSE QUALIFICATIONS, REQUIREMENTS, APPEALS, AND REGULATIONS

In 1995, the Oklahoma Legislature passed the law allowing for the issuance of Self-Defense Act Licenses (hereinafter referred to as a handgun license). In Oklahoma, qualified individuals may obtain a handgun license, which allows the carrying of a concealed or open carry handgun on their person for any lawful purpose. To obtain a handgun license, a person must meet certain requirements and submit an application to the Oklahoma State Bureau of Investigation (OSBI). This chapter deals exclusively with the licensed carry of a handgun in Oklahoma. A handgun license allows for the lawful carry of handguns; the license does not permit the carrying of long guns but does control the carrying of certain edged weapons, knives, and other offensive weapons.

I. The evolution of the Oklahoma concealed carry law

Despite its reputation as being a "gun-friendly state," the laws remained unorganized until 2012 when a comprehensive concealed carry law was passed. On May 15, 2012, Oklahoma State Senate Bill 1733 was signed into law by Governor Mary Fallin and authorized open and concealed carry of handguns by license holders. This law took effect November 1, 2012, and made Oklahoma the 25th state of the United States to allow licensed open carry. From 2009 to 2012, the OSBI issued 126,868 handgun licenses to Oklahoma residents, more than the seven years prior combined. OSBI does not have figures available before 2002.

Oklahoma statutes 21 O.S. § 1290.1, *et seq.*, contain the law on how handgun licenses are administered in Oklahoma. Throughout this chapter, we will discuss the requirements, the application process, as well as the rights given to license holders for carrying a handgun in the State of Oklahoma. At the time of publishing, open carry of handguns in public is permitted under Oklahoma law. Persons holding a valid handgun license may carry a handgun openly, if they choose.

II. How Do I Obtain a Handgun License?

A. Persons who are legally qualified to obtain a handgun license

In this section, we will discuss the requirements to apply for an Oklahoma handgun license as well as potential disqualifications. In addition to the requirements listed below, applicants must also complete state mandated education with an instructor certified by the OSBI and demonstrate proficiency with a semi-automatic handgun, revolver or derringer of .22 caliber or greater.

ELIGIBILITY REQUIREMENTS
Oklahoma Statutes Title 21 § 1290.9

In Oklahoma, a person must:

1. Be a citizen of the United States;
2. Establish a residency in the State of Oklahoma. For purposes of the Oklahoma Self-Defense Act, the term residency shall apply to any person who either possesses a valid Oklahoma driver license or state photo identification card and physically maintains a residence in this state or to any person, including the spouse of such person, who has permanent military orders within this state and possesses a valid driver license from another state where such person and spouse of such person claim residency;
3. Be at least twenty-one (21) years of age;
4. Complete a firearms safety and training course and demonstrate competence and qualifications with the type of pistol to be carried by the person as provided in Section 1290.14 of this title, and submit proof of training and qualification or an exemption for training and qualification as authorized by Section 1290.14 of this title;
5. Submit the required fee and complete the application process as provided in Section 1290.12 of this title; and

6. Comply in good faith with the provisions of the Oklahoma Self-Defense Act.

MANDATORY PRECLUSIONS
Oklahoma Statutes Title 21 § 1290.10

The conditions stated in this section shall preclude a person from eligibility for a handgun license pursuant to the provisions of the Oklahoma Self-Defense Act.

The occurrence of any one of the following conditions shall deny the person the right to have a handgun license pursuant to the provisions of the Oklahoma Self-Defense Act. Prohibited conditions are:

1. Ineligible to possess a pistol due to any felony conviction or adjudication as a delinquent as provided by Section 1283 of this title, except as provided in subsection B of Section 1283 of this title;
2. Any felony conviction pursuant to any law of another state, a felony conviction pursuant to any provision of the United States Code, or any conviction pursuant to the laws of any foreign country, provided such foreign conviction would constitute a felony offense in this state if the offense had been committed in this state, except as provided in subsection B of Section 1283 of this title;
3. Adjudication as a mentally incompetent person pursuant to the provisions of the Oklahoma Mental Health Law, or an adjudication of incompetency entered in another state pursuant to any provision of law of that state, unless the person has been granted relief from the disqualifying disability pursuant to Section 1290.27 of this title;
4. Any false or misleading statement on the application for a handgun license as provided by paragraph 5 of Section 1290.12 of this title;
5. Conviction of any one of the following misdemeanor offenses in this state or in any other state:
   a. any assault and battery, which caused serious physical injury to the victim, or any second or subsequent

assault and battery conviction,

b. any aggravated assault and battery,
c. any stalking pursuant to Section 1173 of this title, or a similar law of another state,
d. a violation relating to the Protection from Domestic Abuse Act, or any violation of a victim protection order of another state,
e. any conviction relating to illegal drug use or possession; or
f. an act of domestic abuse as defined by Section 644 of this title or an act of domestic assault and battery or any comparable acts under the laws of another state. The preclusive period for a misdemeanor conviction related to illegal drug use or possession shall be ten (10) years from the date of completion of a sentence. For purposes of this subsection, "date of completion of a sentence" shall mean the day an offender completes all incarceration, probation, and parole pertaining to such sentence;

6. An attempted suicide or other condition relating to or indicating mental instability or an unsound mind which occurred within the preceding ten-year period from the date of the application for a license to carry a concealed firearm or that occurs during the period of licensure;

7. Currently undergoing treatment for a mental illness, condition, or disorder. For purposes of this paragraph, "currently undergoing treatment for a mental illness, condition, or disorder" means the person has been diagnosed by a licensed physician as being afflicted with a substantial disorder of thought, mood, perception, psychological orientation, or memory that significantly impairs judgment, behavior, capacity to recognize reality, or ability to meet the ordinary demands of life;

8. Significant character defects of the applicant as evidenced by a misdemeanor criminal record indicating habitual criminal activity;

9. Ineligible to possess a pistol due to any provision of law of

this state or the United States Code, except as provided in subsection B of Section 1283 of this title;
10. Failure to pay an assessed fine or surrender the handgun license as required by a decision by the administrative hearing examiner pursuant to authority of the Oklahoma Self-Defense Act;
11. Being subject to an outstanding felony warrant issued in this state or another state or the United States; or
12. Adjudication as a delinquent as provided by Section 1283 of this title, except as provided in subsection B of Section 1283 of this title.

OTHER PRECLUSIONS
Oklahoma Statutes Title 21 § 1290.11

A. The following conditions shall preclude a person from being eligible for a handgun license pursuant to the provisions of the Oklahoma Self-Defense Act for a period of time as prescribed in each of the following paragraphs:
1. An arrest for an alleged commission of a felony offense or a felony charge pending in this state, another state or pursuant to the United States Code. The preclusive period shall be until the final determination of the matter.
2. The person is subject to the provisions of a deferred sentence or deferred prosecution in this state or another state or pursuant to federal authority for the commission of a felony offense. The preclusive period shall be three (3) years and shall begin upon the final determination of the matter;
3. Any involuntary commitment for a mental illness, condition, or disorder pursuant to the provisions of Section 5-410 of Title 43A of the Oklahoma Statutes or any involuntary commitment in another state pursuant to any provisions of law of that state. The preclusive period shall be permanent as provided by Title 18 of the United States Code Section 922(g)(4) unless the person has been granted relief from the disqualifying disability pursuant to Section 3 of this

act;
4. The person has previously undergone treatment for a mental illness, condition, or disorder which required medication or supervision as defined by paragraph 7 of Section 1290.10 of this title. The preclusive period shall be three (3) years from the last date of treatment or upon presentation of a certified statement from a licensed physician stating that the person is either no longer disabled by any mental or psychiatric illness, condition, or disorder or that the person has been stabilized on medication for ten (10) years or more;
5. Inpatient treatment for substance abuse. The preclusive period shall be three (3) years from the last date of treatment or upon presentation of a certified statement from a licensed physician stating that the person has been free from substance use for twelve (12) months or more preceding the filing of an application for a handgun license;
6. Two or more convictions of public intoxication pursuant to Section 8 of Title 37 of the Oklahoma Statutes, or a similar law of another state. The preclusive period shall be three (3) years from the date of the completion of the last sentence;
7. Two or more misdemeanor convictions relating to intoxication or driving under the influence of an intoxicating substance or alcohol. The preclusive period shall be three (3) years from the date of the completion of the last sentence or shall require a certified statement from a licensed physician stating that the person is not in need of substance abuse treatment;
8. A court order for a final Victim Protection Order against the applicant, as authorized by the Protection from Domestic Abuse Act, or any court order granting a final victim protection order against the applicant from another state. The preclusive period shall be three (3) years from the date of the entry of the final court order, or sixty (60) days from the date an order was vacated, canceled or withdrawn;
9. An adjudicated delinquent or convicted felon residing in

the residence of the applicant which may be a violation of Section 1283 of this title. The preclusive period shall be thirty (30) days from the date the person no longer resides in the same residence as the applicant; or

10. An arrest for an alleged commission of, a charge pending for, or the person is subject to the provisions of a deferred prosecution for any one or more of the following misdemeanor offenses in this state or another state:

a. any assault and battery which caused serious physical injury to the victim or any second or subsequent assault and battery,
b. any aggravated assault and battery,
c. any stalking pursuant to Section 1173 of this title, or a similar law of another state,
d. any violation of the Protection from Domestic Abuse Act or any violation of a victim protection order of another state,
e. any violation relating to illegal drug use or possession, or
f. an act of domestic abuse as defined by Section 644 of this title or an act of domestic assault and battery or any comparable acts under the law of another state.

The preclusive period shall be until the final determination of the matter. The preclusive period for a person subject to the provisions of a deferred sentence for the offenses mentioned in this paragraph shall be three (3) years and shall begin upon the final determination of the matter.

B. Nothing in this section shall be construed to require a full investigation of the applicant by the OSBI.

Persons that are currently receiving psychiatric treatment may be disqualified from holding an Oklahoma handgun license while undergoing treatment. The State of Oklahoma considers the following to constitute evidence that a person has a psychiatric disorder or condition described in Oklahoma Statutes 21 O.S. §§ 1290.10 and 1290.11:

1. Involuntary psychiatric hospitalization,

2. Voluntary psychiatric hospitalization,
3. Inpatient substance abuse treatment,
4. Two or more public intoxication convictions for alcohol, or
5. Treatment for a mental illness, condition, or disorder which required medication or supervision.

B. If you don't disclose, you can expect your application to be delayed or denied!

The qualifying factor that probably delays the majority of applications revolves around a person's failure to fully disclose material facts. *See* 21 O.S. § 1290.10(4). To qualify for an Oklahoma handgun license, a person must not make any material misrepresentation or fail to disclose any material fact in his or her application. The application is signed under oath, in person, before the sheriff. Dire consequences may result from making a false or misleading statement on the application. Most often, this is due to a person failing to disclose a criminal conviction of one nature or another. The application process is serious business and one should be very careful about the answers given to ensure full and complete compliance with disclosure requirements.

Many applicants forget about things that may have happened many years ago, but which require disclosure in the application. The best practice is: when in doubt, disclose! Otherwise, a person may face unwanted delays, denial, or criminal sanctions for making a false or misleading statement on their application.

Note: be very careful in the wording of your disclosures. I have seen many applicants encounter difficulties in not using precise descriptions of their legal history, medical condition, *etc.* Be careful with your words!

C. What is a "deferred sentence?"

Under 22 O.S. § 991c of the Oklahoma Code of Criminal Procedure, "Upon a verdict or plea of guilty or upon a plea of nolo contendere, but before a judgment of guilt, the court may, without entering a judgment of guilt and with the consent of the defendant, defer further proceedings upon the specific conditions prescribed by the court not to exceed a ten-year period." Therefore, a deferred sentence is the legal act of either accepting culpability for a crime or refusing to contest the culpability of a crime without actually being convicted of the crime. A deferred sentence is effectively a form of probation—a defendant is released back into society under the condition that the defendant will stay out of legal trouble for a period of time imposed by a judge. At the conclusion of the probationary period, the judge will dismiss the charges against the defendant and the defendant will not be convicted.

D. What if I received a "deferred sentence?" Can I get a handgun license?

If a person received a "deferred sentence" as a result of a criminal charge, that person may still be eligible for a handgun license under specific conditions. 21 O.S. § 1290.11(2) states that a deferred sentence against a person for a felony offense will not prevent a person from possessing a handgun license after a three-year preclusive period upon final determination of the matter. Compare this section with § 1290.10(5(e)) which states a misdemeanor conviction relating to illegal drug use or possession has a preclusion period of ten years from the date of completion of sentence.

If a person has been arrested or charged with a crime which resulted in an order of a deferred sentence prior to his or her application for a handgun license and the crime for which the person received a deferred sentence was for the following misdemeanor offenses, then the person may be eligible to apply for a handgun license after a preclusive period of three years beginning upon the final determination of the matter. Persons who received a deferred sentence for any of the following misdemeanor offenses will qualify for a handgun license after the three-year period of preclusion:

a. any assault and battery which caused serious physical

injury to the victim or any second or subsequent assault and battery,

b. any aggravated assault and battery,
c. any stalking pursuant to Section 1173 of this title, or a similar law of another state,
d. any violation of the Protection from Domestic Abuse Act or any violation of a victim protection order of another state,
e. any violation relating to illegal drug use or possession, or
f. an act of domestic abuse as defined by Section 644 of this title or an act of domestic assault and battery or any comparable acts under the law of another state.

What this means is that persons who have received deferred sentences in Oklahoma or the equivalent from other states for any of the criminal offenses listed above may be eligible to apply for and possess an Oklahoma handgun license three years from the date that their deferred sentence was completed.

E. Suspension and revocation of a handgun license

1. What is the difference between suspension and revocation?

A suspension is only temporary and a person's license may be reinstated without the necessity of submitting a new application. This means that a person will not have to repeat the rigors of the application process or the classroom requirements in order to regain their handgun license.

A revocation means that the OSBI has decided that a person's license shall be terminated. In order for that person to ultimately regain the license, he or she must reapply from step one by attending a handgun license class and submitting the application and the applicable fees.

2. Under what circumstances can the OSBI suspend or revoke a handgun license?

21 O.S. § 1290.17, Suspension and Revocation of License, governs handgun license suspension and revocation and states

that a person's license may be suspended or revoked:

A. The discovery of or the occurrence of any condition pursuant to Section 1290.11 of this title, after a license has been issued, shall cause a suspension of the handgun license for a period of time as prescribed for the condition. Any provision of law that requires a revocation of a handgun license upon a conviction shall cause the Bureau to suspend the handgun license upon the discovery of the arrest of the person for such offense until a determination of the criminal case at which time the Bureau shall proceed with the appropriate administrative action. A licensee may voluntarily surrender a license to the Oklahoma State Bureau of Investigation at any time. Such surrender of a handgun license will render the license invalid.

C. Any law enforcement officer of this state shall confiscate a handgun license in the possession of any person and return it to the Oklahoma State Bureau of Investigation for appropriate administrative proceedings against the licensee when the license is no longer needed as evidence in any criminal proceeding, as follows:

1. Upon the arrest of the person for any felony offense;
2. Upon the arrest of the person for any misdemeanor offense enumerated as a preclusion to a handgun license;
3. For any violation of the provisions of the Oklahoma Self-Defense Act;
4. When the officer has been called to assist or is investigating any situation which would be a preclusion to having a handgun license; or
5. As provided in subsection D of Section 1290.8 of this title.

Any handgun license which is subsequently suspended or revoked must be immediately returned to the Oklahoma State Bureau of Investigation upon notification. Any person who fails to return a license after this notification of its suspension or revocation commits a misdemeanor offense.

4. What happens if my handgun license expires while it is suspended?

If you are unfortunate enough to have your Oklahoma handgun license expire during your period of suspension, you must apply for an Oklahoma handgun license as a new applicant once your suspension period ends. *See* 21 O.S. § 1290.17(E).

5. Procedure for revocation or suspension of a handgun license

Handgun licenses are not automatically suspended or revoked even if one of the elements of revocation or suspension discussed above apply. The revocation or suspension requires law enforcement action before it actually occurs. Oklahoma law allows a law enforcement officer to seize the physical card of a person who the officer suspects will be subject to revocation or suspension. A law enforcement officer may seize the physical card and send it to OSBI. OSBI will then make a decision on whether to revoke or suspend the license. If OSBI decides to proceed with the revocation or suspension, it will send the license holder notification stating the reason for revocation or suspension and require the license holder to surrender his or her license to OSBI. After notification, the person must surrender the license. Refusal to surrender the license after notification by OSBI makes the person subject to a misdemeanor punishable by a $500 fine and/or imprisonment of six months. The person shall also be subject to an additional administrative fine of five hundred dollars.

6. If my handgun license is denied, revoked, or suspended, can I appeal?

A person whose license has been suspended or revoked or against whom a fine has been assessed shall be entitled to an appeal through a hearing in accordance with the Administrative Procedures Act. Any administrative hearing on suspensions, revocations or fines shall be conducted by a hearing examiner appointed by the Bureau. The hearing examiner's decision shall be a final decision appealable to a district court in accordance with the Administrative Procedures Act. *See* 21 O.S. § 1290.17(A). You have a right to appeal. Written appeal requests should be sent to:

Oklahoma State Bureau of Investigation
ATTN: SDA Unit
6600 North Harvey Place
Oklahoma City, Oklahoma 73116

Please note that the appeal process is governed by the Oklahoma Administrative Procedures Act found at 75 O.S. § 250 *et seq*. Should you be the object of any adverse ruling by the OSBI, please consult an attorney to be certain of any relevant appeal times. The appeal time runs from the adverse decisions of the OSBI regarding suspension, revocation or denial of the handgun license. The OSBI website allows for 60 days to appeal the decision of the OSBI, however, the Oklahoma Administrative Procedures Act does not specifically mention 60 days for appeal from an adverse ruling. In order to avoid confusion or waiving rights to appeal, please consult an attorney.

III. The application and process

A. The handgun license application

Completion of an Oklahoma handgun license application packet containing all required information is necessary to obtain a license. *See* 21 O.S. § 1290.12. The packet must be completed and submitted to the sheriff in the county where the applicant resides. The packet can be downloaded and printed out by visiting the OSBI website. For individuals who elect to complete the application online, the training certificate (or exemption) from the training class must be received before you apply. The application requires personal identification information including a valid driver's license or identification card, current demographic, address, contact information, residential status, employment information, as well as personal background information including information regarding any psychiatric, drug, alcohol, or criminal history from the applicant as described in section 1290.18 of the Oklahoma Self-Defense Act. Certain parts of the application process must be completed in person at the county sheriff's office where one resides. Specifically, fingerprints will be taken by the sheriff's office. The sheriff's office will then submit your fingerprints to the OSBI.

B. Handgun license class and shooting test

In order to obtain an Oklahoma handgun license, applicants must complete a state-mandated education course taught by an Oklahoma certified instructor. These classes generally consist of classroom instruction and a firearm safety test followed by training regarding gun handling and a shooting test. The student must demonstrate proficiency with their handgun. Total time for instruction and the shooting test is eight hours. Once an applicant successfully completes the class, the instructor will certify that he or she has established proficiency and the applicant will be ready to submit his or her application to the OSBI for approval and licensing.

CHAPTER NINE

LAW OF CONCEALED CARRY: PART II WHAT, HOW, AND WHERE YOU CAN LEGALLY CARRY WITH A HANDGUN LICENSE

The law concerning carrying a firearm is found in 21 O.S. § 1290.1 through § 1290.24; commonly referred to as the Oklahoma Self-Defense Act. Without a handgun license, a person may carry a handgun on property owned, leased, rented, or otherwise legally controlled by the person. Section 1272, the law prohibiting the carrying of a pistol or revolver, requires that concealed or open carry be done in compliance with the Self-Defense Act. The possession of a handgun license allows the license holder to legally assert that 21 O.S. § 1272 does not apply to them. The handgun license acts as a defense or exception to the general prohibition as set forth in section 1272, along with other exceptions discussed later. It is very important to remember, that the license holder does not receive the benefit of the license's protections if they are not in actual physical possession of their handgun license while they are carrying a handgun either concealed or unconcealed.

Section 1290.2(A)(1) defines "concealed handgun" as "a loaded or unloaded pistol, the presence of which is not openly discernible to the ordinary observation of a reasonable person". Section 1290.2(A)(2) defines an "unconcealed handgun" as "a loaded or unloaded pistol carried upon the person in a belt holster or shoulder holster that is wholly or partially visible, or carried upon the person in a scabbard or case designed for carrying firearms that is wholly or partially visible."

I. Handguns must be concealed or carried in a specific manner openly!

When a pistol is carried in a concealed manner, it does not need to be in a holster, a scabbard or a case designed for carrying a firearm. This means that if your handgun fits in your blue jeans' pocket, you may lawfully carry it in that manner without the handgun being in any type of holster (For safety purposes, is this a good idea? Not at all).

On the other hand, if the pistol is carried openly, it cannot be tucked into a waistband, carried on one's body supported by a string or lanyard, taped to one's body, or carried in hand. To lawfully carry a handgun openly, it must be carried in a belt or shoulder holster, in a scabbard, or a case designed for carrying a firearm. It will be very difficult for an attorney to argue that a person was in compliance with section 1290.2(A)(2) with a straight face if their client glues a tissue box to their person and calls it a holster!

Oklahoma law does not restrict the number of handguns a person can carry concealed or openly. Further, the law allows a handgun license holder to carry both concealed handguns and visibly holstered handguns simultaneously.

A. Willfully brandishing a handgun is a crime

Disturbance by Loud or Unusual Noise or Abusive, Violent, Obscene, Profane or Threatening Language
21 O.S. § 1362

If any person shall willfully or maliciously disturb, either by day or night, the peace and quiet of any city of the first class, town, village, neighborhood, family or person by loud or unusual noise, or by abusive, violent, obscene or profane language, whether addressed to the party so disturbed or some other person, or by threatening to kill, do bodily harm or injury, destroy property, fight, or by quarreling or challenging to fight, or fighting, or shooting off any firearms, or brandishing the same, or by running any horse at unusual speed along any street, alley, highway or public road, he shall be deemed guilty of a misdemeanor, and, on conviction thereof, shall be fined in any sum not to exceed

> One Hundred Dollars ($100), or by imprisonment in the county jail not to exceed thirty (30) days, or by both such fine and imprisonment, at the discretion of the court or jury trying the same.

While a person with a license can open carry, it becomes a crime when a concealed or unconcealed handgun is "willfully" brandished. This means an unintentional, accidental display of a concealed handgun (in other words, "not willful") should not get the police called on you! However, the willful display of a handgun could result in one of several criminal charges. For instance, it is a misdemeanor offense to willfully or maliciously threaten to kill, do bodily harm or injury, or brandish a firearm. 21 O.S. § 1362. Additionally, it is a felony offense to point a handgun, even if it is unloaded, at any person for the purpose of threatening that person. 21 O.S. § 1289.16. The exact same act could possibly end up as a misdemeanor or felony charge! It all depends on what law enforcement recommends and ultimately what an assistant district attorney decides!

This is an area of the law that rightfully concerns many handgun license holders. These incidents are incredibly fact specific. The likelihood of a charge or even a conviction are all fact dependent. Law enforcement will collect witness statements as to how the handgun was displayed, whether it was holstered or unholstered, what sort of verbal threats were made, and other relevant facts surrounding the incident. Additionally, since brandishing has no statutory definition, it will take a test case to figure out exactly what that word means (and hopefully that test case isn't you!). An interesting question that often comes up is – can I be charged with a crime if my gun never leaves the holster? YES! Any willful brandishing of a handgun, whether it is holstered or not, is a violation of the law. There is no exception in Oklahoma law allowing a person to threaten another with a handgun if it is carried in a holster.

Example:

Gordon is wearing his ripped jeans in the law office where he works. Edwin has warned Gordon several times to never wear those jeans to the office. Edwin is lawfully carrying his Glock 19 in a belt holster, and tells Gordon "If you don't get out of this office right now, I'm gonna...!" and points to his holstered handgun.

Has Edwin committed a crime by pointing to his handgun? Probably yes! Edwin threatened Gordon with his handgun by pointing to it and insinuating that he was going to use it against Gordon for wearing ripped jeans in the law office.

B. Unintentional displays of a handgun are not a crime

What do you do if a gust of wind picks up your shirt and shows off your 1911 handgun? What about when your pants accidentally split revealing your Spiderman underwear and your Sig Sauer? How about if your purse comes accidentally open, flashing your Glock? The good news is that none of these incidents are crimes under Oklahoma law.

If a handgun license holder's concealed handgun becomes unconcealed inadvertently, such as by "flashing" or "printing," the handgun license holder may not be breaking the law. If it is carried in a way such that it is lawful open carry, then no crime has occurred, as the person has just switched from one mode of lawful carry to another. If it isn't, Oklahoma law prohibits the "willful brandishing," which means that accidental displays are not prohibited.

C. What is "printing" and is it a crime?

What is printing? First, printing is not a legal term, but printing may be a crime. The word printing does not appear in the Oklahoma statutes. Printing is a common street term. It generally refers to when the outline or characteristics of a handgun become visible under the clothing of a person.

Imagine a person in a skin-tight spandex outfit who is carrying a full-size Glock 9mm pistol under the outfit. The outline of the gun would be clearly visible; and in Oklahoma, a handgun is not considered concealed if it is "openly discernable to the ordinary observation of a reasonable person." Therefore, it would be up to a jury to decide whether or not this was a concealed handgun.

II. Where can a handgun license holder legally carry a concealed handgun?

A person in possession of a handgun license may legally carry their handgun concealed any place where it is not illegal for them to possess a concealed handgun under either state or federal law. The places prohibited under Oklahoma law are located in section 1277 of the Oklahoma Statutes. In addition, because a handgun license is issued by the State of Oklahoma and not the federal government, a handgun license holder may not legally carry their concealed handgun on federal property unless specifically authorized by federal law.

A. Prohibited places for handgun license holders

1. Oklahoma Business Owner's Right to Exclude

If a person, business owner, tenant, employer, or place of worship wants to exclude handgun license holders from legally carrying on their property, he or she has that legal right pursuant to Oklahoma Statutes § 1290.22. Notice to handgun license holders is required in order to lawfully prohibit carrying. A person may become subject to a $250 citation if they refuse to leave the property, and the police are summoned.

Sign and oral notice to exclude handgun license holders

Two forms of legal notice are required that a handgun license holder is trespassing on the premises if he or she carries on that property. Under this law, a property owner must post a sign and give oral legal notice that the carrying of a handgun on the owner's property without permission is prohibited. For example, if a handgun license holder sees and walks past a "no gun" sign, is verbally told to leave the property, and refuses to leave, the license holder has committed a criminal trespass.

What if I did not see the sign?

A very common question with regard to signs for handgun license holders is, "What if I did not see the sign—am I breaking the law if I have my handgun?" A handgun license holder possessing a handgun but who does not see a posted sign at a place is not committing a crime. Additionally, the handgun license holder who walks past the sign and has the opportunity to leave the property before a peace officer is called, avoids a citation. The critical element of section 1290.22 is that the sign provides "notice" to a handgun license holder that the carrying of a handgun is prohibited and that an oral warning to leave is also required. A person who does not see the sign because it was not visible, because it was placed in a location where a person would not ordinarily see it, or for any other reason, has an opportunity to leave the property without breaking the law after he or she receives the oral warning to vacate the property. It is important to keep in mind, however, that the purpose of the law is to provide notice, and such notice can be received in different ways. Because an oral admonition is sufficient to provide notice, it is possible for the licensee to vacate the premises without causing a legally actionable offense. Remember that general trespass laws may apply here even without the requirement of posting a sign.

What if the sign is confusing or illegible?

Oklahoma law, under section 1290.22, allows a property owner, tenant, employer, place of worship or business entity to post signs on their property to prohibit carrying inside of a building. If a sign is unclear as to whether an individual may lawfully carry, and oral notice to leave is given plus the police are summoned to issue a citation, there is a fact issue present whether you received notice from the sign. The fact issue is whether a person was given proper notice handguns are prohibited by the sign. This would be an issue determined by a judge or jury as to whether the sign gave proper notice to the individual. It is important to remember that if a person carrying a handgun refuses to leave the premises based on oral notice *alone*, they may be charged with general criminal trespass as opposed to a citation issued under the authority of 1290.22.

Can I take my gun back to my motor vehicle?
Yes! A property owner, tenant, employer, place of worship or business entity cannot stop a person from taking their gun back to their locked motor vehicle parked in the business's parking lot.

What happens if I violate section 1290.22?
A violation may result in a citation punishable by up to a $250 fine. It will not subject you to any scrutiny by the Oklahoma State Bureau of Investigations or put your license to carry at risk. It is important to point out that a violation of section 1290.22 requires that a property owner who provided valid notice to call a peace officer who will issue a citation for the crime.

2. Business establishment whose primary purpose is the sale of alcoholic beverages
Oklahoma Statute Title 21 § 1272.1 makes it a crime for a handgun license holder to carry their handgun on the premises of an establishment that has the sale of alcoholic beverages or low point beer as its primary purpose of the business. Carefully note that just because an establishment has a bar and sells alcoholic beverages does not necessarily mean that the establishment's primary purpose is to sell alcohol. It is perfectly legal for a license holder to carry a handgun into a restaurant that serves alcohol as long as its primary purpose is not the sale of alcohol.

Unfortunately, there is no method for determining a business' "primary purpose," so when in doubt, take your handgun back to the car. It is a felony crime to carry your handgun into a bar! This means that you could lose all of your firearms rights if convicted!

Handgun Prohibited Where Liquor Consumed: 21 O.S. § 1272.1

It shall be unlawful for any person to carry or possess any weapon designated in Section 1272 of this title in any establishment where low-point beer, as defined by Section 163.2 of Title 37 of the Oklahoma Statutes, or alcoholic beverages, as defined by Section 506 of Title 37 of the Oklahoma Statutes, are consumed. This provision shall not apply to a peace officer, as defined in Section 99 of this title, or to private investigators with a firearms authorization when acting in the scope and course of employment, and shall not apply to an owner or proprietor of the establishment having a pistol, rifle, or shotgun on the premises. Provided however, a person possessing a valid handgun license pursuant to the provisions of the Oklahoma Self-Defense Act may carry the concealed or unconcealed handgun into any restaurant or other establishment licensed to dispense low-point beer or alcoholic beverages where the sale of low-point beer or alcoholic beverages does not constitute the primary purpose of the business.

3. Sporting events and school property

Oklahoma law prohibits the concealed or unconcealed carry of a handgun on the premises of any publicly owned or operated sports arena or venue during a professional sporting event. 21 O.S. § 1277(A)(4). Additionally, Oklahoma prohibits the concealed or unconcealed carry of a handgun on the premises of an elementary or secondary school. 21 O.S. § 1277(A)(5). For private schools, it is an exception to both of these laws that if the location has a policy in place that allows carry, a handgun licensee may carry there. Sporting arenas or venues during sporting events will get a similar policy exception as of November 1, 2016. This means that a handgun license holder cannot carry his or her concealed handgun at a public high school football game, or professional sports game where there is no policy allowing carry. 21 O.S. § 1277(E) prohibits the concealed or unconcealed carry of a handgun into or upon any college, university, or technology center school property unless permission has been given. This means that a license holder could not carry his or her handgun to a college sporting event.

What about events that are not so obvious? Because Oklahoma statutes do not define "professional sporting event," it can be hard to determine whether an event falls under the category. Some events, like professional football, baseball, or basketball games are easily identified as qualifying "professional sporting events." Therefore, for any sports that seem "iffy" as to whether or not they are professional, and they are taking place at a sports arena or venue, it will be a good idea to take your gun back to the car.

The law also provides an exception, 21 O.S. § 1277(B) for any areas designated for parking; so if you find yourself at a public school, or at a professional baseball game at a sporting venue, you may take your handgun back out to your vehicle and be considered legal. For a more in depth look at school zones *see* Chapter 10's discussion.

4. Correctional facilities

Handgun Prohibited in Correctional Facilities
21 O.S. § 1277(A)(2)

A. It shall be unlawful for any person in possession of a valid handgun license issued pursuant to the provisions of the Oklahoma Self-Defense Act to carry any concealed or unconcealed handgun into any of the following places:
2. Any prison, jail, detention facility or any facility used to process, hold, or house arrested persons, prisoners or persons alleged delinquent or adjudicated delinquent;

A license holder is not permitted to carry a concealed or unconcealed handgun into a prison, jail, detention facility, or any facility used to process, hold, or house arrested persons, prisoners, or persons alleged delinquent or adjudicated delinquent under Oklahoma law. However, 21 O.S. § 1277(B)(1) specifically excludes parking lots from this prohibition. This means that a license holder could carry a handgun in the parking lot or other areas outside of the correctional facility.

5. Government owned or controlled building

21 O.S. § 1277(A)(1) prohibits a license holder from carrying a concealed or unconcealed handgun into any structure, building, or office space owned or leased by any governmental authority for the purpose of conducting business with the public. This means that a license holder could not carry into a governmental building that is open and doing business with the public. Finally, after November 1, 2016, courthouses and courtrooms will be specifically added to this list of prohibited areas.

6. Pari-mutuel wagering

Prior to November 1, 2016, carrying a handgun is prohibited at any place where pari-mutuel wagering is authorized by law. As of November 1, 2016, the law will be expanded to state that any place where gambling is authorized by law is prohibited, unless allowed by the property owner.

B. When a license holder is under the influence of alcohol or drugs

21 O.S. § 1289.9 states that a person cannot be **under the influence** of: intoxicating liquors, beer, any hallucinogenic, or drugs which have aftereffects of such consumption that affect mental, emotional or physical processes to a degree that would result in abnormal behavior (whether prescribed or not) while in possession of a shotgun, rifle, or pistol.

Section 1289.9 does not explicitly define "under the influence" or "abnormal behavior." However, other Oklahoma Statutes may provide guidance:

47 O.S. § 11-902, which seeks to define "Persons Under the Influence of Alcohol or Other Intoxicating Substances" provides

the following measures of intoxication in subsection A:

(1) A blood or breath alcohol concentration of (0.08) or more;
(2) Under the influence of alcohol;
(3) Having any amount of a Schedule I chemical or controlled substance blood, saliva, urine or any other bodily fluid;
(4) Under the influence of any intoxicating substance other than alcohol which may render such person incapable of safely driving or operating a motor vehicle;
(5) Under the combined influence of alcohol and any other intoxicating substance which may render such person incapable of safely driving or operating a motor vehicle.

From these definitions, one could gather that "under the influence" occurs when an individual consumes so much of a substance (such as drugs or alcohol, but can include almost any substance) that it adversely impacts that person's mental or physical abilities. Typically, one beer or one glass of wine would not rise to the level of impairment, however, because each individual can react to drugs or alcohol differently, it is best to exercise caution.

C. Concealed carry or open carry on buses

21 O.S. § 1903(D) prohibits the carry of firearms on public buses by any individual who is not an authorized law enforcement officer. Any person who is convicted of violating this subsection will be guilty of a felony and could be imprisoned for not more than ten years, fined no more than $10,000, or both. A person discovered to have such an item may also have the item confiscated and transferred into the custody of law enforcement officers.

D. Employer/employee parking lot rules

Under 21 O.S. § 1289.7a(A), any person, except a convicted felon, is allowed to conceal his or her handgun within his or her locked, privately-owned motor vehicle in an employee parking lot, garage, or other parking area provided by an employer. No person, property owner, tenant, employer, or business entity can enforce any policy or rule that effectively prohibits any person, except convicted felons, from transporting or storing firearms or ammunition in a locked motor vehicle . . . on any property set aside for any motor vehicle.

The law provides a private right of action to sue the employer or person who breaks the law. Section 1289.7a allows an individual to bring a civil action against a person, property owner, tenant, employer, or business for violating this section. If the plaintiff is successful, the court can award damages, enjoin further violations of this section, and award court costs and attorney's fees to the prevailing plaintiff.

E. Automobiles, watercraft, and other places

1. May a person carry a concealed handgun in an automobile?

Under 21 O.S. § 1289.7, yes. A handgun license holder in Oklahoma can legally carry a concealed handgun in their vehicle. Note that a person does not need a handgun license to possess an unloaded open handgun in their vehicle, in a vehicle under their control, or when the handgun is being transported for legal purposes.

Oklahoma also allows you to have an openly carried, unloaded handgun when going to or from your vehicle, or a vehicle in which you are riding as a passenger, to a place designated or authorized for:

- Firearms repairs or reconditioning;
- Firearms trade, sale, barter, or a gunsmith;
- Hunting animals or fowl;
- A hunter safety course;
- Target shooting, or skeet or trap shooting; or
- Any lawfully recognized firearms activity or event.

What does the law say if a person doesn't have a handgun license, but someone else in the vehicle does? Any person operating a vehicle, or who is a passenger in a vehicle wherein there is another person who is licensed to carry, may have a handgun in the vehicle as long as the licensee is in or near the vehicle.

What are "lawfully recognized firearm activities?" 21 O.S. § 1289.6 provides that a person is entitled to possess a loaded or unloaded handgun for certain legal purposes, such as:

1. When hunting animals or fowl;

2. During competition in or practicing in a safety or hunter safety class, target shooting, skeet, trap or other recognized sporting events;

3. During participation in or in preparation for a military function of the state military forces to be defined as the Oklahoma Army or Air National Guard, Federal Military Reserve and active military forces;

4. During participation in or in preparation for a recognized police function of either a municipal, county or state government as functioning police officials;

5. During a practice for or a performance for entertainment purposes;

6. For lawful self-defense and self-protection or any other legitimate purpose in or on property that is owned, leased, rented, or otherwise legally controlled by the person; or

7. For any legitimate purpose not in violation of the Oklahoma Firearms Act of 1971 or any legislative enactment regarding the use, ownership and control of firearms.

Section 1272 also allows the proper use of guns and knives for hunting, fishing, and educational or recreational purposes. A handgun license holder may not only use the above mentioned instruments but is also legally allowed to carry. For the rules governing non- handgun license holders, *see* Chapter 10.

2. May a person legally carry a concealed handgun in a commercial vehicle?
Yes. There are no specific Oklahoma or federal regulations regarding carrying in a commercial shipping vehicle beyond those regulations which may be imposed by the operator's employer. While carrying may be a breach of company policy in certain instances, it is not against the law and is therefore not a crime.

3. May a person carry a handgun on a boat or watercraft?
Yes, if the person holds a valid handgun license from Oklahoma or any other state. 63 O.S. § 4210.3 permits any persons who hold a valid handgun license from Oklahoma or another state to carry, concealed or unconcealed, a firearm in a boat or watercraft. Non-license holders may only carry such weapons for the purposes of hunting animals or fowl under the same section. Section 1290.8 also allows a person with a handgun license to possess a handgun while bow hunting or fishing.

4. May a person with a handgun license carry a handgun in a state or municipal park?
Yes. 21 O.S. § 1277(B)(4) specifically allows for handgun carry on "any property designated by a city, town, county, or state governmental authority as a park recreational area, or fairgrounds." However, stay out of the buildings, because a person cannot carry into buildings in state or municipal parks under 21 O.S. § 1277(A)(1).

5. Can a handgun license holder carry in a restaurant?
Maybe. As discussed earlier, if a restaurant's primary purpose is the sale of alcohol, then the carrying of any weapon is prohibited under 21 O.S. § 1272.1(A). However, if the primary purpose is not the sale of alcohol, then a handgun license holder may carry a concealed or unconcealed handgun subject to the provisions discussed in this chapter.

Restaurants are also private businesses and may post signs as described in 21 O.S. § 1290.22(C). If a restaurant has posted "no gun" signs, the carrying of a handgun by a license holder is prohibited by the owner, but not by law. If the primary purpose of the restaurant is not the sale of alcohol and there are no posted signs prohibiting firearms, then a license holder is legally able to carry their handgun into a restaurant.

6. Can a person have their gun in a hotel?
Hotels are private businesses governed by 21 O.S. § 1290.22(C), meaning they can post a "no gun" sign to prohibit the entry of a person carrying a handgun. So make sure you check for signs or any policy before you check in!

F. Federal Property
A handgun license and its rights are the product of state law and convey no rights to the handgun license holder under federal law. However, in certain instances, the federal government recognizes these state rights on federal property.

1. Federal buildings: firearms are prohibited
Under 18 U.S.C. § 930(g)(1), a "federal facility" refers to any building or part of a building that is owned or leased by the federal government and is a place where federal employees are regularly present for the purpose of performing their official duties. However, this statute does not apply to "the lawful performance of official duties by an officer, agent, or employee of the United States, a State, or a political subdivision thereof, who is authorized by law to engage in or supervise the prevention, detection, investigation, or prosecution of any violation of law," nor does it apply to federal officials or members of the armed forces who are permitted to possess such a firearm by law, or the lawful carrying of a firearm incident to hunting or "other lawful purposes." 18 U.S.C. § 930(d). This assumption does not apply generally to handgun license holders. This statute does not govern the possession of a firearm in a federal court facility.

Firearms Prohibited in Federal Facilities:
18 U.S.C. § 930(a)

...whoever knowingly possesses or causes to be present a firearm or other dangerous weapon in a Federal facility (other than a Federal court facility), or attempts to do so, shall be fined under this title or imprisoned not more than 1 year, or both.

2. National parks

Handgun license holders are permitted to carry in Oklahoma National Parks but not buildings within the park, such as ranger stations because these are federal buildings. Under federal law, for firearms purposes, all federal parks are subject to the state law of the state in which the park is located. *See* 16 U.S.C. § 1a-7b. Oklahoma allows individuals to carry in Oklahoma State Parks under 21 O.S. § 1277. A handgun license holder may, therefore, carry a handgun in a federal park, but not in federal buildings in the park.

3. VA Hospitals: firearms prohibited

One place where many law-abiding handgun license holders fall victim is at the VA Hospital. Unlike the Oklahoma law allowing for the carrying within a hospital, the VA Hospital System is governed by federal law which prohibits the carrying of any firearm while on VA property. This includes the parking lot, sidewalk, and any other area which is the property of the VA.

Firearms Prohibited at Veterans Affairs Hospitals:
38 CFR § 1.218(a)(13)

No person while on property shall carry firearms, other dangerous or deadly weapons, or explosives, either openly or concealed, except for official purposes.

Under federal law, 38 CFR § 1.218(a)(13) states that "no person while on property shall carry firearms, other dangerous or deadly weapons, or explosives, either openly or concealed, except for official purposes." The "official purposes" specified refer specifically to the VA Hospital Police. The area where this specific law gets good people in trouble is that the Department of Veterans Affairs has its own set of laws and guidelines and is not controlled strictly by the Gun Control Act and the general provisions regarding the prohibition of firearms on federal property. The VA law is much more restrictive, and many veterans have found themselves in trouble when they valet-park their vehicle and the valet discovers a handgun in the console or in the door storage area. How rigidly this law is enforced is determined by the individual hospital administrators as described in 38 CFR § 1.218(a), however, regardless of how strictly the law is enforced firearms are still prohibited under the law and the VA police are very aggressive in enforcing them.

4. United States Post Offices: firearms prohibited

Firearms Prohibited at Post Offices:
39 CFR § 232.1(l)

Notwithstanding the provisions of any other law, rule or regulation, no person while on postal property may carry firearms, other dangerous or deadly weapons, or explosives, either openly or concealed, or store the same on postal property, except for official purposes.

Under this regulation, firearms or other deadly weapons are prohibited on postal property which includes not only the building, but all property surrounding the building where a post office is located. This includes the parking lot (*e.g.*, a person's vehicle where a firearm may be stored), as well as the sidewalks and walkways. Recently, there was a decision by a Tenth Criminal Court of Appeals addressing this issue in Colorado. The Appeals Court overturned a U.S. District Court decision allowing a handgun license holder to have a handgun in his car while in the parking lot of the U.S. Post Office for the town of Avon, Colorado. This case reaffirmed that post office parking lots are prohibited places within the states that fall under the jurisdiction of the 10th Circuit Court of Appeals, which includes Oklahoma, the prohibition to possess firearms on United States Post Office property in Oklahoma is valid.

5. Military bases and installations: firearms generally prohibited
Military bases and installations are treated much like the VA Hospital and U.S. Post Offices in that they have, and are governed by, a separate set of rules and regulations with respect to firearms on the premises of an installation or base and are generally prohibited. Military installations are governed by the federal law under Title 32 of the Code of Federal Regulations. Moreover, the sections covering the laws governing and relating to military bases and installations are exceedingly numerous. There are, in fact, sections which are dedicated to only certain bases such as 32 CFR § 552.98 which only governs the possessing, carrying, concealing, and transporting of firearms on Fort Stewart/Hunter Army Airfield, in the State of Georgia.

G. Can municipalities restrict firearms rights?
1. Can cities or other governmental agencies enact firearms laws or regulations regarding carrying of a handgun by handgun license holders that are more restrictive than state law?
No, because municipalities are restricted by the Oklahoma Legislature from passing ordinances further restricting the carry of a handgun by a handgun license holder. 21 O.S. § 1289.24 states that municipalities cannot even touch the field of firearms, knives, components of such, or ammunition. This means that a municipality cannot enact laws or regulations that are more restrictive than state law. However, there are two exceptions. First, a municipality may adopt an ordinance pertaining to the discharge of firearms within a municipality. Second, a municipality may allow the issuance of a traffic citation for transporting a firearm improperly. Everything else firearm related is off-limits to municipal regulation!

2. General Preemption laws not specific to handgun license holder

In addition, Oklahoma Statute section 1289.24 prohibits municipalities from enacting regulations relating to the "transfer, private ownership, keeping, transportation, licensing, or registration of firearms" for any person—not just handgun license holders.

H. How big of a handgun can a handgun license holder legally carry?

A .45 caliber handgun is the largest bore allowed for concealed or open carry under the Self-Defense Act. However, the actual bore size was approved by Attorney General Scott Pruitt's Opinion 2012-15 to be less than .460.

This is an area of law where Oklahoma law and federal law differ. It is illegal under Oklahoma law to carry a .50 caliber gun, however it is legal under federal law if the proper procedure is followed. As we mentioned in Chapter 2, federal law dictates that any firearm which has any barrel with a bore of more than one-half inch in diameter (.50 caliber) is a "destructive device" and is subject to the National Firearms Act (except for certain shotguns). Possession of any such firearm without the proper paperwork associated with NFA firearms is a federal crime whether a person is a handgun license holder or not. For more information on destructive devices and the NFA, *see* Chapter 14. Even though possession may be legal under federal law, it is still a crime under Oklahoma law to carry such a firearm in public!

III. Handgun license holders dealing with law enforcement

A. Do I legally have to present my handgun license to a police officer if they ask for my identification and I am carrying a gun?

Yes, there is a legal penalty if you fail to inform the police of your gun and the fact that you have a handgun license. Oklahoma law, specifically 21 O.S. § 1290.8, is very clear on this topic. A person must identify that they are in actual possession of a concealed or unconcealed handgun pursuant to the Self-

Defense Act when that person first comes into contact with any law enforcement officer. No duty to inform the officer arises unless the license holder is in possession of the handgun. Let's take an example. You are a license holder and are pulled over for speeding down the highway in your brand new sports car that is too small to accommodate your 9mm Glock. When the officer makes initial contact, there is no duty to inform him or her that you are a license holder because the handgun is not in the car! If there is a handgun in the car, a person must present their handgun license along with identification.

A person, carrying a firearm, may be arrested for failing to identify themselves as carrying a gun pursuant to the Self-Defense Act! Keep in mind, a person's handgun license may be suspended for 6 months and up to a $100 fine. Failure of the handgun license holder to inform may alarm the police officer and cause an already stressful situation to become more stressful. In short, you will regret not telling the police officer that you are a handgun license holder who is carrying a handgun.

B. Can a police officer legally take a handgun license holder's handgun away?

No! Police are not allowed to disarm handgun license holders unless the handgun license holder does not have his handgun license on him at the time of the stop. 21 O.S. § 1290.8 also states that a police officer can disarm a handgun license holder and confiscate the handgun license of a person he has arrested upon reasonable and articulable suspicion that another crime was committed.

If the officer arrests the handgun license holder due to suspicion of criminal activity and confiscates the gun, it will eventually be returned, however, if there is a conviction for a felony, the gun will not be returned. Keep in mind, however, that the statutes do not dictate the manner in which the officer must return the firearm which means a person may receive their firearm back unloaded, or disassembled.

C. What are passengers with a handgun license in a vehicle legally obligated to do when the driver is stopped by law enforcement?

If a person is a passenger in a vehicle that is pulled over, and comes into contact with a police officer during the stop, that person is required to identify themselves as a handgun licensee if they are carrying. Keep in mind, if a police officer asks whether a passenger is carrying, it is against the law to lie to the police officer!

IV. Reciprocity

A. Can I carry a handgun in other states if I have an Oklahoma handgun license?

Yes, the following states recognize the Oklahoma handgun license:

Alabama	Alaska	Arizona	Arkansas	Colorado*
Delaware	Florida*	Georgia	Idaho	Indiana
Iowa	Kansas	Kentucky	Louisiana	Maine*
Minnesota	Michigan*	Mississippi	Missouri	Montana
Nebraska	Nevada	New Hampshire	New Mexico	North Carolina
North Dakota	Ohio	Pennsylvania	South Carolina*	South Dakota
Tennessee	Texas	Utah	Vermont	Virginia
Washington	West Virginia	Wyoming		

**Indicates only recognizes Oklahoma handgun license for Oklahoma residents*

Reciprocity either exists between Oklahoma and these states or they have unilaterally decided to recognize Oklahoma handgun license. Every state has the authority to determine whether or not their state will recognize a carry license or permit issued by another state. Reciprocity is where states enter into an agreement with each other, in this case, to recognize each other's carry licenses. However, states are not required to have reciprocity with one another nor are they required to recognize another state's carry license.

There are many states that issue their own licenses, but refuse to recognize a carry license from another state. Conversely, there are states that choose to recognize some or all other states' carry licenses. Since each state is allowed to choose what other states' carry license will be recognized, there are several states that have carry licenses that Oklahoma recognizes, but those states do not recognize Oklahoma. There are also several states that recognize an Oklahoma handgun license, as of the date of writing, an Oklahoma handgun license is recognized by 38 other states.

B. Which out-of-state handgun licenses does Oklahoma recognize?

Oklahoma honors all out-of-state handgun licenses and permits. An out-of-state handgun license holder must follow Oklahoma law while in Oklahoma just like an Oklahoma handgun license holder must follow the laws of the state he or she is located in when traveling. For example, a Florida Concealed Weapons or Firearms License will allow a person to carry a concealed handgun, knife, electric weapon, billy club, and tear-gas gun while in Florida. However, a person with a Florida license will only be allowed to carry a handgun in Oklahoma according to law, and not be legally allowed to carry the exact same weapons allowed in Florida.

C. What state's laws apply to me when using my Oklahoma handgun license in another state?

Anytime an Oklahoma handgun license holder is in another state that recognizes an Oklahoma handgun license, the law of the state where the person is currently located will be the law which governs that person's firearms possession and use. If a person is traveling to another state, they must abide by that state's law. Any non-Okie visiting Oklahoma must follow Oklahoma law. Many of the common laws Oklahoma residents should be aware of are the requirement to present a license and the places that are off-limits to handgun license holders, as most of the time they vary from state to state. For example, while a handgun license holder having a handgun will get quick entry into the Texas State Capitol, it will get a person carrying a gun a quick trip to jail in Louisiana and Oklahoma.

D. Can persons who are not Oklahoma residents obtain an Oklahoma handgun license?

No, 21 O.S. § 1290.9 sets out the eligibility requirements and authorizes the Oklahoma State Bureau of Investigation to issue Oklahoma handgun licenses only to persons who are legal residents of the State of Oklahoma.

CHAPTER TEN

POSSESSING, CARRYING, AND TRANSPORTING FIREARMS WITHOUT AN OKLAHOMA HANDGUN LICENSE

In the previous chapter, we discussed where an individual can lawfully carry a handgun, rifle, or shotgun when they are in possession of an Oklahoma handgun license or a handgun license issued by another state authority. This chapter will discuss when and where a person may possess, carry, or transport a firearm if they do not have an Oklahoma handgun license or another state's Oklahoma-recognized handgun carry license or permit. A person with an Oklahoma handgun license or another state's handgun license generally may carry a firearm unless specifically prohibited by an Oklahoma statute. This chapter has the opposite premise, a person who does *not* have an Oklahoma handgun license or another state's handgun license is generally prohibited from carrying a firearm unless an Oklahoma statute specifically allows a firearm to be carried. The fourth provision of the Oklahoma Self Defense Act clearly states, "As provided by Section 1272 of this title, it is unlawful for any person to carry a concealed or unconcealed handgun in this state, except as authorized by the provisions of the Oklahoma Self-Defense Act or as may otherwise be provided by law." 21 O.S. § 1290.4.

Therefore, this chapter will examine the exceptions to this general prohibition. The laws discussed in this chapter are found primarily in 21 O.S. § 1272 and § 1289.6, generally referred to as the Oklahoma Self-Defense Act and the Oklahoma Firearms Act of 1971. These statutes contain various exceptions to the general rules and govern where and when firearms can be possessed and carried in Oklahoma without the need of a handgun license.

I. Where are firearms (long guns and handguns) prohibited under Oklahoma law?

Under Oklahoma Statute section 1272, it is unlawful for a person to carry any loaded or unloaded firearm including handguns, rifles, shotguns, as well as other weapons, such as daggers, bowie knives, dirk knives, sword canes, blackjacks, loaded canes, billies, hand chains, metal knuckles, or any other types of offensive weapons. However, as of this writing, the Oklahoma legislature removed daggers, bowie knives, dirk knives, and sword canes from the list of prohibited weapons, and such law becomes effective November 1, 2016. Further, it is illegal to carry any of these weapons regardless of whether or not they are concealed or unconcealed. There are a limited number of exceptions listed in 21 O.S. § 1272A. The exceptions that apply to individuals who are not members of law enforcement or judges are:

> "1. The proper use of guns and knives for hunting, fishing, educational or recreational purposes;
> 2. The carrying or use of weapons in a manner otherwise permitted by statute or authorized by the Oklahoma Self-Defense Act; and
> 5. The carrying and use of firearms and other weapons provided in this subsection when used for the purpose of living history reenactment. For purposes of this paragraph, "living history reenactment" means depiction of historical characters, scenes, historical life or events for entertainment, education, or historical documentation through the wearing or use of period, historical, antique or vintage clothing, accessories, firearms, weapons, and other implements of the historical period."

Further, 21 O.S. § 1289.6, entitled "Conditions Under Which Firearms May Be Carried" allows a person without a handgun license to carry loaded or unloaded shotguns, rifles, and pistols, as long as they are carried openly under the following circumstances:

1. When hunting animals or fowl;
2. During competition in or practicing in a safety or hunter safety class, target shooting, skeet, trap or other recognized sporting events;
3. During participation in or in preparation for a military function of the state military forces to be defined as the Oklahoma Army or Air National Guard, Federal Military Reserve and active military forces. As of November 1, 2016, The Oklahoma Army or National Guard personnel with proper authorization and performing a military function may carry loaded or unloaded and concealed weapons on Oklahoma Military Department facilities in accordance with rules promulgated by the Adjutant General;
4. During participation in or in preparation for a recognized police function of either a municipal, county or state government as functioning police officials;
5. During a practice for or a performance for entertainment purposes;
6. For lawful self-defense and self-protection or any other legitimate purpose in or on property that is owned, leased, rented, or otherwise legally controlled by the person; or
7. For any legitimate purpose not in violation of the Oklahoma Firearms Act of 1971 or any legislative enactment regarding the use, ownership and control of firearms.

Further, subsection B of § 1289.6 states:

> A person shall be permitted to carry unloaded shotguns, rifles and pistols, open and not concealed and without a handgun license as authorized by the Oklahoma Self-Defense Act pursuant to the following conditions:
>
> 1. When going to or from the person's private residence or vehicle or a vehicle in which the person is riding as a passenger to a place designated or authorized for firearms repairs or reconditioning, or for firearms trade, sale, or

barter, or gunsmith, or hunting animals or fowl, or hunter safety course, or target shooting, or skeet or trap shooting or any recognized firearms activity or event and while in such places; or

2. For any legitimate purpose not in violation of the Oklahoma Firearms Act of 1971.

Additionally, subsection C of § 1289.6 states, "The provisions of this section shall not be construed to prohibit educational or recreational activities, exhibitions, displays or shows involving the use or display of rifles, shotguns or pistols or other weapons if the activity is approved by the property owner and sponsor of the activity."

So let us look closer at these areas where firearms are permitted for everyone (except felons).

II. Where are firearms permitted?

A. Hunting, fishing, recreational, or educational activities

The general possession of handguns and long guns is prohibited, however, the several statutes that prohibit firearm possession have specifically provided that loaded or unloaded firearms, as well as knives, are legal when they are carried for hunting, fishing, recreational, or educational purposes. This exception can be found in several places in Oklahoma law, the Oklahoma Firearms Act in section 1272, and the Oklahoma Self-Defense Act in section 1289.6(A)(1), section 1289.6(A)(2), and section 1289.6(C). It appears to be the clear intent of the Oklahoma legislature to allow people in the State to be able to lawfully carry both loaded and unloaded firearms while they are hunting, fishing, skeet shooting, trap shooting, target shooting, or taking a hunter safety course. Further, 21 O.S. § 1289.6(B)(1), allows a person who does not have a handgun license to transport a firearm from their residence to a vehicle to a place designated for hunting, target shooting, *etc.*, as long as it is transported in an unloaded and open fashion. This exception also allows a firearm to be carried openly and unloaded to sell it, purchase it, repair it, or have any gun-smith work done to it.

B. A person's own premises or premises under their control

The most fundamental place a person is lawfully allowed to possess a firearm is on their own property. Interestingly, this exception to the general rule appears to be buried in the Oklahoma Self-Defense Act in section 1289.6(A)(6). A person who may legally possess a firearm may possess a firearm for lawful self-defense purposes or any other legitimate purpose on property that they own, lease, rent, or otherwise legally control. The handgun, rifle, or shotgun may be loaded or unloaded, concealed or unconcealed. This language covers a vast scope of real property and real property improvements. Houses, barns, yards, pastures, and acreage fall under the broad umbrella of "property." Also, this includes rented spaces such as apartments, offices, or commercial spaces.

1. Open carrying of handguns on own premises

Oklahoma law does not make it a crime to openly carry a handgun on your own premises; therefore, it is legal. However, as a practical legal matter, a person may not engage in loud or profane behavior, shoot off any firearms, or brandish the same, and it disturb a city of the first class, town, village, neighborhood, family, or person. If a person carries on in this manner, the person could be charged with a crime under 21 O.S. § 1362. So shouting and shooting your gun, in your front yard when O-U scores a touchdown could be a no-no if you are living in the city.

2. When is an RV considered a "residence/dwelling" or premises?

If the RV is not operating as a vehicle and is parked at an owned or leased site, then the argument may be easily made that the RV is a mobile home that has become the premises controlled by the owner of the RV. The difficulty arises when the RV is mobile and on the public road. A person without a handgun license may not transport a loaded firearm on a land borne vehicle pursuant to 21 O.S. § 1289.13. Therefore, before you hit the highway, if you don't have a license, make sure your firearms are unloaded as discussed in Section D later.

3. May a person keep a firearm in their hotel room?

Yes. A hotel room is considered a temporary residence, or dwelling designed to be occupied by people under 21 O.S. § 1289.25. A temporary residence under a person's control also qualifies as a residence, and the law allows for the unlicensed carrying of a firearm in such place under 21 O.S. § 1289.6 (B)(1), when going to or from the person's private residence or vehicle. However, a hotel, or any private business has the right and ability to prohibit the possession of firearms in or on their property by not just license holders, but also by persons who do not possess a handgun license. Remember that since a hotel is a private business it may provide notice via a sign and oral warning that the possession of firearms is prohibited.

C. Carrying a firearm without a handgun license in a motor vehicle

In Oklahoma there are several statutes that govern how a person without a handgun license can carry a firearm in a motor vehicle. These statutes include 21 O.S. § 1289.7, 21 O.S. § 1289.13, and 21 O.S. § 1289.13A. These statutes specifically refer to "motor vehicle," but also use the term "vehicle" interchangeably.

1. What is the legal definition of a "motor vehicle?"

Interestingly, while none of these statutes actually define "motor vehicle," 21 O.S. § 1289.8 defines a "motor vehicle" as "any automobile, truck, minivan, sports utility vehicle, motorcycle, motor scooter, and any other vehicle required to be registered under the Oklahoma Vehicle License and Registration Act." One question that is often asked is whether or not a personal mobility scooter (like a Rascal) or some other personal mobility device qualifies as a motor vehicle? Under 47 O.S. § 562, a personal mobility device is an off road vehicle and is not required to be registered under the Oklahoma Vehicle License and Registration Act. Therefore, it is a vehicle but not a motor vehicle like a car or a truck. This means that a person who does not have a handgun license is not able to legally carry an unloaded handgun or long gun while traveling on a public highway on such a device because the vehicle is not a vehicle that is allowed to travel on the public highway.

2. How can handguns and long guns be carried in a motor vehicle?
There are specific laws on the manner in which the pistol or long gun must be transported in a vehicle: generally it must be unloaded and unconcealed in the vehicle.

3. May the firearm be magazine loaded or chamber loaded?
Oklahoma law, 21 O.S. § 1289.7 requires that the firearm remain "in plain view," which means it must be in a case designed for carrying firearms, which case is wholly or partially visible, in a gun rack mounted in the vehicle, in an exterior locked compartment or a trunk of a vehicle. The statute section 1289.7 goes on to say that "Any person, except a convicted felon, may transport in a motor vehicle a rifle or shotgun concealed behind a seat of the vehicle or within the interior of the vehicle provided the rifle or shotgun is not clip, magazine or chamber loaded." Section 1289.13 says: "a rifle or shotgun may be transported clip or magazine loaded and not chamber loaded when transported in an exterior locked compartment of the vehicle or trunk of the vehicle or in the interior compartment of the vehicle notwithstanding the provisions of section 1289.7 of this title when the person is in possession of a valid handgun license pursuant to the Oklahoma Self-Defense Act."

4. May I keep a long gun in my vehicle under Oklahoma law?
Yes, and the long gun has to be in plain view, in a gun case or in a gun rack, in an exterior locked compartment or in the trunk. However, openly displaying a long gun in one's vehicle may attract thieves—particularly when the car is parked and unattended!

A handgun cannot be loaded and carried inside a vehicle. The law does not allow the handgun to be loaded or accessible—it must be inside of a gun case unloaded or in the trunk.

Practical Legal Tip:

If you carry a handgun in your vehicle, don't allow yourself to be drawn into a road-rage incident, no matter how minor. Someone who calls 911 to report that you pointed a gun at them, even though it was really just your middle finger, may get you arrested and charged with a crime. So, if you carry a gun in the car, forget how to flip the bird! –Robert

5. How does the law define "When going to or from the person's private residence or vehicle?"

"When going to or from the person's private residence or vehicle" means to travel directly to a vehicle. The more a person strays from a direct route to their vehicle, the less likely it will look like they are going to or from their vehicle. There is, however, no case law drawing bright lines in determining this issue.

6. May I keep a handgun in my vehicle if there are children in the car?

Yes, having children in the car does not change the law on whether a person is able to possess a handgun in the vehicle legally. Be aware that 21 O.S. § 1273 makes it a crime for a parent or an adult to allow a child to possess any of the prohibited weapons listed in section 1272; it is unlawful for a child to possess the weapons listed in section 1272 except for certain activities noted in the section. Section 1289.7 requires that the handgun remain unloaded, cased, and in plain view. It is also a violation of the law if a parent allows a child to possess a firearm resulting in injury to the child; thus, the parent would be guilty of permitting the injury to the child. The person could be charged with child endangerment, 21 O.S. § 852.1.

7. May I possess a long gun while riding in another person's vehicle?
Yes.

8. Is it legal for an occupant of a vehicle who does not have a handgun license to have a loaded handgun in the vehicle when another person with a handgun license is present?
Under 21 O.S. § 1289.7, the legal requirement is that a person who does not have a handgun license may have a handgun in a vehicle if another person with a handgun license is present in the same vehicle.

D. Boats and guns
In reference to boats, vessels and watercraft, Oklahoma Statute Title 63 O.S. § 4210.3, controls. This statute makes it unlawful for a non-licensee to transport a long gun or pistol in a vessel except for the purposes of hunting animals or fowl, and in compliance with existing state and federal laws, however, the holder of a valid handgun license may transport a pistol in a vessel. The same rules which allow the possession and carrying of a long gun in a vehicle do not apply to boats and other watercraft. 63 O.S. § 4210.3 prohibits the transporting of a firearm or discharge of the firearm from a vessel/boat/watercraft except for the purpose of hunting animals or fowl. However, anyone possessing a handgun license may carry a handgun on the vessel in compliance with the Oklahoma Self-Defense Act.

III. Long guns
A. Long guns shall not be carried openly in public except according to law
Oklahoma law does not authorize a person with or without a handgun license to carry a long gun in public, except under

limited circumstances, as previously discussed; nor does the law allow that a long gun be carried for self-defense purposes under the Self Defense Act in public. Oklahoma statute 21 O.S. § 1272 generally prohibits the carrying of firearms in public. The statutes that address the manner in which a long gun may be carried in public are §§ 1289.6 and 1289.7.

1. Manner in which long guns may be displayed in public

A person may legally display a long gun in public for any legitimate purpose not in violation of the Firearms Act of 1971. 21 O.S. § 1289.6. The intention of §§ 1289.6 and 1289.7 is to allow the display of firearms as an exception to the general rule. For example: A merchant may display a long gun for sale to the public. The buyer may purchase the weapon and take it home, to the range for target practice, or to the field for hunting. However, there are strict conditions for carrying a long gun in public.

Example:

> *Tim is walking down the street from his home to a shooting range with his AR-15 in a sling pointed down to the ground on his back, coffee in one hand, and range tote bag in the other. Tim is stopped by a police officer.*

Has Tim engaged in a crime by carrying a rifle in public? Yes. Tim illegally carried his rifle down the street without authorization from an exception to the general rule cited in § 1272. The closest exception to section 1272 is found in § 1289.6 (B)(1). Paragraph B says, "A person shall be permitted to carry unloaded shotguns, rifles and pistols, open and not concealed and without a handgun license as authorized by the Oklahoma Self-Defense Act pursuant to the following conditions: When going to or from the person's private residence or vehicle or a vehicle in which the person is riding as a passenger to a place designated or authorized for firearms repairs or reconditioning, or for firearms trade, sale, or barter, or gunsmith, or hunting animals or fowl, or hunter safety course, or target shooting..."

Tim certainly did not knowingly or intentionally threaten anyone. He was going to the shooting range. However, Tim's mistake was walking to the range. He should have driven. The law focuses on Tim's compliance with the Self-Defense Act and the manner in which the firearm was displayed and transported. The law specifically allows Tim to walk from his house to his car and then transport the weapon to the range in the car. There is no provision for transporting a firearm on foot.

IV. Private property owners

Under 21 O.S. § 1290.22(B), private property owners cannot prevent any person, except a felon, from keeping a firearm in a locked vehicle on their parking lots and driveways.

V. Carrying handguns and alcohol

A. Places where alcohol is sold

In places where alcohol is sold, individuals will often see a sign entitled "Felony Notice" which states that the possession of a weapon, prohibited in § 1272 is a felony under state law. This sign applies to individuals who possess a handgun license and to individuals who do not possess a handgun license. *See* 21 O.S. § 1272.1.

B. Carrying while under the influence of alcohol

Carrying a firearm while intoxicated is strictly prohibited by 21 O.S. § 1289.9.

VI. Traveling across state lines with firearms

Many people vacation and travel outside of Oklahoma. Naturally, no Oklahoman wants to travel unarmed if they can help it, but, unfortunately, not every state shares the same views on gun ownership and gun rights as we do in the Sooner State. This is especially true in the northeast corner and west coast of the United States. How then does a person pass through states that have restrictive firearms laws or those different from Oklahoma? For example, how does a person legally pass through a state that prohibits the possession of a handgun without a license from that state? The answer: safe-passage legislation.

A. Federal law: qualifying for firearms "Safe Passage"

Traveling across state lines with a firearm means that a person may need to use the provisions of the federal law known as the "Safe Passage" provision. Federal law allows individuals who are legally in possession of firearms in their state (the starting point of traveling) to travel through states that are not as friendly. This protection is only available under federal law to transport such firearms across state lines for lawful purposes, as long as they comply with the requirements of the Firearm Owners Protection Act, 18 U.S.C. §926A, nicknamed the "Safe Passage" provision. The first requirement to qualify for the Federal "Safe Passage" provision is that throughout the duration of the trip through the anti-firearm-state, the firearm must be unloaded and locked in the trunk, or locked in a container that is out of reach or not readily accessible from the passenger compartment. The ammunition also must be locked in the trunk or a container. Note that for the storage of both firearms and ammunition, the glove box and center console compartment are specifically not allowed under the statute.

1. "Safe Passage" requires legal start to legal finish

To get protection under federal law, a gun owner's journey must start and end in states where the traveler's possession of the firearm is legal; for instance, a person traveling with their Glock 17 starting in Oklahoma and ending in Vermont. Even though a person must drive through New York and possibly even Massachusetts to get to Vermont, as long as the person qualifies under the "Safe Passage" provision then they may legally pass through. However, if the start point was Oklahoma and the end point was New York (a place where the handgun would be illegal), there is no protection under the federal law. Safe-passage requires legal start and legal finish.

Although traveling across state lines naturally invokes federal law, it is important to remember that whenever a person finally completes their journey and reaches their destination state, the laws of that state control the possession, carrying, and use of the firearm. Federal law does not make it legal or provide any protection for possession of a firearm that is illegal under the laws of the destination state (*i.e.*, the end state of your travels).

2. What is the definition of "traveling" for "Safe Passage" provisions?

The final requirement for protection under the federal law is that individuals MUST be "traveling" while in the firearm hostile state. The legal definition of "traveling" is both murky and narrow. The "Safe Passage" provision protection has been held in courts to be limited to situations that strictly relate to traveling and nothing more. Traveling is a term that is not defined in the federal statute; however, it has received treatment in the courts that is indicative of what one can expect. Generally speaking, if a person stops somewhere for too long they cease to be "traveling" and, therefore, lose their protection under the "Safe Passage" provision. How long this time limit is has not been determined either statutorily or by case law with any definitiveness.

While stopping for gas or restroom breaks may not disqualify a person from the "traveling" protection, any stop for an activity not directly related to traveling could be considered a destination and thus you would lose the legal protection. For example, in Chicago anyone in the city for more than 24 hours is not considered to be traveling under local policy. In an actual case, stopping for a brief nap in a bank parking lot in New Jersey caused a Texan driving back home from Maine to lose the "traveling" protection. He received 5 years in prison for possession of weapons that are illegal under New Jersey law. Of course, if the driver would have made it to Hershey, Pennsylvania, he would have been safe. The moral of the story is to travel through these gun-unfriendly states as fast as you can (without breaking the speed limit, of course)!

3. Protection under federal law does not mean protection from prosecution in unfriendly states

To make matters even worse for firearms travelers, even if a person qualifies for protection under the federal "Safe Passage" provision, New Jersey and New York seem quite proud to treat this protection as an affirmative defense. This means that someone can be arrested even though he or she met all of the requirements of the federal statute. Then, they would have to go to court to assert this defense. In other words, while a person could beat the rap, they will not beat the ride! This becomes even more troublesome in the instance of someone who is legally flying with their firearm, and then due to flight complications, must land in New Jersey or New York, as travelers in this position have been arrested or threatened with arrest.

Once again, the "Safe Passage" provision only applies while a person is traveling; as soon as they arrive at their destination and cease their travels, the laws of that state control a person's actions. Remember: check all applicable state firearms laws before you leave for your destination!

VII. Air travel with a firearm at municipal airports

Generally, neither handgun license holders nor non-license holders are allowed to bring firearms or other weapons into any building owned by a governmental entity. The airports in Oklahoma, such as the Will Rogers World Airport, which is owned by Oklahoma City, are owned by municipalities. While there is no specific statutory exception for air travel with firearms, this law does not appear to be enforced against travelers who are taking firearms into government owned airports when they are packed for travel. In fact, the travel tips issued by the Will Rogers World Airport include a reference to packing "hunting guns" in accordance with Transportation Safety Administration ("TSA") regulations. Therefore, it appears if the firearm is unloaded and packed in a person's checked baggage it can be brought into the airport for travel as long as there is compliance with the TSA. Remember, when traveling by airplane to another state, check the destination state's laws to make sure you are not committing a crime when you take possession of your firearm as you get your luggage at baggage claim.

A. How do I legally travel with a firearm as a passenger on a commercial airline?

It is legal to travel with firearms on commercial airlines so long as the firearms transported are unloaded and in a locked, hard-sided container as checked baggage. Under federal law, the container must be completely inaccessible to passengers. Further, under U.S. Homeland Security rules, firearms, ammunition and firearm parts, including firearm frames, receivers, clips, and magazines, are prohibited in carry-on baggage. The TSA also requires that "realistic replicas of firearms are also prohibited in carry-on bags and must be packed in checked baggage. Rifle scopes are permitted in carry-on and checked bags."

1. Firearms must be inaccessible

Federal law makes it a crime subject to fine, imprisonment for up to 10 years, or both, if a person "when on, or attempting to get on, an aircraft in, or intended for operation in, air transportation or intrastate air transportation, has on or about the individual or the property of the individual a concealed dangerous weapon that is or would be accessible to the individual in flight." 49 U.S.C. § 46505(b). Additionally, under 49 U.S.C. § 46303(a) "[a]n individual who, when on, or attempting to board, an aircraft in, or intended for operation in, air transportation or intrastate air transportation, has on or about the individual or the property of the individual a concealed dangerous weapon that is or would be accessible to the individual in flight is liable to the United States Government for a civil penalty of not more than $10,000 for each violation."

2. Firearms must be checked in baggage

The following guidelines are put out by the TSA for traveling with firearms on airlines:

"To avoid issues that could impact your travel and/or result in law enforcement action, here are some guidelines to assist you in packing your firearms and ammunition:

- All firearms must be declared to the airline during

the ticket counter check-in process.

- The term firearm includes: (Please see, for instance, United States Code, Title 18, Part 1, Chapter 44 for information about firearm definitions.)
- Any weapon (including a starter gun) which will, or is designed to, or may readily be converted to expel a projectile by the action of an explosive.
- The frame or receiver of any such weapon.
- Any firearm muffler or firearm silencer.
- Any destructive device.
- The firearm must be unloaded.
- As defined by 49 CFR § 1540.5, 'A loaded firearm means a firearm that has a live round of ammunition, or any component thereof, in the chamber or cylinder or in a magazine inserted in the firearm.'
- The firearm must be in a hard-sided container that is locked. A locked container is defined as one that completely secures the firearm from being accessed. Locked cases that can be pulled open with little effort cannot be brought aboard the aircraft.
- If firearms are not properly declared or packaged, TSA will provide the checked bag to law enforcement for resolution with the airline. If the issue is resolved, law enforcement will release the bag to TSA so screening may be completed.
- TSA must resolve all alarms in checked baggage. If a locked container containing a firearm alarms, TSA will contact the airline, who will make a reasonable attempt to contact the owner and advise the passenger to go to the screening location. If contact is not made, the container will not be placed on the aircraft.
- If a locked container alarms during screening and is

not marked as containing a declared firearm, TSA will cut the lock in order to resolve the alarm.

- Travelers should remain in the area designated by the aircraft operator or TSA representative to take the key back after the container is cleared for transportation.
- Travelers must securely pack any ammunition in fiber (such as cardboard), wood or metal boxes or other packaging specifically designed to carry small amounts of ammunition.
- Firearm magazines and ammunition clips, whether loaded or empty, must be securely boxed or included within a hard-sided case containing an unloaded firearm.
- Small arms ammunition, including ammunition not exceeding .75 caliber for a rifle or pistol and shotgun shells of any gauge, may be carried in the same hard-sided case as the firearm, as long as it follows the packing guidelines described above.
- TSA prohibits black powder or percussion caps used with black-powder.
- Rifle scopes are not prohibited in carry-on bags and do not need to be in the hard-sided, locked checked bag."

See www.tsa.gov.

3. May I have a firearm in a private aircraft that stays in Oklahoma?

Generally, yes. For purposes of Oklahoma state law, a private aircraft is treated like any other motorized vehicle. For more information concerning firearms in vehicles, see our earlier discussion in Section II of this chapter.

4. May I have a firearm in a private aircraft that travels from Oklahoma to another state?

In situations where a private aircraft is taking off from one state and landing in another, the law will simply view this as traveling interstate with firearms. Where no other statutes apply to the person's flight, the person will be subject to the provisions of 18 U.S.C. § 926A regarding the interstate transportation of a firearm: "any person who is not otherwise prohibited by this chapter from transporting, shipping, or receiving a firearm shall be entitled to transport a firearm for any lawful purpose from any place where he may lawfully possess and carry such firearm to any other place where he may lawfully possess and carry such firearm if, during such transportation the firearm is unloaded, and neither the firearm nor any ammunition being transported is readily accessible or is directly accessible from the passenger compartment of such transporting vehicle."

This statute allows a person to transport firearms between states subject to the following conditions: that the person can lawfully possess the firearm at his or her points of departure and arrival, and that the firearm remain unloaded and inaccessible during the trip. However, what if the person is a handgun license holder and wants to carry between states? Fortunately, 18 U.S.C. § 927 states that section 926A does not pre-empt applicable state law. Thus, if a person can lawfully carry a weapon in the state in which he or she boards the aircraft and in the state in which he or she lands, the handgun license holder is not subject to the unloaded and inaccessible restrictions of section 926A.

For operations of private aircraft within one state, a person will only be subject to the laws of the state within which he or she is operating. The person will need to review their state's statutes to determine whether they impose any restrictions on possession of firearms within non-secure areas of airports. The person will also need to be familiar with the airports he or she will be visiting to determine whether each airport has any restrictions (*e.g.*, posting to prohibit concealed carry, *etc.*).

VIII. Understanding gun free school zone laws

The discussion of gun free school zones is one that covers many different areas of the law and affects both persons who hold a handgun license as well as persons who do not. That is because the "Gun Free School Zone" law and its meaning cause a lot of confusion. Signs warning about being in a "gun free school zone" are common around schools, but what does this mean to people lawfully in possession of firearms? There are actually both Oklahoma and federal "gun free school zone" laws, each with very different meanings and consequences. For this reason, we will explain the applicable rules to individuals who possess and do not possess a handgun license in this chapter, although the chapter has been dedicated to possessing or carrying a firearm without a license.

A. Oklahoma gun law for schools

In addition to the laws that generally prohibit a person without a handgun license from carrying a firearm, 21 O.S. § 1277(A)(3) also prohibits a handgun license holder from carrying a handgun into "any public or private elementary or public or private secondary school..." However, this law has an exception for any property that is used for parking by Oklahoma handgun license holders to carry handguns in their motor vehicles. Under Oklahoma law this includes in the parking lots, streets adjacent to schools, and premises adjacent to schools. Further, this law does not prohibit them from carrying on their person a concealed weapon adjacent to the premises of a school. Also, under Oklahoma law a private school may adopt a policy that allows a handgun license holder to carry a handgun onto school property and in school vehicles.

B. Federal "Gun Free School Zone" law: 18 U.S.C. § 922(q)

The school law that creates the most concern for lawful firearms owners is the federal "Gun Free School Zone" law found in 18 U.S.C. § 922(q). This law states that it is a federal crime for a person to possess a firearm that has moved through interstate commerce (this includes virtually all firearms), on the grounds of or within 1,000 feet of a public, parochial, or private school. As surprising as it may seem, under this federal law, the mere possession of a firearm by the occupant of a motor vehicle while driving past a school or dropping off a child, is a federal crime.

However, federal law provides seven exceptions:

1. *Exception one*: if the possession is on private property which is not part of the school grounds. This means that a person living within 1,000 feet of a school can keep a firearm in their house.
2. *Exception two*: if the individual possessing the firearm is licensed to do so by the state in which the school zone is located or a political subdivision of the state, and the law of the state or political subdivision requires that, before an individual obtains such a license, the law enforcement authorities of the state or political subdivision verify that the individual is qualified under law to receive the license. This means that a handgun license holder may legally carry a firearm into a "gun free school zone." However, there is one important note about the statute: a person can only lawfully carry in a school zone located in the state that issued the firearms license. Therefore, if a person has an Oklahoma handgun license they can only carry through Oklahoma school zones. If that Oklahoma license holder is traveling through another state, the exception under federal law does not apply to them, and they are in violation of this law. It also means that an Oklahoma resident, who holds a non-resident handgun carry license or permit from another state does not benefit from this exception and is in violation of the law if they take a firearm into a school zone.
3. *Exception three*: if the firearm is not loaded, and is in a locked container, or a locked firearms rack that is on a motor vehicle. This means that if a firearm is unloaded and carried in a locked case, or other type of locked container, such as a glove box or trunk, there is no violation of the federal law.
4. *Exception four*: if the firearm is carried by an individual for use in a program approved by a school in the school

zone. This exception covers school-sponsored shooting activities, such as an ROTC program.

5. *Exception five*: if the firearm is carried by an individual in accordance with a contract entered into between a school in the school zone and the individual or an employer of the individual. This means that school security guards can carry firearms while on the job.
6. *Exception six*: if the firearm is carried by a law enforcement officer acting in his or her official capacity. This exception covers police officers while on-duty only. It does not appear to cover them while they are off-duty, even if they are required by state law to carry while off-duty.
7. *Exception seven*: if the firearm is unloaded and is in the possession of an individual while traversing school property for the purpose of gaining access to public or private lands open to hunting, if the entry on school premises is authorized by school authorities. This means that if a hunter must cross school property to get to a lawful hunting ground, they must have the permission of the school, and the firearm must be unloaded.

C. Is a person legally permitted to possess a firearm in their vehicle in the parking lot of a college or university?

Yes, all individuals with a handgun license may possess a firearm in a vehicle the person owns or is under their control in a college or university parking lot as the parking lot does not constitute the "premises" of the institution. *See* 21 O.S. § 1277(F)(1-3). As of November 1, 2016, this law is found in 21 O.S. § 1277(E)(1).

CHAPTER ELEVEN

RESTORATION OF FIREARMS RIGHTS: THE LAW OF PARDONS AND EXPUNGEMENTS

I. Is it possible to restore a person's right to bear arms?

What happens after a person has been convicted of a crime, is it possible to later clear their name and/or criminal record? If possible, then what is the process for removing a conviction and restoring a person's right to purchase and possess firearms? This chapter will explain how a person under very limited circumstances can have arrest records, criminal charges, and even criminal convictions removed or nullified. But words of caution, success in this arena may be rare. Further, each state has different rules concerning these issues as well as a completely different set of rules under federal law. Before we begin a meaningful discussion, it is important to explain two terms and concepts: clemency and expungement.

A. What is clemency?

Clemency is the action the government, usually the chief executive (*e.g.,* the President on the federal level or a governor on the state level), takes in forgiving or pardoning a crime or canceling the penalty of a crime, either wholly, or in part. Clemency can include full pardons after a conviction, full pardons after completion of deferred sentence, conditional pardons, pardons based on innocence, commutations of a sentence, emergency medical reprieves, and family medical reprieves. Clemency can be granted at both the federal and state level.

B. What is expungement?

Expungement is the physical act of destroying or purging government criminal records, unlike sealing which is simply hiding the records from the public. Under certain circumstances, a person may have their criminal record either expunged or sealed.

Practical Legal Tip:

While our intention is to provide you with as much information as possible as to how you can have your firearms rights restored if you are convicted of a crime, it's also important to make sure you are aware of how rarely pardons, expungements, and restorations of firearms rights are granted. While it's certainly worth the effort to apply for a pardon in the event you receive one, be careful not to get your hopes up, because they are seldom granted.
-Robert

II. Federal law

A. Presidential pardon

Under Article II, Section 2 of the United States Constitution, the President of the United States has the power "to grant reprieves and pardons for offenses against the United States, except in cases of impeachment." The President's power to pardon offenses has also been interpreted to include the power to grant conditional pardons, commutations of sentence, conditional commutations of sentence, remission of fines and forfeitures, respites, and amnesties. However, the President's clemency authority only extends to federal offenses; the President cannot grant clemency for a state crime.

1. How does a person petition for federal clemency or a pardon?

Under federal law, a person requesting executive clemency must petition the President of the United States and submit the petition to the Office of the Pardon Attorney in the Department of Justice. The Office of the Pardon Attorney can provide petitions and other required forms necessary to complete the application for clemency. *See* 28 CFR § 1.1. Petition forms for commutation of sentence may also be obtained from the wardens of federal penal institutions. In addition, a petitioner applying for executive clemency with respect to military offenses should submit his or her petition directly to the Secretary of the military branch that had original jurisdiction over the court-martial trial and conviction of the petitioner.

The Code of Federal Regulations requires an applicant to wait five years after the date of the release of the petitioner from confinement, or in a case where no prison sentence was imposed, an applicant is required to wait five years after the date of conviction prior to submitting a petition for clemency. The regulation further states that "generally, no petition should be submitted by a person who is on probation, parole, or supervised release." 28 CFR § 1.2. With that in mind, the President can grant clemency at any time, whether an individual has made a formal petition or not. For example, President Gerald Ford granted a full and unconditional pardon to former President Richard Nixon prior to any indictment or charges being filed related to his involvement in Watergate.

2. What should a petition for clemency include?

Petitions for executive clemency should include the information required in the form prescribed by the United States Attorney General. This includes the following information:

a) That the person requesting clemency must state specifically the purpose for which clemency is sought, as well as attach any and all relevant documentary evidence that will support how clemency will support that purpose;
b) That discloses any arrests or convictions subsequent to the federal crime for which clemency is sought;
c) That discloses all delinquent credit obligations (whether disputed or not), all civil lawsuits to which the applicant is a party (whether plaintiff or defendant), and all unpaid tax obligations (whether local, state, or federal); and

d) That includes three character affidavits from persons not related to the applicant by blood or marriage.

In addition, acceptance of a Presidential pardon generally carries with it an admission of guilt. For that reason, a petitioner should include in his or her petition a statement of the petitioner's acceptance of responsibility, an expression of remorse, and atonement for the offense. All of the requirements are contained in 28 CFR §§ 1.1-1.11.

3. What happens after a petition for executive clemency is submitted?

All petitions for federal clemency are reviewed by the Office of the Pardon Attorney in the Department of Justice. A non-binding recommendation on an application is made to the President. Federal regulations also provide for guidelines and requirements to notify victims of the crimes, if any, for which clemency is sought. The President will either grant or deny a pardon. There are no hearings held on the petition, and there is no appeal of the President's decision.

4. What is the effect of a Presidential pardon?

A pardon is the forgiveness of a crime and the cancelation of the penalty associated with that crime. While a Presidential pardon will restore various rights lost as a result of the pardoned offense, it will not expunge the record of your conviction. This means that even if a person is granted a pardon, the person must still disclose their conviction on any form where such information is required, although the person may also disclose the fact that the offense for which they were convicted was pardoned.

B. Expungement of federal convictions

1. No law exists for general federal expungement

Congress has not provided federal legislation that offers any comprehensive authority or procedure for expunging criminal offenses. There exist only statutes that allow expungement in certain cases for possession of small amounts of controlled substances (*see* below) and interestingly, a procedure to expunge DNA samples of certain members of the military wrongfully convicted. Because there is no statutory guidance, federal courts have literally made up the rules and procedures themselves, often coming to different conclusions. Some federal circuit courts have stated they have no power to expunge records. However, other federal courts have indicated that they do have the power to expunge. The federal Tenth Circuit, which includes Oklahoma, has held that under certain limited circumstances federal courts may order expungement both of records held by other branches of the government (*e.g.*, executive branch), and its own court records. *Camfield v. City of Oklahoma City*, 248 F.3d 1214, 1234 (10th Cir. 2001); *United States v. Friesen*, 853 F.2d 816 (10th Cir. 1988). The Supreme Court has passed on hearing cases that would have resolved the split between the circuits. This issue remains legally murky.

2. Possible procedure for federal expungement

There are no statutory guidelines for how to seek an expungement under federal law, however, the place to start would be to file a motion with the federal court that issued the conviction that a person wants to be expunged. However, federal judges very rarely grant these types of motions. Some circuits have adopted a balancing test to decide if a record held by the court may be expunged: "if the dangers of unwarranted adverse consequences to the individual outweigh the public interest in maintenance of the records, then expunction is appropriate." Further, these same courts have freely stated that this balancing test "rarely tips in favor of expungement," and that expungement should be granted in only the most extreme cases. *United States v. Flowers*, 389 F.3d 737 (7th Cir. 2004). The Tenth Circuit requires "a factual showing of harm or 'extreme circumstances'" before a court may begin to consider ordering expungement. *Friesen* at 817. Some of the areas where expungement has worked are in incidents of extreme police misconduct, or where the conviction is being misused against the person. Unless there exist compelling reasons, a federal judge is highly unlikely to grant expungement.

3. Expungement for drug possession: statutory authority

Under a federal law entitled "special probation and expungement procedures for drug possessors," certain persons are allowed to request a federal court to issue an expungement order from all public records. 18 U.S.C. § 3607. Congress intended this order to restore the person to the status he or she "occupied before such arrest or institution of criminal proceedings." 18 U.S.C. § 3607(c).

In order to qualify for the expungement, you must have been under the age of 21 when you were convicted, you must have no prior drug offenses, and your conviction must have been for simple possession of a small amount of a controlled substance.

4. How does a person have firearms rights restored under federal law?

Under the Gun Control Act of 1968, a person who has received a Presidential pardon is not considered convicted of a crime preventing the purchase and possession of firearms subject to all other federal laws. *See* 18 U.S.C. §§ 921(a)(20) and (a)(33). In addition, persons who had a conviction expunged or set aside, or who have had their civil rights restored are not considered to have been convicted for purposes of the GCA "unless the pardon, expungement, or restoration of civil rights expressly provides the person may not ship, transport, possess, or receive firearms." 18 U.S.C. §§ 921(a)(20) and (a)(33).

The GCA also provides the United States Attorney General with the authority to grant relief from firearms disabilities where the Attorney General determines that the person is not likely to act in a manner dangerous to the public safety and where granting relief would not be contrary to the public interest. 18 U.S.C. § 925(c). The Attorney General has delegated this authority to the ATF. Unfortunately, the ATF reports that it has been prohibited from spending any funds in order to investigate or act upon applications from individuals seeking relief from federal firearms disabilities. This means that until the ATF's prohibition has been lifted, a person's best—and most likely—option to have their firearms rights restored is through a Presidential pardon. *See* www.atf.gov.

III. Oklahoma law

A. Clemency by Governor and Oklahoma Pardon and Parole Board

Article VI, Section 10 of the Oklahoma Constitution gives the Governor of Oklahoma the authority to grant pardons, except in cases of impeachment. Unlike the President's widespread authority to grant federal clemency, the authority of the Governor of Oklahoma is limited. The Governor can only grant a pardon if a majority of the members of the Oklahoma Pardon and Parole Board recommend that a pardon be granted.

1. Who is eligible for a pardon in Oklahoma?

Pardons, reprieves, commutations, and/or paroles can be granted to any person who has been convicted of a felony or misdemeanor under the laws of the State of Oklahoma. The applicant must have completed in entirety the sentence for the offense that he wishes to have pardoned, and must have paid all fines, costs, and restitution for that offense in full. Finally, the applicant must not have any charges pending against him at the time of application.

2. How does a person seek a pardon in Oklahoma?

A person seeking a pardon in Oklahoma is required to complete an application which is available from the Oklahoma Pardon and Parole Board. The applicant must include their "full and explicit reasons" for seeking a pardon within this application. Once properly submitted, the file of any applicant eligible for a pardon will be reviewed by the Board.

Once a completed application has been submitted to the Board, the Board will investigate the application and place it on the next available docket for a hearing. The applicant may appear at the hearing, and may choose to testify to the Board on his own behalf for a maximum of two minutes. After the hearing, the Board members vote on case files individually, and an applicant must obtain a majority number of votes of the Board before the application will be sent to the Governor for a final determination. If the majority of the Board recommends a pardon be extended to an applicant, the file is sent to the Governor, who may accept the Board's recommendation and grant a pardon, or reject the recommendation. If the Board votes against recommending a pardon to the Governor, applicants are not able to appeal the decision of the Board. However, applicants may re-apply for clemency one year after the Board's denial and there is no limit on the number of times an applicant may re-apply. For more information, *see* www.ok.gov/ppb/.

3. What is the effect of a pardon in Oklahoma?
Similar to federal clemency, unless the person receiving a pardon has their records expunged, the records of the original conviction continue to exist. A person who has been pardoned must still disclose the conviction on any relevant form seeking such information, however, the person may also state the nature of the clemency received.

B. Oklahoma expungement
22 O.S. §§ 18, 19 and 19a Oklahoma Code of Criminal Procedure control expungement under Oklahoma law. Expungement under these sections is limited, and does not include destruction of a person's criminal records. It simply seals those records from public view, while still allowing full access to the district attorney's office and other law enforcement entities.

1. Who is eligible for expungement?
Section 18 of the Code of Criminal Procedure provides for when a person is entitled to expungement. Section 18 allows expungement for persons who were acquitted or pardoned, had charges dismissed, were convicted as a juvenile for being delinquent or for an alcohol-related offense. The list of persons qualifying for an expungement is lengthy and is set out fully

below:

1. The person has been acquitted;
2. The conviction was reversed with instructions to dismiss by an appellate court of competent jurisdiction, or an appellate court of competent jurisdiction reversed the conviction and the district attorney subsequently dismissed the charge;
3. The factual innocence of the person was established by the use of deoxyribonucleic acid (DNA) evidence subsequent to conviction, including a person who has been released from prison at the time innocence was established;
4. The person has received a full pardon on the basis of a written finding by the Governor of actual innocence for the crime for which the claimant was sentenced;
5. The person was arrested and no charges of any type, including charges for an offense different than that for which the person was originally arrested, are filed and the statute of limitations has expired or the prosecuting agency has declined to file charges;
6. The person was under eighteen (18) years of age at the time the offense was committed and the person has received a full pardon for the offense;
7. The person was charged with one or more misdemeanor or felony crimes, all charges have been dismissed, the person has never been convicted of a felony, no misdemeanor or felony charges are pending against the person, and the statute of limitations for refiling the charge or charges has expired or the prosecuting agency confirms that the charge or charges will not be refiled; provided, however, this category shall not apply to charges that have been dismissed following the completion of a deferred judgment or delayed sentence;
8. The person was charged with a misdemeanor, the charge was dismissed following the successful completion of a deferred judgment or delayed sentence, the person has

never been convicted of a misdemeanor or felony, no misdemeanor or felony charges are pending against the person, and at least one (1) year has passed since the charge was dismissed;

9. The person was charged with a nonviolent felony offense, not listed in Section 571 of Title 57 of the Oklahoma Statutes, the charge was dismissed following the successful completion of a deferred judgment or delayed sentence, the person has never been convicted of a misdemeanor or felony, no misdemeanor or felony charges are pending against the person, and at least ten (10) years have passed since the charge was dismissed;

10. The person was convicted of a misdemeanor offense, the person has not been convicted of a felony, no felony or misdemeanor charges are pending against the person, and at least ten (10) years have passed since the end of the last misdemeanor sentence;

11. The person was convicted of a nonviolent felony offense, not listed in Section 571 of Title 57 of the Oklahoma Statutes, the person has received a full pardon for the offense, the person has not been convicted of any other felony, the person has not been convicted of a separate misdemeanor in the last fifteen (15) years, no felony or misdemeanor charges are pending against the person, and at least ten (10) years have passed since the felony conviction; or

12. The person has been charged or arrested or is the subject of an arrest warrant for a crime that was committed by another person who has appropriated or used the person's name or other identification without the person's consent or authorization.

2. What is the procedure for obtaining an expungement?

To obtain an expungement, a petitioner is required to file a petition for expungement in the district court. There are two procedures, one under section 18 which requires the filing of a motion and the other under section 19 which requires the filing of a petition. The section 18 motion is filed in the criminal case and the section 19 petition is filed as a civil case. Even though expungement proceedings are governed by the Code of Criminal Procedure, expungement itself is a civil matter and, therefore, is a matter addressed by civil district courts. Once the proper paperwork is filed, the district court will set the matter for a hearing, and notice the district attorney's office, the arresting agency, the Oklahoma State Bureau of Investigation, and anyone else who may have relevant information regarding the sealing of the criminal record.

Expungement petitions under 22 O.S. §§ 18 and 19 can become adversarial proceedings involving one or more parties, including the State, which may object to the court granting an order of expungement. The court will hold a hearing to consider the reason for expungement and any State objections. If after the hearing, the court finds that harm to the privacy of the person or danger of unwarranted adverse consequences outweighs the public interest in the availability of the records, the court will issue an order to seal records.

Section 19a of the Oklahoma Code of Criminal Procedure also governs expungement procedure, however, this section is applicable only to victims of identity theft seeking an expungement. For more information, *see* 22 O.S. § 19a.

3. Expungement might not be the end of the story!

Remember, expungement in Oklahoma is simply the *sealing*, not *destruction*, of criminal records. Oklahoma law enforcement officials can still see the information, and it can still be used against you to impeach your credibility during a legal proceeding. To make matters worse, any time after an expungement is granted the State can file a motion to unseal the records. The court will schedule a hearing, and if the court determines that there has been a change in conditions or there is a compelling reason to unseal the records, the court may issue an order mandating that some or all of the records be unsealed!

C. How does a person have firearms rights restored under Oklahoma law?

The only method to recover firearms rights in Oklahoma is to receive a full pardon; by the President for a federal offense, or the governor of the state of conviction for a state level offense. Oklahoma Statute Title 21 § 1283 prohibits any individual convicted of a felony offense, federal or arising in any state, from possessing "any pistol, imitation or homemade pistol, machine gun, sawed-off shotgun or rifle, or any other dangerous or deadly firearm." Not only can the convicted felon not have a firearm, it is also illegal for that person to be a passenger in a car where there is a firearm present, or live in a home where there is a firearm, even if the firearm does not belong to the felon and is never in their possession! The only way to remove this prohibition and restore firearms rights is for the President or governor to pardon the offense.

CHAPTER TWELVE

I'M BEING SUED FOR WHAT?
CIVIL LIABILITY IF YOU HAVE USED YOUR GUN

I. What does it mean to be sued?

The term "lawsuit" refers to one party's assertion in a written filing with a court that another party has violated the law. In the context of firearms, typically the party suing has been injured and wants a ruling or judgment from the court that will entitle the person suing to receive damages, usually in the form of money.

A. What is a civil claim or lawsuit?

A civil "lawsuit" or "suit" refers to the actual filing of written paperwork with a court (1) asserting that another party violated the law, and (2) seeking some type of redress. A "claim" can exist without the filing of a lawsuit. A claim is simply the belief or assertion that another party has violated the law. Many parties have claims they never assert, or sometimes parties informally assert the claim in hopes of resolving the dispute without the filing of a lawsuit. Also, another term commonly used is "tort" or "tort claim." A tort is a civil claim arising out of a wrongful act, not including a breach of contract or trust, that results in injury to another's person, property, reputation, or the like. The claims described in this chapter are tort claims.

B. Difference between "civil claims" and "criminal charges"

To start with the basics, there are two different aspects of the legal system that gun owners may face after the use of a firearm: criminal and civil. There are several names and descriptive terms used for each (*e.g.*, civil lawsuit, criminal actions, civil claims, criminal proceedings, *etc.*), but regardless of the terms, the same breakdown applies; cases are either criminal or civil. There is another subgroup of proceedings called administrative actions. Those actions are not covered by this chapter but can sometimes impact handgun license holders. For example, appealing the denial of an Oklahoma handgun license is an administrative act. *See* Chapter 8 for more information. With that said, the three primary differences between a criminal action and a civil proceeding are: (1) who or what is bringing the action or lawsuit, (2) what are they seeking, and (3) what is the burden of proof.

1. State versus individual bringing claims

In a criminal case, the party bringing the action is the "sovereign," meaning the United States, state, municipality, county, *etc.*, that believes that a person violated their laws. Even if an individual calls the police, fills out a criminal complaint, or even asks the district attorney to file charges, the party that actually brings a criminal action is the state, county, *etc.*, not an individual.

A civil action is usually filed by any individual, business, or other entity (partnership, LLC, trust, *etc.*). The entity bringing the claim is called the "plaintiff." Even governmental entities can bring civil claims; *i.e.*, if you negligently shoot a county propane tank causing a fire, the county can sue you civilly for those damages. The typical gun case, though, will involve an individual filing a lawsuit against another individual for damages caused by the firearm. If the incident occurs at a place of business, the plaintiff may also sue the business claiming that it is in some way at fault for the incident. The party being sued is typically called the "defendant."

2. Relief sought/awarded

In a criminal case, the entity prosecuting the case is usually seeking to imprison or fine you. Most crimes are punishable by a term of days, months, or years in prison or jail, and a fine not to exceed a statutory maximum amount.

By contrast, the plaintiff in the civil case is almost always seeking a monetary award. Several other types of relief are available (declaratory, injunctive, specific performance), but for the most part, gun cases will involve the plaintiff seeking monetary damages.

3. Burden of proof

In a criminal case, the standard is "beyond a reasonable doubt." In civil cases, however, a plaintiff must prove a person is liable for damages by a "preponderance of the evidence" standard. A preponderance of the evidence is a much lower standard than the criminal standard of beyond a reasonable doubt. It generally means that the party with the greater weight of credible evidence wins that issue. The preponderance of the evidence has been described as more than half, that is, if the evidence demonstrates that something "more likely occurred than not," this meets the burden of proof. Whereas in a criminal case, if there exists any "reasonable doubt," the burden of proof is not met. These levels of proof do not necessarily mean the party with the most exhibits or greater number of witnesses will prevail. It is possible that one highly credible witness can prevail over the testimony of a dozen biased, shady witnesses.

Example:

> *John mistakes a utility meter reader for a burglar due to his disheveled appearance, tool bag, and because he appears to be snooping around John's house. John fires a shot without warning and injures the meter reader.*

Possible criminal liability: the State of Oklahoma could bring criminal charges against John for a number of crimes (aggravated assault and battery, shooting with intent to kill, or discharging a firearm). The State would be seeking to imprison or fine John for his conduct, and it would be required to prove that John committed the crime at issue "beyond a reasonable doubt."

Possible civil liability: the meter reader could also file a civil lawsuit against John alleging that John was negligent or committed the tort of assault and battery. The meter reader would seek monetary damages and be required to prove his claims by a "preponderance of the evidence."

C. Impact of result in one court upon the other

1. Can a result in a criminal trial be used in a civil trial?

Yes, because of the legal doctrines of *res judicata* and collateral estoppel. These two legal doctrines govern the impact of a ruling or judgment in one case, upon a separate case involving the same set of facts and circumstances. For the present discussion, if a person is found guilty of a crime in a criminal proceeding, because that court uses a higher standard of "beyond a reasonable doubt" than the civil requirement of "preponderance of the evidence," the finding of the criminal court may be used for purposes of establishing civil liability. Entire chapters in law books have been written on these topics, so, suffice to say, this section is a brief overview of these laws.

The criminal concept of *nolo contendere* or "no contest" often generates confusion in this area. In a criminal case, a plea of *nolo contendere* or no contest means that the defendant does not admit guilt but does not contest the state's case against him. The plea, however, still results in a judgment that the defendant is guilty of the crime, but that judgment cannot be used as evidence to establish the defendant's liability in a separate civil case.

Example:

> *Phil and Jeremy become involved in a road rage incident, and an altercation follows. Phil shoots Jeremy, wounding him. When all is sorted out, Phil is found guilty of criminal assault and receives punishment from the court (remember, criminal trials use the "beyond a reasonable doubt" standard).*

If Jeremy later sues Phil because of the injuries he received when Phil shot him, Jeremy, in his civil action, will very likely be allowed to use the finding of guilt in the criminal case (because it used the higher standard of beyond a reasonable doubt) to establish his burden in the civil case (the lower preponderance of the evidence standard) that he is owed damages or money in the civil case. This is an example of collateral estoppel; Phil will not be permitted to re-litigate his guilt in the civil case.

Both doctrines are based on the concept that a party to a legal proceeding should not be able to endlessly litigate issues that have already been decided by the legal system. At its most basic level, it means that a party to a legal proceeding, who receives a final ruling on a particular issue, win or lose, cannot attempt to have another trial court or even the same court decide the same issue.

Note about appeals: collateral estoppel and *res judicata* are different concepts than an appeal, or asking the court in the first proceeding to reconsider its ruling, or grant a new trial. An appeal is a request to a higher court to review the decision of a lower court. Likewise, in any given case, the parties will have numerous opportunities to ask the current court to reconsider its rulings, or even ask for a new trial after a trial is completed. Collateral estoppel and *res judicata* come into play after a judgment is final and is no longer subject to appeal or revision by the trial court.

Example:

> *Michele is sued for accidentally shooting Nancy. Nancy wins a judgment of $350 against Michele, much less than Nancy believed she was damaged.*

In that case, Nancy can appeal the decision, or even ask that trial court for a new trial. However, Nancy cannot file another new lawsuit regarding the same incident and attempt to recover more in the second case because of the doctrine of *res judicata*. In order for the doctrine to apply, the facts, circumstances and issues must be the same.

Example:

> *Justin fires his hunting rifle from his deer blind, hitting Peter with one round. Peter files a civil*

> *suit against Justin and loses at trial. The court awards Peter no damages. Peter appeals and loses the appeal also.*

Peter is legally barred from recovering in another lawsuit against Justin involving the same incident. However, Peter is not barred from filing suit against Justin for damages arising out of another set of facts and circumstances, for example, if the two are involved in a car wreck on a different day.

Practical Legal Tip:

Unlike criminal cases where a unanimous jury verdict is required to convict someone, to prevail in a civil suit in Oklahoma, only nine of the twelve jurors (or five out of six, depending upon the court where your case is pending) must agree to render a verdict. In a criminal case, many times the goal of the defendant is to avoid conviction by convincing a single juror that the State cannot prove its case at the higher "beyond a reasonable doubt" standard. By contrast, in a civil lawsuit a plaintiff can prevail and recover damages, even if three of the jurors vehemently believe the defendant should prevail, as long as the remaining nine jurors believe that the plaintiff has proven his case by the lower "preponderance of the evidence" standard. *–Robert*

2. Civil case result impact on criminal case

Suppose you lose a civil suit and a judgment is entered against you arising out of a shooting incident. Can that judgement be used to establish that you committed a crime? No. The burden of proof is much higher in the criminal context than the civil case. The plaintiff proved his civil case by a "preponderance of the evidence." This does not mean that he proved his case "beyond a reasonable doubt," meaning a separate criminal trial is required to make that determination.

The one area where a civil case can impact a criminal case is the potential overlapping use of evidence and testimony. Your admission in one case can almost always be used against you in another case. Meaning, your sworn testimony in the civil case ("yes, I shot the guy") can almost always be used against you in the criminal case, and vice versa.

II. What might you be sued for? Gun related claims in civil courts

A. Liability for unintentional discharge

This section deals with accidental or unintentional discharges of your firearm. Common unintentional discharges are associated with hunting and cleaning accidents or the mishandling of a weapon. Intentional shootings are addressed in the following section.

With that said, the following are the types of civil claims that may be asserted in connection with an unintentional discharge.

1. Negligence/gross negligence

Most civil cases for damages resulting from an accidental discharge will include a negligence or gross negligence claim. What does this mean and what does a plaintiff have to prove before they can win? Under Oklahoma law, negligence is defined as the failure to use ordinary care, that is, failing to do that which a person of ordinary prudence would have done under the same or similar circumstances, or doing that which a person of ordinary prudence would not have done under the same or similar circumstances. If a person fails to use ordinary care, then they have acted negligently and will be liable for damages resulting from their conduct. "Ordinary care" means that degree of care that would be used by a person of ordinary prudence under the same or similar circumstances. This is an "objective standard," meaning, the test is not whether you believed you acted prudently, but whether the judge or jury believes you acted as a person of ordinary prudence would have acted. Of course, this is the definition of negligence in the civil context. There is actually a different definition of criminal negligence, which is beyond the scope of this book's discussion.

What is gross negligence and how is it different than "regular" negligence? Many gun cases will include a claim for "gross negligence" by the plaintiff. The primary reason for this is that if a plaintiff establishes gross negligence by a defendant, the plaintiff may be entitled to additional types or amounts of money that are legally available if more than mere negligence is established. The Oklahoma Supreme Court and the Oklahoma Legislature have defined gross negligence. The Oklahoma Supreme Court, in *Fox v. Oklahoma Memorial Hosp.*, 774 P.2d 459, 461 (Okla. 1989) (citations omitted) stated that, "Oklahoma recognizes three degrees of negligence - slight, ordinary and gross. Gross negligence is defined by 25 O.S. § 6 as the lack of slight care and diligence. The question is whether the negligence of the [defendants] was either so flagrant, so deliberate, or so reckless that it is removed from the realm of mere negligence. The intentional failure to perform a manifest duty in reckless disregard of the consequences or in callous indifference to the life, liberty or property of another, may result in such a gross want of care for the rights of others and of the public that the finding of a willful, wanton, deliberate act is justified."

The Oklahoma Legislature also defined the degrees of negligence for an act or omission in 25 O.S. § 6:

> Slight negligence consists in the want of great care and diligence; ordinary negligence in the want of ordinary care and diligence; and gross negligence in the want of slight care and diligence.

The defendant's state of mind is also a key difference between negligence and gross negligence. Negligence involves an objective standard—how would a reasonable person have acted? Gross negligence applies a subjective component—was this particular person lacking slight care related to the risk involved?

Example:

Jessica has practiced her shooting at a private range on her country property for 20 years, without incident. Jessica shoots towards an area where she has never seen another person, and she believes the range of her guns cannot reach her property line. One day, a neighbor is hit by a shot as he is strolling through the woods just off of Jessica's property.

Result: Jessica might be liable for negligence if a jury determines, for example, that a reasonably prudent person would have acted differently, tested the range of her guns, or built a different type of back stop or berm, *etc.* However, Jessica was not subjectively aware of an extreme degree of risk so there would be no evidence of gross negligence. However, change Jessica's awareness and it changes the result.

Example:

Jessica has received several complaints over the years about bullets leaving her property and hitting her neighbor's property. Nevertheless, Jessica ignores the complaints and continues practicing in the direction that she typically shoots. One day while practicing, her bullet leaves her property and hits her neighbor. She is later sued by the neighbor for gross negligence.

Result: Jessica may very well be liable for gross negligence because she intentionally failed to perform a manifest duty in reckless disregard of the consequences. Additionally, Jessica was aware that there was a risk to the life, liberty or property of her neighbor, but was callously indifferent; she continued to shoot without changing direction or building a back stop or berm and someone was injured as a result.

2. Negligent entrustment of a firearm

Oklahoma recognizes a claim for entrusting (*e.g.*, giving, lending, transferring) a firearm to another person. Negligent entrustment occurs when a person permits a third person (including their own children) to use a thing (such as a firearm) or to engage in an activity which is under the control of the actor, if the actor knows or should know that such person intends or is likely to use the thing or to conduct himself in the activity in such a manner as to create an unreasonable risk of harm to others. *See Vance By and Through Vance v. Thomas*, 716 P.2d 710 (Okla. Crim. App. 1986). Let's look at some examples.

> Example:
>
> *Shaun lets his adult grandson Gordon borrow a shotgun to take on a fishing trip because he knows there are water moccasins in the spot where they plan to fish. Gordon has never been in trouble with the law, has repeatedly been trained in firearms safety, and has never had an incident with a gun. However, while on the trip, Gordon accidentally shoots a fellow fishing buddy with Shaun's shotgun. The fishing buddy, now turned plaintiff, sues Gordon for negligence and Shaun for negligent entrustment of a firearm.*

Can the plaintiff win his claim for negligent entrustment? Probably not. Shaun might get sued for giving the shotgun to his grandson, but the facts described do not meet the elements necessary to establish negligent entrustment under Oklahoma law, and Shaun should prevail in any lawsuit. First, there are no facts that suggest Shaun knew Gordon intended to create an unreasonable risk of harm to others. Further, there are no facts showing knowledge by Shaun that Gordon was either incompetent or reckless to the point where loaning him the gun would create an unreasonable risk of harm to others. Thus, the negligent entrustment claim would legally fail.

Many plaintiffs have urged Oklahoma appellate courts to adopt a "strict liability" standard when looking at gun cases. In other words, if you give someone your gun, you are automatically liable for whatever happens. Barring certain circumstances regarding minor children, Oklahoma appellate courts have uniformly rejected a strict liability standard.

3. Is negligent storage of a firearm recognized in Oklahoma?

A question commonly asked by gun owners is "if someone steals my gun, am I liable if they shoot someone?" In other words, if I store my gun and a criminal or another less-than-responsible person gets the gun, am I liable if they shoot someone? As of the date of this publication, the answer in Oklahoma is unresolved. This means that there has not been an appellate court that has had an opportunity to definitively state whether or not such a tort could exist as a matter of Oklahoma law.

21 O.S. § 1273, entitled Allowing Minors to Possess Firearms, states that it is generally unlawful for any parent or guardian to "...permit his or her child to possess any of the arms or weapons designated in Section 1272 of this title, including any firearm...". There are circumstances under which the law will create liability for a parent to permit a child to access/possess firearms/prohibited weapons. However, there are also circumstances where a parent may lawfully allow a minor to possess a firearm. *See* Section VII discussed later in this Chapter. As a result, it remains extraordinarily important to exercise due care in the storage of your firearms.

B. Intentional discharge: a person intended to shoot

1. Negligence/gross negligence

Just because you intend to shoot someone, or otherwise "use" your gun, does not necessarily mean that the plaintiff will not assert negligence or gross negligence claims. In other words, you may have fully intended to pull the trigger, but the plaintiff may claim that you were negligent for any number of reasons; for example, you mistook the mailman for a burglar. The negligence and gross negligence claims, as defined above, can be brought even if you intended to pull the trigger. Many times claims of negligence are couched in language that will qualify a home liability insurance policy to cover the claim, because most liability insurance policies exclude intentional acts including the intentional act of self-defense.

2. Civil assault and battery

If a person has shot at or shot someone, they may be sued for a claim of assault and/or battery. This is an intentional act, not an accident nor a claim based on a deviation from a standard of care. An assault, as defined in section 21 of the Second Restatement of Torts, occurs if a:

1. Defendant acted either with the intent of making a harmful/offensive contact with the person of Plaintiff, or with the intent of putting Plaintiff in apprehension of such a contact; and
2. Plaintiff was placed in apprehension of an immediate harmful/offensive contact with his/her person by the conduct of Defendant; or Plaintiff was caused to suffer fright and terror.

Further, if a dangerous instrumentality is used in the assault such as a firearm, then the civil claim could be modified to Assault with a Dangerous Weapon. *See Vaughn v. Baxter*, 488 P.2d 1234, 1237 (Okla. 1971).

Battery, under section 13 of the Second Restatement of Torts, occurs whenever a person acts intending to cause a harmful or offensive contact with the person of the other, or a third person, or creates an imminent apprehension of such contact, and a harmful contact with the person of the other directly or indirectly results.

Example:

Bill is startled while driving. Martha is standing next to his passenger window at a light screaming that he cut her off in traffic, but taking no action to indicate she intends to harm Bill or do anything besides verbally lodging her complaints. In response, Bill fires a shot at Martha to make her go away, and hits her in the leg.

In this situation, Bill has committed both a civil assault and battery with a dangerous weapon. He intended to and did cause serious bodily injury to Martha with no legal justification. Therefore, a civil jury would likely find Bill liable and award damages to Martha.

Example:

Bill is startled while driving. Martha is standing next to his passenger window at a light screaming that he cut her off in traffic, but taking no action to indicate she intends to harm Bill or do anything besides verbally lodging her complaints. In response, Bill points his gun at Martha and says "You're dead!" He fires his gun but misses.

Bill has committed a civil assault with a dangerous weapon. He knowingly threatened Martha with imminent bodily injury with no legal justification. However, since there was no direct or indirect contact, he would likely not be liable for a civil battery.

C. False imprisonment: being sued for detaining people

What if a gun owner detains someone at gun point? If the person who was detained later decides to sue, it will likely include a claim for "false imprisonment." Oklahoma recognizes a civil claim for false imprisonment. This claim can arise when someone detains persons waiting for police, *e.g.* homeowners detaining burglars, *etc.* However, it can also come up commonly in shoplifting cases (*see* Chapter 7). The elements of false imprisonment are: (a) the detention of a person against his (or her) will and (b) the unlawfulness of the detention. Merchants are constantly at risk for false imprisonment claims when they detain suspected shoplifters. At common law, a merchant who detained someone on a reasonable *but ultimately mistaken belief* that the person had stolen some merchandise, would have been subject to a claim for false imprisonment. However, the Oklahoma legislature modified this common law rule through its enactment of 22 O.S. §§ 1343 and 1344. Section 1343 protects from civil and criminal liability a merchant who (a) has *reasonable grounds* or *probable cause* to believe that a person has wrongfully shoplifted merchandise and (b) detains that person in a *reasonable manner* and *for a reasonable length of time*. Section 1344 creates a presumption of probable cause to believe that concealed unpurchased merchandise was shoplifted. *Walters v. J.C. Penney Company, Inc.,* 82 P.3d 578 (Okla. 2003). Remember, this exception is for merchants only, non-merchants are still subject to civil suits for false imprisonment.

Example:

> *Emily fears she is about to be attacked in a grocery store parking lot by Randall. Randall follows her step-by-step through the parking lot and stops right next to Emily's car. Emily draws her .380 and tells Randall to "stay right there while I call the police." Randall complies, and Emily holds him at gunpoint until the police arrive. When the police arrive, they determine that Randall was an out-of-uniform store employee tasked with rounding up the grocery carts in the parking lot and was no threat to Emily.*

If a jury determines that Emily acted without justification (*i.e.*, she was not reasonably in fear of death or bodily injury), Emily could be civilly liable for falsely imprisoning Randall and owe him damages.

D. Wrongful death

If a person is in the unfortunate position that they have shot and killed another individual and a civil suit occurs because of the shooting, it likely will include a claim for wrongful death. In Oklahoma, when one's death is caused by the wrongful act or omission of another, the personal representative of the deceased may maintain an action against the latter, or his or her personal representative if he or she is also deceased. The action must be commenced within the two-year statute of limitations. *See* 12 O.S. § 1053.

III. What can the plaintiff recover?

If a person is sued in civil court and the plaintiff convinces a jury that the defendant was liable for damages, what and how much can a plaintiff get? There are scores of cases discussing the details of each category of damages that a plaintiff can recover in a civil lawsuit. The following is a brief description of two very important concepts: (1) "proximate cause," which is essential to recover damages in most circumstances, and (2) the basic types of damages that a plaintiff may typically seek in a gun case.

A. Proximate cause

One basic concept that is important to most civil claims, and is usually required to recover damages, is "proximate cause." Virtually every tort claim will require the plaintiff to prove that his damages were proximately caused by the defendant. "Proximate cause" is defined as enough evidence to sufficiently establish a causal connection between the alleged negligence of defendant and the injury incurred by the plaintiff. *Missouri K. & T. Ry. Co. v. Perino*, 247 P. 41 (Okla. 1926). In a suit for personal injuries, the question whether defendant's negligence is the proximate cause of the injury sustained, should be left to the jury where the evidence is conflicting, or where men of ordinary intelligence might differ as to the effect of the evidence on the point. *Incorporated Town of Sallisaw v. Wells*, 215 P. 118 (Okla. 1923).

For a gun owner, the most obvious cases of proximate cause are pulling the trigger on a firearm and hitting the person or thing you aimed at. A jury will likely hold that your action proximately caused whatever physical damage the bullet did to persons or property. But what about those circumstances where the use of the gun is far removed from the damages claimed? This is where the doctrine of proximate cause will cut off liability. If the damage is too far removed from the act, then the act cannot be a proximate cause of that damage.

Example:

> *Anthony is cleaning his AR-15 one night in his apartment and is negligent in his handling of the rifle. He has an accidental discharge and the bullet goes through the wall of his apartment and strikes his neighbor, Ray, in the leg. Ray, although in massive pain, received prompt medical care from his wife, Gail, and made a speedy recovery.*

If Anthony is later sued by Ray and his wife Gail, Anthony's negligence undoubtedly "proximately caused" damages for things like Ray's medical bills, hospital stay, and perhaps even lost wages. But what if Gail claims that because of her having to treat Ray's wounds that she missed a big job interview and lost out on a big raise in pay and that she wants Anthony to pay that as a component of damages? A jury would hold that Gail likely could not recover damages for her lost raise in pay because the loss would not be "proximately caused" by the act being sued for. In that case, there will be no recovery for the plaintiff, Gail. Proximate cause must be established in every case and may appear to be arbitrary legal line drawing because it is.

As discussed later in this chapter, Oklahoma law also recognizes a doctrine that unforeseen criminal conduct breaks the causal link between an action and a third-party's injuries.

B. What types of damages can a plaintiff recover?

The following is merely a brief snapshot of the types of damages recoverable in a firearms case. To recover any of the damages below, the plaintiff must first prove one of the previously discussed claims by a preponderance of the evidence. For example, if the jury determines a defendant was not negligent, a plaintiff cannot recover his or her medical costs, no matter how severe the plaintiff's injuries. Some of the damages a plaintiff can try to recover include:

- Lost Wages
- Medical Costs
- Permanent Disability
- Pain & Suffering (Physical, Mental & Emotional)
- Funeral and Burial Costs
- Disfigurement
- Loss of Companionship
- Loss of Household Services
- Lost Future Wages
- Future Medical Costs
- Punitive or exemplary damages (Note: the standard of proof in Oklahoma for punitive/exemplary damages is "clear and convincing evidence," which is higher than a "preponderance of the evidence." Punitive damages are also only available in cases of intentional or reckless conduct, or gross negligence.)

Remember, these damages require evidence to establish recovery. A court can find the defendant 100% at fault, but award no damages because the plaintiff failed to prove damages by a preponderance of the evidence. For example, a plaintiff who seeks reimbursement for medical expenses but has no evidence that they ever went to a doctor or hospital, will very likely be unable to recover those medical expenses.

Practical Legal Tip:

Most people don't know that civil courts in Oklahoma have no independent means of sifting through the thousands of lawsuits filed every year to determine which are frivolous and which are meritorious and should go forward. The civil justice system is "user driven," meaning that unless one side or the other asks the judge to rule on a particular issue (usually called a "motion"), no one at the courthouse, including the judge, is going to take any action to examine the merit, or lack thereof, of a lawsuit. *-Robert*

IV. How good are Oklahoma civil immunity laws for gun owners?

A. No immunity from lawsuits

There is a common misunderstanding that there exists a law that if you are legally justified in using your gun that you can't be sued. This is just not the case. First, if a person has the filing fee, anyone can sue anyone else in the State of Oklahoma. There is no one stopping anyone else from filing a lawsuit. Winning a lawsuit is a different issue entirely. If someone files the lawsuit, no matter how frivolous, it still must be dealt with, and it still must be shown to the court that there is a defense that bars this lawsuit. This process can take significant time, money, and legal energy even for the most frivolous cases. In short, lawyers will need to be paid and even if you beat the "rap," you still have to take the civil "ride." So, if there is no immunity to lawsuits for gun owners, what protection is there?

B. Immunity for certain claims

Most important for gun owners if they find themselves included in a civil suit after a justified use of force will be Oklahoma Statute 21 O.S. § 1289.25(F), that provides civil immunity in situations where the person has used force or deadly force under § 1289.25(B) which includes what is commonly called the "castle doctrine" and § 1289.25(D) which is commonly called the "stand your ground" law.

> ***Immunity from Damages***
> **21 O.S. § 1289.25(F)**
>
> F. A person who uses force, as permitted pursuant to the provisions of subsections B and D of this section, is justified in using such force and is immune from criminal prosecution and civil action for the use of such force. As used in this subsection, the term "criminal prosecution" includes charging or prosecuting the defendant.

The Oklahoma law of immunity from criminal prosecution or civil action is an absolute defense. This statute does not prevent lawsuits; it just makes the ones filed harder to win. Immunity from civil action is an affirmative defense, but it is brought before trial as a pre-trial motion, so you are saved some of the pain a civil suit may cause an innocent defendant. So how does an innocent defendant invoke the statutory immunity of § 1289.25(F)?

In order to answer this question we can look at the recent case of *State of Oklahoma v. Ramos*, decided by the Oklahoma Court of Criminal Appeals on June 9, 2015. Even though this is a criminal case where the Ramos brothers claimed that they were immune from criminal prosecution because they killed a man in self-defense, it is applicable to the civil analysis because the statute includes both criminal and civil immunity. Another interesting twist to this case is that it is an unpublished opinion which normally means that it holds no value as legal precedent, however the Oklahoma Court of Criminal Appeals explicitly states in the opinion itself, "These procedures shall govern future cases." *State v. Ramos*, Case Nos. S-2013-509, S-2013-510 (Okla. Crim. App., June 9, 2015), at page 11.

According to the Oklahoma Court of Criminal Appeals, a person who has been accused of unlawfully using force or deadly force against another will have to show that they are entitled to immunity by asserting it before trial or else it is waived. The defendant must file a pre-trial motion to dismiss the claim and ask for an evidentiary hearing. At the hearing the judge should take evidence and argument then determine by a preponderance of the evidence whether or not the defendant's use of force or deadly force was proper under either subsection B (Castle Doctrine) or subsection D (Stand Your Ground). In the event that the judge rules against the defendant, they may appeal this decision to an appellate court for a review. It is very important to remember, it is the innocent defendant who must assert the protection of civil immunity prior to trial, otherwise the immunity is waived and cannot be used. This area of law is relatively new and should continue to evolve and become more clear and concrete.

The Oklahoma Legislature was very protective of people who justifiably use force and deadly force to protect themselves by not only providing them with the shield of immunity, but also the sword of recompense so that they can be compensated for being wrongfully sued. Subsection H of section 1289.25 will give consolation to the defendant who is wrongfully sued after having immunity. The law states:

> H. The court shall award reasonable attorney fees, court costs, compensation for loss of income, and all expenses incurred by the defendant in defense of any civil action brought by a plaintiff if the court finds that the defendant is immune from prosecution as provided in subsection F of this section.

Because subsection H allows the victorious, immune party, if they win, to collect attorney fees and costs, is a clear indication that the immunity granted under section 1289.25 is not immunity from a lawsuit itself, but immunity from paying damages after enduring the filing and defending against a civil lawsuit during a pre-trial hearing.

Example:

> *John is the victim of a home invasion. He fires several shots at the intruder. The intruder is hit and stopped. One shot, however, misses the intruder and hits a propane tank at the house across the street. The propane tank explodes and burns down the neighbor's home.*

The resulting damage is neither personal injury nor death, however subsection F does not limit civil immunity only to cases involving personal injury or death, the statute says a person who "uses force, as permitted...is justified in using such force and is immune from... prosecution." It is likely that the immunity statute will provide John with protection from a civil suit by the neighbor for the damages to the house.

C. Justification

All of the justifications and defenses under Oklahoma statutes can also be asserted as affirmative defenses in a civil action. This means, for example, if you shoot someone in defense of yourself, others, or your property and are sued as a result, you may assert the applicable sections of the Oklahoma statutes, Title 21, as a defense to the civil claims. If the judge or jury agrees that you acted in self-defense, or properly used force to defend others or property, the plaintiff will be barred from recovery. *See* Chapters 4 through 7.

D. Statute of limitations for civil claims

The statute of limitations is a doctrine in Oklahoma (and almost every other jurisdiction) that requires civil claims to be brought within a certain period of time after the incident. If the claim is not brought within the statute of limitations period, it is barred. There are a number of issues relating to *when* the statute of limitations starts to run in many cases, but for the most part, limitations will start to run immediately after a shooting incident. The statute of limitations can vary from claim to claim, most, however, are between one and two years. In Oklahoma, the limitations period most likely to apply to gun cases is going to be two years. Negligence, and wrongful death claims all provide two-year limitations periods; however, assault and battery and false imprisonment have a one year statute of limitations. Be aware that any claims against a government entity have special statutes of limitation as governed by the government tort claim act. Special notices to the government are required and many cases against the government for negligence or intentional torts are dismissed because the short statute of limitations expired.

What does this mean for gun owners? If you "use" your gun, the plaintiff must bring a civil suit against you within the applicable one or two year statute of limitations of the incident in almost all cases or the claim will be barred.

E. Superseding or intervening criminal conduct

Oklahoma law recognizes a doctrine that absolves someone from responsibility for conduct that might otherwise be a tort (*e.g.*, negligence) if a criminal act breaks the causal connection between the tort and the injury. Generally, a third party's criminal conduct is a superseding cause which relieves the negligent actor from liability. However, the actor's negligence will not be excused where the criminal conduct is anticipated or a foreseeable result of the actor's negligence. *See Long v. Ponca City Hospital, Inc.*, 593 P.2d 1081 (Okla. 1979).

Example:

> *Justin allows his nephew Randall to use his handgun for protection. Justin knows Randall has been in trouble with the law repeatedly and has been accused of armed robbery. While Randall has the handgun, his apartment is burglarized, and the gun is stolen and used in a crime spree. During the crime spree, Melanie is*

shot and injured.

Melanie would not be able to recover from Justin, even though Justin may have been negligent in giving his gun to Randall, because the criminal act of burglarizing Randall's apartment and subsequent crime spree were superseding causes that broke the link between Justin's actions and the resulting injuries.

F. Contributory negligence/comparative liability

Oklahoma has a doctrine called comparative liability. If this defense is applicable and properly raised in court, either the judge or the jury will be asked to determine the percentage of fault or responsibility of the parties involved in the incident. The damages are then apportioned based upon the percentages assigned by the judge or jury.

Example:

> *Richard is a young adult trick-or-treater. He uses a fake gun as a part of his costume and knocks loudly on Nancy's door at 11:30 p.m. on October 31. Nancy, having forgotten about Halloween, is frightened by the knock, the fake gun, and the late hour of Richard's arrival. She fires through the door, injuring Richard.*

In the civil suit that follows by Richard against Nancy, the jury will be permitted to consider whether Richard's negligence, if any, contributed to cause the resulting injuries. The jury could determine that Richard was 0% at fault, 100%, or anything in between. By way of example only, if the jury awarded Richard $100,000.00 in damages, but found he was 30% at fault, and Nancy 70%, Richard would only be able to recover $70,000 of his damages.

In Oklahoma, this rule only applies where the damaged party is 50% or less at fault. In other words, if the plaintiff bringing the lawsuit is determined to be more than 50% responsible for the injuries, he or she cannot recover any damages. This can be important for the average gun owner in that a carjacker/home invader/general troublemaker who is the overwhelming cause of an incident cannot recover just because the judge or jury finds the gun owner made a slight misstep in defending themselves or their home.

V. What about third parties?

Oklahoma law provides a different standard when it comes to injuries to innocent third parties. In this section, a "third-party" generally means someone who is not a party to the encounter with the firearm; *e.g.*, bystanders, witnesses, folks nearby who were not the intended targets.

Oklahoma uses a rule that would allow an injured innocent third-party to recover damages if the person exercising force or deadly force did so in a manner that unnecessarily put others at risk. This rule was adopted from the Restatement of Torts. There is an old case (that is still good law) that restates the rule for Oklahoma. Essentially, the court held:

"'Where a person in lawful self-defense fires a pistol at an assailant, and, missing him, wounds an innocent bystander, he is not liable for the injury, if guilty of no negligence...' Where an act is lawful in itself [referring to self-defense], injury resulting therefrom is not actionable, unless the act is done at a time, or in a manner, or under circumstances indicative of a want of proper regard for the rights of others. [T]his must be the correct rule; and the only qualification thereof that in any case would seem to commend itself is that, where such self-defense is obviously dangerous to others, and the necessity thereof may be avoided by withdrawing from the combat, or in other words, by retreating to the wall, we apprehend it would be for the jury to say whether due care for the safety of bystanders would not require such avoidance." *Shaw v. Lord*, 137 P. 885, 351 (Okla. 1914)(citations omitted), *reaffirmed by Cook v. Hunt*, 63 P. 2d 693 (Okla. 1936).

It appears that only when acts of self-defense are committed under circumstances where the actor should foresee that such acts create an unreasonable risk of causing harm to innocent third parties that such third parties may subject the actor to liability. This means that even if you defend yourself or others, but you create an unreasonable risk to others in doing so, you may be liable if one of those third parties is injured.

Example:

> *Mel shoots Anthony as he unlawfully breaks into Mel's occupied home at night. She fires a single shot with her .22 that narrowly misses Anthony but hits a man washing his car down the street.*

Mel is probably not liable to the man down the street, because her conduct did not unreasonably place third parties at risk.

Example:

> *Ben shoots at Anthony as he unlawfully breaks into Ben's occupied home at night. Ben fires 30 shots with his fully-automatic M-16, missing with the initial burst. Anthony turns and runs. Ben continues to fire haphazardly at Anthony as he runs down the street. One shot hits a man washing his car four houses away.*

Ben could very likely be liable to the man washing his car because he unreasonably placed third parties at risk by haphazardly firing a fully automatic weapon down a neighborhood street.

VI. Traps and spring guns

Oklahoma common law governs the use of "devices" to protect land or tangible movable property. In *City of Shawnee v. Cheek*, 137 P. 724 (Okla. 1913), the court stated that any trap, including spring guns, that cause "wanton" injury will incur liability, even if the person injured is a trespasser! What are "wanton" injuries? The court gave us the following definition: "A mere omission, involving a reckless disregard for the safety of merely technical and reasonably anticipated trespassers or bare licensees, in respect to seriously dangerous artificial condition of premises which is obvious to such owner may amount to wantonness in him; and the artificiality, the attractiveness, and the accessibility of such dangerous place or thing thereat, together with the probability of such trespassers or licensees, the gravity of the danger, the length of time it has existed, the smallness of the cost or inconvenience and of the deprivation of beneficial use involved in eliminating same, and the reasonableness of the inference that the landowner, as a person of ordinary sensibility and prudence, knew or should have known of and, under all the facts and circumstances of the case, should have eliminated such danger, are proper considerations in determining whether there was such reckless disregard for the safety of such trespassers or bare licensees, or, in other words, whether there was wantonness."

As you can see, wanton injuries are extremely fact and scenario specific, so it will ultimately be up to a jury to decide whether your trap caused mere injury, or whether it caused a "wanton" injury. However, if you want to stay on the safe side, don't set any traps!

VII. Will insurance cover it if I shoot someone?

A. Homeowners' insurance

With few exceptions, almost every homeowner's insurance policy excludes coverage for intentional acts. The act of using your firearm in self-defense is almost always an intentional act. You intended to stop the threat. Plaintiffs' attorneys will very likely assert a negligence claim against a homeowner in an attempt to fall within the coverage, but at the end of the day, if the only evidence is that you intentionally shot the plaintiff because you intended to stop a threat, it is likely that any insurance policy with an intentional act exclusion will not provide coverage for any damages awarded.

B. Auto insurance

Scores of cases around the country exist where the parties allege that a gun incident is covered by automobile insurance merely because the use of the firearm occurs in or involves an automobile. Almost universally, courts have held that these incidents are not covered merely because the discharge occurs in or involves a car.

Example:

Justin is cleaning his 9mm handgun in the car. It accidentally discharges causing his passenger Edwin severe injuries.

This event will almost certainly not be covered by Justin's auto insurance policy!

Example:

Justin discharges his 9mm handgun in the car at Edwin during an attempted carjacking, causing Edwin severe injuries and also hitting a bystander.

This event will almost certainly not be covered by Justin's auto insurance policy either.

For an injury to fall within the "use" coverage of an automobile policy (1) the accident must have arisen out of the inherent nature of the automobile, as such, (2) the accident must have arisen within the natural territorial limits of an automobile, and the actual use must not have terminated, (3) the automobile must not merely contribute to cause the condition which produces the injury, but must itself produce injury.

VIII. What civil liability does a person face if their children access their firearms?

A. Parents are not responsible for minor children's actions merely because they are parents!

As a general rule, minors are civilly liable for their own torts (that is, their wrongful actions such as negligence, gross negligence, assault, *etc.*). 76 O.S. § 1.1. The mere fact of paternity or maternity does not make a parent liable to third parties for the torts of his or her minor children. *Stumpf v. Montgomery*, 226 P. 65 (Okla. 1924). Under this general rule, barring certain circumstances outlined later, parents are not responsible for their minor children's tortious actions when the minor child commits a tort and the parent had no direct relationship to the child's action, such as providing a firearm in a negligent manner, failing to supervise the child, or allowing the child to engage in behavior the parent knows is dangerous or risky.

B. Parents who "negligently entrust" their guns may become responsible

While a parent who has no direct relationship to a minor child's tortious actions is generally not liable for that child's injurious actions, a parent may be liable if the parent's negligence made the injury possible. Most often parental liability is sought to be imposed where the parent entrusts his child with an instrumentality which, because of the youth or inexperience of the child, may become a source of danger to others. A parent may be liable if he or she is negligent in entrusting a dangerous weapon or instrumentality to a child who, because of his age or inexperience, might use the instrumentality in such a way as to endanger the person of another.

Oklahoma recognizes claims of "negligent entrustment." Liability occurs when a person permits a third person (including their own children) to use a thing (such as a firearm) or to engage in an activity which is under the control of the actor, if the actor knows or should know that such person intends or is likely to use the thing or to conduct himself in the activity in such a manner as to create an unreasonable risk of harm to others. *See Vance By and Through Vance v. Thomas*, 716 P.2d 710 (Okla. Crim. App. 1986). Let's look at some examples.

Example:

> *Jon, your 17-year-old son, has been hunting since he was 11 and has taken several firearms training courses.*

If you take Jon hunting, and for some reason Jon accidentally discharges his shotgun, injuring another person, it is highly unlikely that you, the parent, will be civilly liable for an accident that occurs while hunting. This is because you had no reason to know this would occur, due to the training and experience of Jon. Consider this situation, though:

Example:

> *Gordon, your 12-year-old son, has never handled a gun or taken a firearms training course. You decide to take him to the range for the first time, but you are both asked to leave the range after Gordon repeatedly fires into the ceiling and the floor. Fed up, you take Gordon to another range with no additional instruction or training.*

If Gordon shoots and injures someone at the second range, it is likely that you will be liable, because you permitted Gordon to use the gun, knowing that he is likely to conduct himself in such a manner as to create an unreasonable risk to others.

C. Parents may be liable for criminal acts of children

In addition to the situations described in the preceding section where parents may become liable for a minor child's actions when the parent's own actions (or lack, thereof) played a role, Oklahoma has a statute that also provides limited parental liability for the criminal acts of a child. Oklahoma Statute Title 23 § 10 provides in its first subsection that a parent is liable for any bodily injury or property damage caused by any child under the age of 18 who lives with their parents, arising out of criminal or delinquent acts that result in bodily injury to a person or damage to property belonging to the state, county, city, school district, person, corporation or organization, the damages not to exceed $2,500.

In the second subsection, the statute states that any victim or the victim's representative in the event of the victim's death, shall be entitled to recover damages in a court of competent jurisdiction from any person convicted of a violation of subsection B of section 1273 of Title 21 of the Oklahoma

Statutes (*see* possession of firearms by minors earlier in this book) or as otherwise allowed by law.

The first subsection creates sweeping liability applying to many types of criminal activities or delinquencies a child can get into. Note, however, that it creates liability only for *criminal* activity or delinquency; this means that the civil standard of negligence, which is a lower burden of proof than "criminal negligence," would not lead to liability. *Glidden v. Higgs*, 839 P.2d 680 (Okla. Crim. App. 1992). For example, if your 16-year-old child takes your car for a spin, and seeks to recreate some scenes from their favorite action movie by purposefully driving through fruit carts or panes of glass, you may very well be liable for up to $2,500 worth of damage. This is because they intentionally destroyed the property of others, which is a crime. However, if they take your car out for a leisurely drive, forget to use a turn signal, and cause an automobile accident, under this specific statute you may not be liable even if a civil court finds their actions to have been negligent. Unless they were criminally negligent in their actions, a much higher standard than mere civil negligence, it does not meet the requirements of the statute.

The statute also creates additional liability for parents or guardians who have intentionally, knowingly, or recklessly permitted their child to possess firearms or weapons if the parent or guardian is aware of a substantial risk that the child will use the weapon to commit a criminal offense, and that child then causes some manner of recoverable injury to a person or property. There is also liability if the child has been adjudicated a delinquent or convicted of any criminal offense that contains as an element the threat or the use of physical force against the person of another, and causes some manner of recoverable injury.

Example:

In preparation for the annual family hunting trip, Frank took his 16-year-old son Billy to the

> *outdoor shooting range. As happens every year, while at the range, Billy was haphazard and intentionally unsafe in his handling of his firearm. Billy, who refuses to take anything seriously, repeatedly pointed his firearm in the direction of other persons, and even discharged his gun into the air three times while ululating. Frank scolded Billy by telling him that it is "not nice" to point guns at other people. During the hunting trip, Billy randomly fired his shotgun for no apparent reason into the trees. Billy's last shot hit a fellow hunter standing among the trees.*

Is Frank liable for his minor son Billy's acts? Probably yes. Frank was well-aware of the fact that Billy handled firearms in a dangerous manner, and there was a substantial risk he would commit a criminal offense (such as discharge of a firearm, assault, or murder) and Frank intentionally, knowingly, and/or recklessly allowed Billy to possess the firearm.

Example:

> *Bobby, a 14-year-old boy, does not like his neighbor. One day, he retrieves the family 12-gauge shotgun and decides to shoot the neighbor's fence. Bobby's parents know nothing about this behavior and Bobby has never had trouble with a firearm in the past. As a result of the shooting, a number of pickets from the fence were destroyed, three windows were broken, and numerous pockmarks were left in the brick façade of the home.*

Under subsection A of 23 O.S. § 10, Bobby's parents would be liable for the damage Bobby caused to his neighbor's property up to $2,500, because Bobby was under the age of 18, lived with his parents, and his actions were a criminal or delinquent act. However, under the second subsection of this statute, since they were not aware of any substantial risk of criminal activity, they will most likely not incur additional liability beyond $2,500.

CHAPTER THIRTEEN

BEYOND FIREARMS:
KNIVES, BILLY CLUBS, AND TASERS

I. Introduction

In addition to Oklahoma's many firearms laws, there also exist state laws governing the possession and use of "other weapons." This includes any object that is not a firearm but could be used as a weapon. This chapter will briefly discuss the laws governing these other weapons, including weapons that are unlawful to carry in public under the law, weapons that are illegal to carry, and exceptions to the laws prohibiting the carrying of unlawful weapons.

II. Unlawful carry weapons

A. What is an unlawful to carry weapon?

Oklahoma statute 21 O.S. § 1272, which is entitled "Unlawful Carry," states "It shall be unlawful for any person to carry upon or about his or her person, or in a purse or other container belonging to the person" certain prohibited weapons. Section 1272 has been interpreted to prohibit public carrying of the prohibited weapons but there are exceptions including possessing or carrying one of the prohibited weapons while hunting, fishing, educational or recreational purposes, or during a living history reenactment.

B. Changes in the law

1. As of November 1, 2016, more knives are legal to carry!

On and after November 1, 2016, bowie knives, dirks, daggers, and sword canes are legal to possess and carry! Oklahoma law does not expressly define any of the knives listed above. However, the bowie is defined in general terms as a large sheath knife with a crossguard and a clip point. A dagger is traditionally defined as a short knife with a pointed and double edged blade. A dirk generally is defined as a long straight-bladed dagger. Finally, a sword cane generally is defined as a

bladed dagger. Finally, a sword cane generally is defined as a cane in which a sword blade is concealed.

Dagger

Switchblades are no longer illegal!

Also once listed as a prohibited weapon, switchblades were removed from the list in 2015. Oklahoma statute section 1272 previously prohibited push button or spring assisted knives. However, that particular design of knife has been removed from the list of prohibited weapons and is now legal.

C. What weapons are unlawful to carry under Oklahoma law?

The list of prohibited weapons is found in 21 O.S. § 1272. Prior to November 1, 2016, this section prohibited the carrying of fourteen different weapons or classes of weapons, including firearms. As of November 1, 2016, daggers, bowie knives, dirks, and sword canes will be removed from the prohibited weapons list. What items are specifically prohibited after November 1, 2016? Section 1272 states, "...any pistol, revolver, shotgun or rifle whether loaded or unloaded or any blackjack, loaded cane, billy, hand chain, metal knuckles, or any other offensive weapon, whether such weapon be concealed or unconcealed..."

1. Metal knuckles

The term "metal knuckles" is not specifically defined in Oklahoma statutes. However, the term is generally understood to mean an instrument that consists of finger rings or guards made of a hard substance designed for the purpose of inflicting serious bodily injury or death by striking a person. The common use of "knuckles" typically refers to "brass knuckles." However, the statute covers more than just "brass" knuckles and includes all metal knuckles.

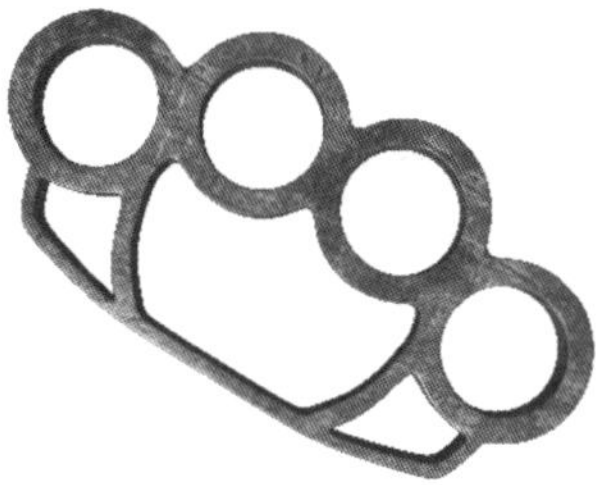

Traditional "Brass Knuckles"

Other objects which may be held in the hand used to augment the strength of a punch as an offensive weapon, such as a "fist filler" (pictured below), are not "knuckles" as defined by Oklahoma law and should not be considered prohibited weapons, however, the item may be considered an "other offensive weapon."

Commercial "Fist Filler"

Roll of Coins

2. Billy

A "billy," also called a billy club, is traditionally defined as a heavy wooden stick used as a weapon. The term can include blackjacks, nightsticks, mace, and tomahawks. The carrying of a billy club on one's person in public is prohibited by section 1272 unless one can qualify under an exception.

Blackjack

Nightstick

Mace

Tomahawk

When do ordinary items become illegal clubs?

Many ordinary items that a person may find in the home or vehicle may be considered an offensive weapon/billy club if the item has been adapted to serve a different purpose than originally intended. For instance, a baseball bat is designed to be used for playing baseball. However, if a person takes a baseball bat and hammers a few nails through the end of the bat, the baseball bat has been adapted to become a mace/other offensive weapon.

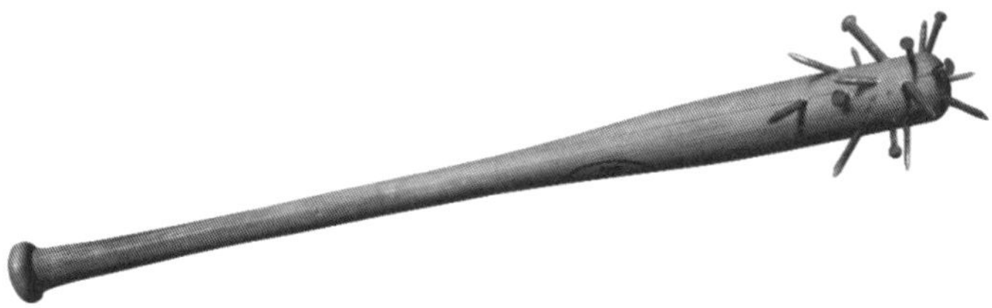

Baseball Bat adapted as a Mace

Practical Legal Tip:

Some weapons are combinations of the items we've talked about throughout this chapter such as brass knuckles combined with a dagger, or a taser-billy (baton). Even though such a weapon includes a legal item such as a taser, if it incorporates any illegal item (such as knuckles, or billies), it is still illegal! *-Robert*

3. Chemical dispensing devices are not specifically prohibited, but may be classified as an "other offensive weapon"

Under Oklahoma law, pepper spray is not by name or description an unlawful carry. There is no statute banning the carrying or possession of any size chemical dispensing devices, so pepper spray, tear gas, mace and other sprays are legal to carry. However, 21 O.S. § 1272.3 makes it a felony to discharge the deleterious agents, including tear gas, mace, and pepper mace, against a peace officer, corrections officer, probation officer, firefighter, E.M.T., or paramedic acting in the course of official duty. Misusing pepper spray against a person or using any similar weapon for an illegal purpose may result in felony charges of assault with a dangerous weapon.

It is important to note however that any tool, like a machete, chainsaw or ice pick used for offensive purposes may be classified a dangerous weapon prohibited under 21 O.S. § 1272.

4. Additional weapons requiring NFA compliance

Oklahoma allows the possession of the following NFA regulated weapons and devices provided that NFA requirements are met. These are discussed in greater detail in Chapter 14, "National Firearms Act":

- Explosive weapons

- Machine guns
- Short-barreled firearms
- Firearm silencers and suppressors

III. Exceptions to unlawful carry

21 O.S. § 1272 prohibits the carrying of any pistol, revolver, shotgun or rifle whether loaded or unloaded or any blackjack, loaded cane, billy, hand chain, metal knuckles, or any other offensive weapon. The question is open as to whether these items (with the exception of firearms) may be carried on one's private property or possessed in one's home. *Pierce v. State*, 42 Okla .Crim. App. 272 (1929) gives some guidance on this issue. That court stated, "I do not believe that the intention of the Legislature, when it enacted the law regulating the carrying of weapons, intended to abridge the sacred right of a citizen of the state by prohibiting him from doing a certain thing within the walls of his home..." The analysis may be argued in reference to blackjacks, loaded canes, billies, hand chains, metal knuckles, or other offensive weapons. Presently, 21 O.S. § 1289.6(6) allows the carrying of firearms on property that one owns, leases or legally controls. A good argument can thus be made that if one can carry firearms for self-defense on one's property, one can carry on one's property all the prohibited weapons listed in section 1272. However, it is unknown whether this would be a winning argument in court!

1. Specific exceptions to the law prohibiting the carrying of a billy

For those individuals who are required to carry weapons normally prohibited under section 1272, Oklahoma law provides an exception to the prohibition of carrying an illegal billy club and other weapons so long as the person meets the specific requirements of each exception. The Oklahoma Security Guard and Private Investigator Act found at 59 O.S. § 1750.1-1750.14, authorizes and regulates security guards who are not peace officers while 70 O.S. § 1750.1 regulates peace officers.

Exception for Police Officers and Other Persons Authorized by Law:
59 O.S. § 1750 .1-.14

Section 1272 does not apply to a person who possesses a weapon while in the actual discharge of official duties as:
3. The carrying, possession and use of any weapon by a peace officer or other person authorized by law to carry a weapon in the performance of official duties and in compliance with the rules of the employing agency.

The provision of Section 1272 prohibiting the carrying of a billy club does not apply to an unarmed security guard in Oklahoma who carries a billy club, nightstick or similar club, and who is licensed as a security guard. The difference between an "armed security guard" and a "security guard" is that the former is authorized to carry a firearm on duty. An "unarmed security guard" shall have training not to exceed 40 hours of instruction.

The training requirements, in addition to the employment requirement, of this exception are very specific and strict. A security officer can only carry during the course of employment for his or her "employing agency." An "employing agency" is a security company or employer of the person carrying the billy club during hours of employment. A security officer cannot carry a billy club while off duty.

2. Living history reenactment
Oklahoma section 1272(5) provides a specific exception to the law prohibiting the illegal carrying or transportation of accessories, firearms, weapons, and other implements of the historical period if the weapon is used in a "living history reenactment," defined as a "depiction of historical characters, scenes, historical life or events for entertainment, education, or historical documentation through the wearing or use of period, historical, antique or vintage clothing, accessories, firearms, weapons, and other implements of the historical period."

3. Defense for persons authorized by law to carry weapons
Under section 21 O.S. § 1272(A)(3), peace officers or "other person[s] authorized by law to carry a weapon in the performance of official duties" are exempt from the prohibitions of 21 O.S. § 1272. This explains why, most commonly, one would see a police officer have or use a billy or blackjack, and not be charged with a crime for breaking the law regarding prohibited weapons.

The exception provided in this portion of the statute is general and applies to Peace Officers, employees of the Department of Corrections and those members of the armed forces or employees of a penal institution as they carry out their duties.

4. Recreational purposes
Under section 21 O.S. § 1272(A)(1), this statute dealing with unlawful carry does not prohibit "the proper use of guns and knives for hunting, fishing, educational or recreational purposes."

5. Local knife ordinances are preempted by Oklahoma law and cannot be more restrictive than the general state law!
Like firearms, there is preemption by state law of local knife ordinances. This means that local municipalities, government agencies, and other regulatory bodies cannot enact laws, ordinances, and rules which are more restrictive than Oklahoma law. *See* 21 O.S. § 1289.24A(1).

IV. Tasers

It is perfectly legal for persons to purchase, sell, carry, and use conductive energy weapons (such as tasers or stun guns) under Oklahoma law. However, 21 O.S. § 1287 governs carrying or use of conductive energy weapons when committing a felony. Section 1287 provides a felony enhancement for committing or attempting to commit a felony while carrying a host of different weapons in addition to the prohibited and named weapons listed in section 1272, such as conductive energy weapon.

The use of weapons such as tasers is not without controversy and danger. Most frequently, tasers are used by law enforcement officers as a method of subduing a suspect without the use of a firearm. Unfortunately, in some instances, the use of a taser has amounted to lethal force. In Oklahoma, the use of a taser in a defensive situation may sometimes be misconstrued by law enforcement, thus resulting in charges of assault with a dangerous weapon. *See* 21 O.S. § 645, assault and battery with a dangerous weapon (conductive energy weapon).

Oklahoma statutes refer to conductive energy weapons but do not provide a blanket definition, *see* 21 O.S. § 1272.3 (referring to felony enhancement for carrying a conductive energy weapon during the commission of a felony). In fact, the term "taser" is not used anywhere in the Oklahoma statutes, because Taser is a brand name, just like Phazzer is a brand name.

Handheld "Stun Gun" Taser brand

Cartridge Taser

At the time of this writing, there are few Oklahoma appellate cases which mention the words "stun gun", "taser", or "conductive energy weapon". These cases describe fact situations where stun guns are part of felonious activities and none of these cases involve when or how a stun gun may be used legally. For that reason, it is important to be aware that the use of a stun gun/taser will subject a person to the same standards of self-defense as outlined in Chapters 4 through 6 of this book in that a person will need to be justified in using either force or deadly force before the use of a stun gun/taser will also be justified. Because the law does not clearly classify or define a stun gun/taser in any way and because there are no cases on this subject addressing the use of a stun gun, how a prosecutor, judge, or jury will view a person's use of a taser as being either mere force or deadly force is unknown. Although a taser is not designed to kill, you should be aware that under certain circumstances and when used in a manner other than designed (such as prolonged use), a taser may cause or play a part in a person's death.

CHAPTER FOURTEEN

SILENCERS, SHORT-BARRELED WEAPONS, AND MACHINE GUNS: THE NATIONAL FIREARMS ACT

Can an individual in Oklahoma legally own a silencer or suppressor, short-barreled shotgun, short-barreled rifle, machine gun, or "destructive device?" Yes, if all NFA regulations are satisfied. This chapter deals with the laws regarding the possession and use of firearms that are subject to the provisions of the National Firearms Act (NFA) codified in 26 U.S.C. Chapter 53, specifically, silencers, short-barreled firearms, machine guns, and firearms that are otherwise illegal. These firearms are illegal to purchase or possess without possessing the proper paperwork and a "tax stamp." In this chapter, we will discuss the purpose behind the NFA, what firearms are regulated by the Act, as well as the process and procedure for legally possessing weapons that are subject to the Act's provisions.

I. What is the National Firearms Act?

The National Firearms Act was enacted in 1934 in response to gangster crimes. Prior to the Act's passage, any person could go to the local hardware store and purchase a Thompson Submachine Gun or shorten the barrel on their rifle or shotgun. President Roosevelt pushed for the passage of the NFA in an attempt to diminish a gangster's ability to possess and carry dangerous and/or easily concealable firearms, such as machine guns and short-barreled rifles and shotguns.

NFA is firearms regulation using a registration and tax requirement

The NFA requires both the registration of and a tax on the manufacture and transfer of certain firearms. The law created a tax of $200 on the transfer of the following firearms: short-barreled shotguns, short-barreled rifles, machine guns, silencers, and destructive devices. The tax is only $5 for firearms that are classified as "Any Other Weapons" or AOWs. Back in 1934, a $200 tax was the approximate equivalent to about $3,500 today!

Five years after the NFA's passage, the Supreme Court held in *United States v. Miller* that the right to bear arms can be subject to federal regulation. Miller brought suit against the government stating that the NFA infringed upon his Constitutional right to bear arms under the Second Amendment. While the Court agreed that the Constitution does guarantee *a right* to bear arms, it held that the right does not extend to every firearm. *See United States v. Miller*, 307 U.S. 174 (1939).

II. What firearms does the NFA regulate?

A. Short-barreled rifles and shotguns

In order to be possessed legally, short-barreled shotguns and rifles must be registered, and a tax paid on the firearm. What is a short-barreled shotgun? Under both federal and Oklahoma law, short-barreled shotguns have one or more barrels less than 18 inches in length and the overall length is less than 26 inches. What is a short-barreled rifle? It is any rifle with one or more barrels less than 16 inches in length, and the overall length of the rifle is less than 26 inches. *See* 27 CFR § 478.11 and 21 O.S. § 1289.18.

Short-barreled shotguns and rifles may be purchased from an FFL who deals in NFA items. Also, short-barreled firearms are very popular for individuals to build and/or modify on their own. This is legal if the person has properly registered the firearm to be modified into a short-barreled firearm with the ATF and paid the tax before it is modified. Once approved, a person may alter or produce a short-barreled firearm and must engrave legally required information on the receiver of the firearm such as manufacturer, location, *etc*. *See* discussion later in this chapter for detailed requirements.

B. Machine guns

Machine guns are generally illegal under federal and state law.

However, if the requirements of the NFA are satisfied, machine guns may be legally owned by individuals. First, what is a machine gun? Federal law defines a machine gun as "any weapon which shoots, is designed to shoot, or can be readily restored to shoot, automatically more than one shot, without manual reloading, by a single function of the trigger. The term shall also include the frame or receiver of any such weapon, any part designed and intended solely and exclusively, or combination of parts designed and intended, for use in converting a weapon into a machine gun, and any combination of parts from which a machine gun can be assembled if such parts are in the possession or under the control of a person." 27 CFR § 478.11. As a result of this definition, the individual metal components that make a firearm a machine gun, such as a full-auto sear, individually meet the federal definition of machine gun. The parts for the machine gun do not have to be assembled to meet the definition.

Under Oklahoma law, the term "machine gun" is not defined. The only mention of a machine gun is 21 O.S. § 1283 A and D, convicted felons and delinquents are prohibited from possessing or controlling a machine gun. Traditionally, however, a machine gun is defined as an automatic gun that fires bullets in rapid succession for so long as the trigger is pressed.

No new manufacturing of machine guns for private ownership
Because of a federal law that effectively disallows private ownership (not military, police department, *etc.*) of any machine gun manufactured after May 19, 1986, machine guns available for private ownership are limited to the legally registered machine guns that existed prior to May 19, 1986. Thus, the number of machine guns in the private market is very limited and prices, as a result, are very high.

C. Firearm suppressors
What is a suppressor? It is just a muffler for a firearm and is legal to possess if all NFA requirements are met. In legal terms,

a firearm suppressor is defined in 27 CFR § 478.11 as "any device for silencing, muffling, or diminishing the report of a portable firearm, including any combination of parts, designed or redesigned, and intended for use in assembling or fabricating a firearm silencer or firearm muffler, and any part intended only for use in such assembly or fabrication." The Oklahoma definition is similar to the federal one as "any device which noticeably suppresses noise from a firearm, commonly known as a suppressor." *See* 29 O.S. § 5-201. Interestingly enough, the definition of a suppressor is found in the Oklahoma Wildlife Conservation Code.

Firearm suppressors are very practical instruments. They are great for hunting and recreational shooting not only because they suppress gunshots in a way so as to not alarm other animals being hunted nearby, but also because they lessen the impact on the shooter's ears. However, firearms owners should be carefully aware that the definition of a suppressor is very broad whether under federal or Oklahoma law. Suppressors do not need to be items manufactured specifically for use as a suppressor. There are some ordinary, every-day items that could be easily converted into a suppressor such as a water bottle or an automotive oil filter. Possession of otherwise legal items when used or modified to be used as a suppressor is illegal.

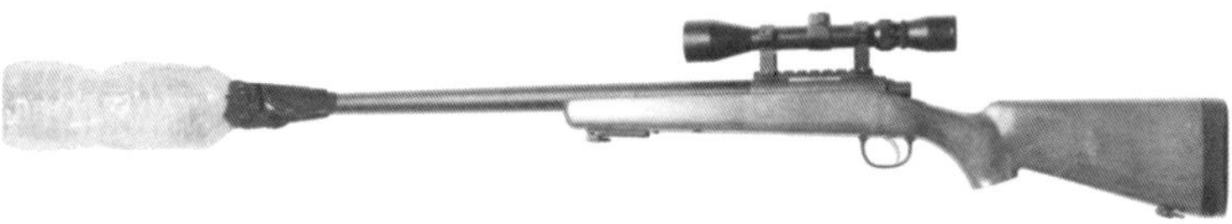

D. Destructive devices

The term "destructive device" is a legal term given to certain firearms, objects, and munitions that are illegal under the NFA. The "destructive devices" as defined in the statute are effectively broken down into three categories: explosive devices, large caliber weapons, and parts easily convertible into a destructive device.

Destructive Devices – Part A
27 C.F.R. § 478.11

Any explosive, incendiary, or poison gas (1) bomb, (2) grenade, (3) rocket having a propellant charge of more than 4 ounces, (4) missile having an explosive or incendiary charge of more than one-quarter ounce, (5) mine, or (6) device similar to any of the devices described in the preceding paragraphs of this definition.

Destructive Devices – Part B
27 C.F.R. § 478.11

Any type of weapon (other than a shotgun or shotgun shell which the Director finds is generally recognized as particularly suitable for sporting purposes) by whatever name known which will, or which may be readily converted to, expel a projectile by the action of an explosive or other propellant, and which has any barrel with a bore of more than one-half inch in diameter.

Destructive Devices – Part C
27 C.F.R. § 478.11

Any combination of parts either designed or intended for use in converting any destructive device described in [part] (A) and (B) of this section and from which a destructive device may be readily assembled.

The first portion of the definition of a destructive device deals with explosive, incendiary and poison gas munitions. The definition specifies that any explosive, incendiary, or poison gas bomb, grenade, mine or similar device is a destructive device. In addition, the definition includes a rocket having a propellant charge of more than four ounces and a missile (projectile) having an explosive or incendiary charge of more than one-quarter ounce. These topics and the regulations thereof are beyond the scope of this book's discussion.

The second section of the definition addresses large caliber weapons and states that any type of weapon that has a bore diameter of more than one-half inch in diameter is a destructive device with the exception of shotguns (and shotgun shells) that are suitable for sporting purposes. Thus, any caliber in a rifle or handgun more than .5 inches or fifty caliber is classified as a destructive device. Shotguns are exempt from this prohibition on size unless the ATF rules it is not for "sporting purposes." How do you know if a shotgun is suitable for sporting purposes? The ATF keeps a list and has issued rulings classifying specific shotguns as destructive devices because they are not considered to be particularly "suitable for sporting purposes" including the USAS-12, Striker-12, Streetsweeper, and 37/38mm Beanbags. The ATF does not provide any specific definition of what constitutes being "suitable for sporting purposes" nor does it specify the methodology in which it determines what makes a particular shotgun suitable for sporting purposes. Ultimately, one will have to check with the ATF lists to see whether a particular shotgun with a larger bore-diameter is classified as a destructive device or not.

Finally, a destructive device does not need to be a completed and assembled product to fall under the federal definition and regulation of the NFA. Much like machine guns, if a person possesses parts that can be readily assembled into a destructive device then whether or not the device has actually been constructed is irrelevant—by law, it's already a destructive device.

Although these firearms, munitions, and devices are prohibited by the law on its face pursuant to the National Firearms Act, a person may nevertheless receive permission to possess them so long as they possess the correct legal authorization.

E. "Any Other Weapons" or AOWs

The AOW category under the NFA pertains to firearms and weapons that may not fit the traditional definition of some of the firearms discussed elsewhere in this book due to the way in which they are manufactured or modified. Under federal law, an AOW is "any weapon or device capable of being concealed on the person from which a shot can be discharged through the energy of an explosive, a pistol or revolver having a barrel with a smooth bore designed or redesigned to fire a fixed shotgun shell, weapons with combination shotgun and rifle barrels 12 inches or more, less than 18 inches in length, from which only a single discharge can be made from either barrel without manual reloading, and shall include any such weapon which may be readily restored to fire. Such term shall not include a pistol or a revolver having a rifled bore, or rifled bores, or weapons designed, made, or intended to be fired from the shoulder and not capable of firing fixed ammunition." 26 U.S.C. § 5845(e).

1. Concealable weapons and devices

Weapons capable of being concealed from which one shot can be discharged are AOWs. This includes weapons such as a pengun, knife gun, or umbrella gun. Oklahoma law does not use the term AOW but rather makes "homemade pistol" fall outside of the Self-Defense Act, thus prohibiting the carry or possession of one under Section 1272.

Pengun

Knife gun

Umbrella gun

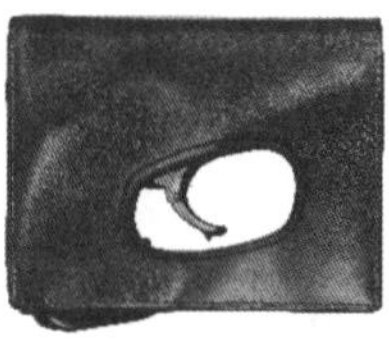

Wallet gun

2. Pistols and revolvers having a smooth-bore barrel for firing shotgun shells

Pistols and revolvers that have a smooth bore (no rifling) that are designed to shoot shotgun ammunition are defined as an AOW. The ATF cites firearms such as the H&R Handy Gun or the Ithaca Auto & Burglar Gun as firearms which fall under the AOW category. *Note:* Handguns with partially rifled barrels such as The Judge do not fall under this category due to the rifling of the barrel.

H&R Handy Gun

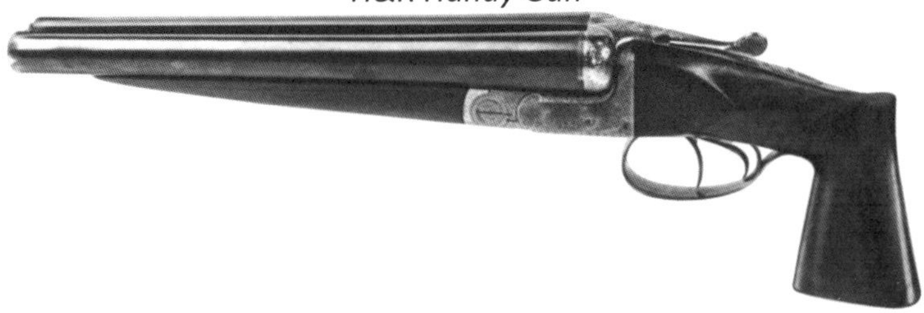

Ithaca Auto & Burglar Gun

3. Weapons with barrels 12 inches or longer and lengths 18 inches or shorter

The definition of Any Other Weapon also includes any weapon that has a shotgun or rifle barrel of 12 inches or more but is 18 inches or less in overall length from which only a single discharge can be made from either barrel without manual reloading. The ATF identifies the "Marble Game Getter" as the firearm most commonly associated with this definition (excluding the model with an 18" barrel and folding shoulder stock).

4. Pistols and revolvers with vertical handgrips

If a pistol is modified with a vertical grip on the front, it will now be legally classified as an AOW and require registration and a paid tax. Note that vertical grips are readily available and are legal to own as long as they are not placed on a handgun. The definition of a handgun is a weapon which is intended to be fired by one hand. The addition of the vertical foregrip makes it so the weapon now is intended to be fired with two hands. This modification changes the weapon from a legal handgun to an AOW that is now a prohibited weapon without the proper documentation.

F. Antique firearms

Firearms that are defined by the NFA as "antique firearms" are not regulated by the NFA. The NFA definition of antique firearm is found in 26 U.S.C. § 5845(g) as "any firearm not designed or redesigned for using rim fire or conventional center fire ignition with fixed ammunition and manufactured in or before 1898 (including any matchlock, flintlock, percussion cap, or similar type of ignition system or replica thereof, whether actually manufactured before or after the year 1898) and also any firearm using fixed ammunition manufactured in or before 1898, for which ammunition is no longer manufactured in the United States and is not readily available in the ordinary channels of commercial trade." Under this statute and for NFA purposes, the only firearms that are antiques are firearms which were both actually manufactured in or before 1898 and ones for which fixed ammunition is no longer manufactured in the United States and is not readily available in the ordinary channels of commercial trade.

With this in mind, the ATF states in its NFA guidebook that "it is important to note that a specific type of fixed ammunition that has been out of production for many years may again become available due to increasing interest in older firearms. Therefore, the classification of a specific NFA firearm as an antique can change if ammunition for the weapon becomes readily available in the ordinary channels of commerce."

Practical Legal Tip:

Some of the items regulated by the NFA simply don't make as much sense as some of the other things it regulates. Suppressors are really nothing more than mufflers for your firearm—they aren't really firearms themselves (notwithstanding the legal definition). Thinking about the utility of the suppressor, if the firearm was invented today, you can be sure that not only would the government not prohibit them, OSHA would probably require them for safety purposes! *-Robert*

G. NFA curio firearms and relics

Under federal law, curios or relics are defined in 27 CFR § 478.11 as "firearms which are of special interest to collectors by reason of some quality other than is associated with firearms intended for sporting use or as offensive or defensive weapons." Persons who collect curios or relics may do so with a special collector's license although one is not required. The impact of an NFA item being classified as a curio or relic, however, is that it allows the item to be transferred interstate to persons possessing a collector's license. The collector's license does not allow the individual to deal in curios or relics, nor does it allow the collector to obtain other firearms interstate as those transactions still require an FFL.

To be classified as a curio or relic, federal law states that the firearm must fall into one of the following three categories:

1. Firearms which were manufactured at least 50 years prior to the current date, but not including replicas thereof;
2. Firearms which are certified by the curator of a municipal, State, or Federal museum which exhibits firearms to be curios or relics of museum interest; or
3. Any other firearms which derive a substantial part of their monetary value from the fact that they are novel, rare, bizarre, or because of their association with some historical figure, period, or event.

See 27 CFR § 478.11.

The ATF maintains a list of firearms that are classified as curios or relics.

H. How can some after-market gun parts make your firearm illegal?

A number of companies manufacture and sell gun products or parts that alter the appearance or utility of a firearm (*i.e.* shoulder stocks, forward hand grips, *etc.*). However, some of these after-market products can actually change the firearm you possess from one type of a weapon to another type of weapon for legal purposes whether you realize it or not. As a result, many individuals make the modifications to their firearms thinking that because there was no special process for purchasing the accessory, any modification would be in compliance with the law. Unfortunately, this is not always the case. Consider the example of short-barreled uppers for AR-15s: selling, buying, or possessing AR-15 "uppers" with barrels less than 16 inches is legal. However, it is illegal to put the upper on a receiver of an AR-15 because this would be the act of manufacturing a short-barreled rifle and is legally prohibited. This is equally true of vertical forward grips on a handgun. Vertical foregrips are legal to buy or possess, however, if you actually install one on a handgun, you have manufactured an

AOW, and it is illegal, unless registered and a tax paid. *Note:* there are other types of braces that are permissible in their proper application and illegal in any application or adaptation that would alter the classification of the weapon. For example, the Sig Arm Brace is legal to attach to an AR Pistol when used as an arm brace, but illegal when used as a shoulder stock.

III. Process and procedure for obtaining NFA firearms

A. Who can own and possess an NFA firearm?

Any person may own and possess an NFA firearm as long as they are legally not disqualified to own or possess firearms and live in a state that allows possession of NFA items. *See* Chapters 2 and 3. The ATF also allows for a non-person legal entity to own these items, such as corporations, partnerships, and trusts, *etc*. On July 13, 2016, a new rule went into effect modifying the process for filing for a transfer or manufacture of an NFA weapon.

B. What are the usual steps for buying or manufacturing NFA items?

Whether a person is buying or making (manufacturing) an NFA firearm, there are several steps in the process. The transfer or manufacture of an NFA firearm requires the filing of an appropriate transfer form with the ATF, payment of any federally-mandated transfer tax, approval of the transfer by the ATF, and registration of the firearm to the transferee. Only after these steps have occurred may a buyer legally take possession of the NFA item, or may a person legally assemble or manufacture the NFA item. In this section, we will walk through the process, step-by-step, of (1) purchasing an NFA item that already exists, and (2) manufacturing an NFA firearm.

Steps for buying an existing NFA item (for example, a suppressor):

1. Select and purchase the item (suppressor) from a transferor who is usually an FFL dealer who is authorized to sell NFA weapons;

2. Assemble appropriate paperwork: ATF Form 4 (*see* Appendix B), fingerprints on an FBI Form FD-258, a passport size photograph, and a payment for the tax ($200);
   (a) If the buyer is an individual they must notify the Chief Law Enforcement Officer of their city or county of residence by serving the CLEO a copy of ATF Form 4;
   (b) If the buyer is a corporation or trust, each "responsible person" of the corporation or trust must complete an ATF Form 5320.23 (*see* Appendix B), including fingerprints and passport photograph, and must notify the Chief Law Enforcement Officer of their city or county by delivering to them the CLEO copy of ATF Form 5320.23;
3. Submit paperwork, fingerprints, and tax to the ATF for review and approval;
4. ATF sends approval (tax stamp affixed to Form 4) to the dealer;
5. FFL dealer notifies the buyer to pick up suppressor.

Steps for manufacturing an NFA item (for example, a short-barreled AR-15 from an 80% lower)

1. Select the item to manufacture or modify (short-barreled AR-15);
2. Assemble appropriate paperwork: ATF Form 1 (*see* Appendix B), fingerprints on an FBI Form FD-258, a passport size photograph, and a payment for the tax ($200);
   (a) If the buyer is an individual they must notify the Chief Law Enforcement Officer of the city or county of their residence by delivering the CLEO copy of ATF Form 1;
   (b) If the buyer is a corporation or trust, each "responsible person" of the corporation or trust must complete an ATF Form 5320.23 (*see* Appendix B), including fingerprints and passport photograph, and must notify the Chief Law Enforcement Officer of their city or county of residence by delivering to them the CLEO copy of ATF Form 5320.23;
3. As "Applicant" you submit paperwork and tax to the ATF for review and approval;

4. ATF sends you the approval (tax stamp affixed to Form 1);
5. You may then legally assemble the AR-15, *i.e.*, put upper with a barrel length of less than 16 inches on a lower receiver, *etc.* The item must now be engraved and identified.

When purchasing an NFA firearm from a dealer, the dealer is required to have the purchaser fill out ATF Form 4473 when the purchaser goes to pick up the item from the dealer.

Practical Legal Tip:

Even if you don't own a machine gun today, that doesn't mean you won't be the intended owner of one later. A person could always leave you their NFA items in a will. If this happens, you must file the appropriate paperwork with the ATF as soon as possible, or at least before probate is closed. *–Robert*

C. How must an NFA item be engraved and identified if I make it myself?

Once you receive ATF approval to manufacture your own NFA item (such as the short-barreled AR-15 in the previous section), federal law requires that you engrave, cast, stamp, or otherwise conspicuously place or cause to be engraved, cast, stamped, or placed on the frame, receiver, or barrel of the NFA item the following information:

1. The item's serial number;
2. The item's model (if so designated);
3. Caliber or gauge;
4. The name of the owner whether individual, corporation, or trust; and
5. The city and state where the item was made.

This information must be placed on the item with a minimum

depth of .003 inch and in a print size no smaller than 1/16 inch. *See* 27 CFR § 479.102.

D. Which way should I own my NFA item? Paperwork requirements for individuals, trusts, or business entities to own NFA items

1. Form 4 and Form 1

The appropriate paperwork that must be assembled and submitted to the ATF under the NFA varies depending on whether an individual or a legal entity, such as a trust, corporation, or partnership, is purchasing or manufacturing the NFA item. The paperwork generally starts either with an ATF Form 4 (used for purchasing an existing item), or an ATF Form 1 which is used if a person wishes to manufacture a new NFA item. All relevant portions of the Form must be completed. Both Form 4 and Form 1 have a requirement that a Chief Law Enforcement Officer's must be notified. Therefore, unlike in the past, a Chief Law Enforcement Officer signature is not necessary.

2. Who is a Chief Law Enforcement Officer who must be notified?

For the purposes of ATF Forms 1 and 4, and the responsible person questionnaire, Form 5320.23, a CLEO is considered to be a chief law enforcement officer who has jurisdiction where the transferor, the applicant, and any "responsible persons" are located. These persons include "the Chief of Police; the Sheriff; the Head of the State Police; or a State or local district attorney or prosecutor."

3. Photograph and fingerprints are required for individual applicants and "responsible persons"

If an individual is purchasing or manufacturing an NFA item, the applicant must submit an appropriate photograph and their fingerprints. An entity such as a trust or corporation must designate "responsible persons" who are allowed to have access to use and possess an NFA weapon. As of July 13, 2016, corporations and trusts must submit the appropriate documents showing its existence, such as the trust or corporate formation documents, the ATF responsible person questionnaire, and fingerprints and passport photographs of these persons.

"Responsible persons" of trusts, partnerships, associations, companies, or corporations, are defined as "any individual who possesses, directly or indirectly, the power or authority to direct the management and policies of the trust or entity to receive, possess, ship, transport, deliver, transfer or otherwise dispose of a firearm for, or on behalf of, the trust or legal entity." The ATF Form 5320.23 provides examples of "responsible persons," including, "settlors/grantors, trustees, partners, members, officers, directors, board members, or owners." Persons who are not "responsible persons" are "the beneficiary of a trust, if the beneficiary does not have the capability to exercise the enumerated powers or authorities."

E. Why are trusts so popular to own NFA items?

There are several major reasons trusts are very popular to own NFA items: paperwork, control, and ease of ownership. A trust is a legal entity that can hold property for the benefit of a third party.

A major reason for having a trust own an NFA item is that it makes owning and using the NFA item easier if more than one person wishes to possess and use the item. If an individual owns the item, then only the registered individual can ever "possess" it. On the other hand, if the item is owned by a trust, all trustees, including co-trustees, are able to possess and use the items contained in the trust. Therefore, co-trustees may be added or removed.

Further, unlike other entities such as corporations, LLCs, *etc.*, a trust requires no filings with the government to create, which saves expenses. Further, these expense savings continue because there are no continuing government fees or compliance requirements. Thus, trusts are one of the best ways currently to own an NFA item.

F. The Tax Stamp

Once the ATF has an applicant's materials in hand, they will be reviewed and checked by NFA researchers and an examiner. The application will then either be approved or denied. A denial will be accompanied by an explanation of why the application was denied and how to remedy it, if possible. If the application is approved, the examiner will affix a tax stamp on one of the submitted Forms 1 or Forms 4 and send the newly-stamped Form to the applicant. The ATF will perform background checks on all applicants and "responsible persons" and determine if each person is lawful to have access to, and the ability to possess an, NFA weapon.

This tax stamp on the appropriate form is a person's evidence of compliance with the NFA's requirements and is a very important document. A copy should always be kept with the NFA item.

G. What documents should I have with me when I am in actual possession of my suppressor, short-barreled firearm, or other NFA item?

If you have an NFA item, always have the proper documentation with you to prove that you legally possess the item. Again, if you are in possession of your suppressor, short-barreled firearm, destructive device, or if you are lucky enough, your machine gun—always have your paperwork showing you are legal, or it may be a long day with law enforcement. To show you are legal, always keep a copy of your ATF Form 4 or Form 1 (whichever is applicable) with the tax stamp affixed for every NFA item in your possession, personal identification, and if the item is held in a trust or corporation, a copy of the trust or articles of incorporation, and the authorization for possession. Care should be given to make sure these documents name the individual so as to show legal ownership, *i.e.*, trust and/or amendments showing the person is a co-trustee or an officer of the corporation.

Practically, individuals should not carry around the original documents as they could be destroyed by wear and tear, rain, or be misplaced, effectively destroying the required evidence of compliance. Photocopies of the stamp and any other pertinent documents, including the ATF Form 5320.23 for "responsible persons," are generally enough to satisfy inquisitive law enforcement officials. The more technologically advanced may take pictures on their phone or other mobile device, or even upload them to a cloud database. Keep in mind that if the phone dies or the cloud cannot be reached, and you have no way to access the documents, your proof is gone and you may have a very bad day ahead of you! We recommend keeping photocopies of the ATF form with the tax stamp affixed and appropriate documents to avoid any problems with technology.

H. Why is the paperwork necessary?

According to 21 O.S. § 1289.18, short-barreled firearms are illegal to possess. However, Oklahoma section 1289.18 states that it is a defense to prosecution that possession was pursuant to the National Firearms Act. This defense is what is known as an affirmative defense; a defense which, if proven, defeats or mitigates the legal consequences of otherwise unlawful conduct. In other words, even though you meet the elements of committing a crime (possessing the listed items), the law provides a defense you can prove to defeat the criminal charges (proving possession pursuant to the NFA). In theory, law enforcement officers could arrest an individual for violating this law. The individual would then be forced to show up to court to prove this affirmative defense. Practically, however, simply showing the proper paperwork to the law enforcement officer is likely sufficient to avoid any further entanglement in the legal system.

APPENDIX

OKLAHOMA STATUTES

CHAPTER 1:

CONFISCATION OF PROPERTY

Title 11 O.S. § 28-121: The municipal criminal court of record, by and through its clerk or judge, shall have power to issue subpoenas, writs of attachment, and summonses, to administer oaths, to verify complaints and other processes and writs issuable by the district judge in criminal proceedings, and to direct the same to the chief of police or other law enforcement officers. The municipal criminal court of record shall have power to compel obedience to its writs and orders in the same manner and to the same extent as the district court. The municipal criminal court of record shall also have power to issue arrest warrants and search and seizure warrants and to hear and determine proceedings for the confiscation of property used in violation of the ordinances of the municipality. A law enforcement officer of the municipality or a county sheriff may serve an arrest warrant issued by the municipal court any place within this state. If the warrant is served by a county sheriff, the municipality shall pay the Sheriff's Service Fee Account a fee of Twenty Dollars ($20.00).

PROHIBITED WEAPONS

Title 21 O.S. § 1272: It shall be unlawful for any person to carry upon or about his or her person, or in a purse or other container belonging to the person, any pistol, revolver, shotgun or rifle whether loaded or unloaded or any dagger, bowie knife, dirk knife, sword cane, blackjack, loaded cane, billy, hand chain, metal knuckles, or any other offensive weapon, whether such weapon be concealed or unconcealed, except this section shall not prohibit.

PENALTY FOR TRANSPORTING A LOADED FIREARM

Title 21 O.S. § 1289.13A: A. Notwithstanding the provisions of Section 1272 or 1289.13 of this title, any person stopped pursuant to a moving traffic violation who is transporting a loaded pistol in the motor vehicle without a valid handgun license authorized by the Oklahoma Self-Defense Act or valid license from another state, whether the loaded firearm is concealed or unconcealed in the vehicle, shall be issued a traffic citation in the amount of Seventy Dollars ($70.00), plus court costs for transporting a firearm improperly. In addition to the traffic citation provided in this section, the person may also be arrested for any other violation of law.

B. When the arresting officer determines that a valid handgun license exists, pursuant to the Oklahoma Self-Defense Act or any provision of law from another state, for any person in the stopped vehicle, any firearms permitted to be carried pursuant to that license shall not be confiscated, unless:

1. The person is arrested for violating another provision of law other than a violation of subsection A of this section; provided, however, if the person is never charged with an offense pursuant to this paragraph or if the charges are dismissed or the person is acquitted, the weapon shall be returned to the person; or

2. The officer has probable cause to believe the weapon is:

a. contraband, or

b. a firearm used in the commission of a crime other than a violation of subsection A of this section.

C. Nothing in this section shall be construed to require confiscation of any firearm.

PREEMPTION

Title 21 O.S. § 1289.24: A. 1. The State Legislature hereby occupies and preempts the entire field of legislation in this state touching in any way firearms, knives, components, ammunition, and supplies to the complete exclusion of any order, ordinance, or regulation by any municipality or other political subdivision of this state. Any existing or future orders, ordinances, or regulations in this field, except as provided for in paragraph 2 of this subsection and subsection C of this section, are null and void.

2. A municipality may adopt any ordinance:

a. relating to the discharge of firearms within the jurisdiction of the municipality, and

b. allowing the municipality to issue a traffic citation for transporting a firearm improperly as provided for in Section 1289.13A of this title, provided however, that penalties contained for violation of any ordinance enacted pursuant to the provisions of this subparagraph shall not exceed the penalties established in the Oklahoma Self-Defense Act.

3. As provided in the preemption provisions of this section, the otherwise lawful open carrying of a handgun under the provisions of the Oklahoma Self-Defense Act shall not be punishable by any municipality or other political subdivision of this state as disorderly conduct, disturbing the peace or similar offense against public order.

4. A public or private school may create a policy regulating the possession of knives on school property or in any school bus or vehicle used by the school for purposes of transportation.

B. No municipality or other political subdivision of this state shall adopt any order, ordinance, or regulation concerning in any way the sale, purchase, purchase delay, transfer, ownership, use, keeping, possession, carrying, bearing, transportation, licensing, permit, registration, taxation other than sales and compensating use taxes, or other controls on firearms, knives, components, ammunition, and supplies.

C. Except as hereinafter provided, this section shall not prohibit any order, ordinance, or regulation by any municipality concerning the confiscation of property used in violation of the ordinances of the municipality as provided for in Section 28-121 of Title 11 of the Oklahoma Statutes. Provided, however, no municipal ordinance relating to transporting a firearm or knife improperly may include a provision for confiscation of property.

D. When a person's rights pursuant to the protection of the preemption provisions of this section have been violated, the person shall have the right to bring a civil action against the persons, municipality, and political subdivision jointly and severally for injunctive relief or monetary damages or both.

CHAPTER 2:

PROHIBITED PERSON, FELON

Title 21 O.S. § 1283: A. Except as provided in subsection B of this section, it shall be unlawful for any person convicted of any felony in any court of this state or of another state or of the United States to have in his or her possession or under his or her immediate control, or in any vehicle which the person is operating, or in which the person is riding as a passenger, or at the residence where the convicted person resides, any pistol, imitation or homemade pistol, altered air or toy pistol, machine gun, sawed-off shotgun or rifle, or any other dangerous or deadly firearm.

B. Any person who has previously been convicted of a nonviolent felony in any court of this state or of another state or of the United States, and who has received a full and complete pardon from the proper authority and has not been convicted of any other felony offense which has not been pardoned, shall have restored the right to possess any firearm or other weapon prohibited by subsection A of this section, the right to apply for and carry a handgun, concealed or unconcealed, pursuant to the Oklahoma Self-Defense Act and the right to perform the duties of a peace officer, gunsmith, or for firearms repair.

C. It shall be unlawful for any person serving a term of probation for any felony in any court of this state or of another state or of the United States or under the jurisdiction of any alternative court program to have in his or her possession or under his or her immediate control, or at his or her residence, or in any passenger vehicle which the person is operating or is riding as a passenger, any pistol, shotgun or rifle, including any imitation or homemade pistol, altered air or toy pistol, shotgun or rifle, while such person is subject to supervision, probation, parole or inmate status.

D. It shall be unlawful for any person previously adjudicated as a delinquent child or a youthful offender for the commission of an offense, which would have constituted a felony offense if committed by an adult, to have in the possession of the person or under the immediate control of the person, or have in any vehicle which he or she is driving or in which the person is riding as a passenger, or at the residence of the person, any pistol, imitation or homemade pistol, altered air or toy pistol, machine gun, sawed-off shotgun or rifle, or any other dangerous or deadly firearm within ten (10) years after such adjudication; provided, that nothing in this subsection shall be construed to prohibit the placement of the person in a home with a full-time duly appointed peace officer who is certified by the Council on Law Enforcement Education and Training (CLEET) pursuant to the provisions of Section 3311 of Title 70 of the Oklahoma Statutes.

E. Any person having been issued a handgun license pursuant to the provisions of the Oklahoma Self-Defense Act and who thereafter knowingly or intentionally allows a convicted felon or adjudicated delinquent or a youthful offender as prohibited by the provisions of subsection A, C, or D of this section to possess or have control of any pistol authorized by the Oklahoma Self-Defense Act shall, upon conviction, be guilty of a felony punishable by a fine not to exceed Five Thousand Dollars ($5,000.00). In addition, the person shall have the handgun license revoked by the Oklahoma State Bureau of Investigation after a hearing and determination that the person has violated the provisions of this section.

F. Any convicted or adjudicated person violating the provisions of this section shall, upon conviction, be guilty of a felony punishable as provided in Section 1284 of this title.

G. For purposes of this section, "sawed-off shotgun or rifle" shall mean any shotgun or rifle which has been shortened to any length.

H. For purposes of this section, "altered toy pistol" shall mean any toy weapon which has been altered from its original manufactured state to resemble a real weapon.

I. For purposes of this section, "altered air pistol" shall mean any air pistol manufactured to propel projectiles by air pressure which has been altered from its original manufactured state.

J. For purposes of this section, "alternative court program" shall mean any drug court, Anna McBride or mental health court, DUI court or veterans court.

FIREARM CONTROL

Title 21 O.S. § 1289.2: The Legislature finds as a matter of public policy and fact that it is necessary for the safe and lawful use of firearms to curb and prevent crime wherein weapons are used by enacting legislation having the purpose of controlling the use of firearms, and of prevention of their use, without unnecessarily denying their lawful use in defense of life, home and property, and their use by the United States or state military organizations and as may otherwise be provided by law, including their use and transportation for lawful purposes.

PISTOL DEFINED OFA 1971

Title 21 O.S. § 1289.3: "Pistols" as used in the Oklahoma Firearms Act of 1971, Sections 1289.1 through 1289.17 of this title, shall mean any firearm capable of discharging a projectile composed of any material which may reasonably be expected to be able to cause lethal injury, with a barrel or barrels less than sixteen (16) inches in length, and using either gunpowder, gas or any means of rocket propulsion, but not to include flare guns, underwater fishing guns or blank pistols.

RIFLE DEFINED

Title 21 O.S. § 1289.4: "Rifles" as used in the Oklahoma Firearms Act of 1971, Sections 1289.1 through 1289.17 of this title, shall mean any firearm capable of discharging a projectile composed of any material which may reasonably be expected to be able to cause lethal injury, with a barrel or barrels more than sixteen (16) inches in length, and using either gunpowder, gas or any means of rocket propulsion, but not to include archery equipment, flare guns or underwater fishing guns. In addition, any rifle capable of firing "shot" but primarily designed to fire single projectiles will be regarded as a "rifle".

SHOTGUN DEFINED

Title 21 O.S. § 1289.5: "Shotguns" as used in the Oklahoma Firearms Act of 1971, Sections 1289.1 through 1289.17 of this title, shall mean any firearm capable of discharging a series of projectiles of any material which may reasonably be expected to be able to cause lethal injury, with a barrel or barrels more than eighteen (18) inches in length, and using either gunpowder, gas or any means of rocket propulsion, but not to include any weapon so designed with a barrel less than eighteen (18) inches in length. In addition, any "shotgun" capable of firing single projectiles but primarily designed to fire multiple projectiles such as "shot" will be regarded as a "shotgun".

SAWED OFF SHOTGUN DEFINED

Title 21 O.S. § 1289.18: A. "Sawed-off shotgun" shall mean any firearm capable of discharging a series of projectiles of any material which may reasonably be expected to be able to cause lethal injury, with a barrel or barrels less than eighteen (18) inches in length, and using either gunpowder, gas or any means of rocket propulsion.

B. "Sawed-off rifle" shall mean any rifle having a barrel or barrels of less than sixteen (16) inches in length or any weapon made from a rifle (whether by alteration, modification, or otherwise) if such a weapon as modified has an overall length of less than twenty-six (26) inches in length, including the stock portion.

C. Every person who has in his possession or under his immediate control a sawed-off shotgun or a sawed-off rifle, whether concealed or not, shall upon conviction be guilty of a felony for the possession of such device, and shall be punishable by a fine not to exceed One Thousand Dollars ($1,000.00), or imprisonment in the State Penitentiary for a period not to exceed two (2) years, or both such fine and imprisonment.

D. It is a defense to prosecution under this section, if the approved application form that authorized the making or transfer of the particular firearm to the defendant, which indicates the registration of the firearm to said defendant pursuant to the National Firearm's Act, is introduced.

NFA DEFENSE

Title 21 O.S. § 1289.18(D): D. It is a defense to prosecution under this section, if the approved application form that authorized the making or transfer of the particular firearm to the defendant, which indicates the registration of the firearm to said defendant pursuant to the National Firearm's Act, is introduced

ILLEGAL BULLETS

Title 21 O. S. § 1289.19 : "Restricted bullet" means a round or elongated missile with a core of less than sixty percent (60%) lead and having a fluorocarbon coating, which is designed to travel at a high velocity and is capable of penetrating body armor.

POSSESSION OF ILLEGAL BULLETS

Title 21 O. S. §1289.21: It shall be unlawful for any person to possess, carry upon his person, use or attempt to use against another person any restricted bullet as defined in Section 1289.19 of this title.

CONCEALED HANDGUN DEFINED

Title 21 O.S. §1290.2(A)(1): A. As used in the Oklahoma Self-Defense Act:

1. "Concealed handgun" means a loaded or unloaded pistol, the presence of which is not openly discernible to the ordinary observation of a reasonable person.

UNCONCEALED HANDGUN DEFINED

Title 21 O.S. §1290.2(A)(2): A. As used in the Oklahoma Self-Defense Act:

2. "Unconcealed handgun" means a loaded or unloaded pistol carried upon the person in a belt holster or shoulder holster that is wholly or partially visible, or carried upon the person in a scabbard or case designed for carrying firearms that is wholly or partially visible;

PISTOL DEFINED SDA

Title 21 O.S. § 1290.2(A)(3)(c): A. As used in the Oklahoma Self-Defense Act:

3. "Pistol" means any derringer, revolver or semiautomatic firearm which:

c. is designed to be held and fired by the use of a single hand, and

PROHIBITED HANDGUN SDA

Title 21 O.S. § 1290.6: Any concealed or unconcealed handgun when carried in a manner authorized by the provisions of the Oklahoma Self-Defense Act and when loaded with any ammunition which is either a restricted bullet as defined by Section 1289.19 of this title or is larger than .45 caliber or is otherwise prohibited by law shall be deemed a prohibited weapon for purposes of the Oklahoma Self-Defense Act. Any person violating the provisions of this section shall be punished for a criminal offense as provided by Section 1272 of this title or any other applicable provision of law. In addition to any criminal prosecution for a violation of the provisions of this section, the licensee shall be subject to an administrative fine of Five Hundred Dollars ($500.00), upon a hearing and determination by the Oklahoma State Bureau of Investigation that the person is in violation of the provisions of this section.

CHAPTER 3:

KNOWINGLY

Title 21 O.S. § 96: The term "knowingly," when so applied, imports only a knowledge that the facts exist which bring the act or omission within the provisions of this code. It does not require any knowledge of the unlawfulness of such act or omission.

SELF DEFENSE

Title 21 O.S. § 733(2) : When committed in the lawful defense of such person or of another, when the person using force reasonably believes such force is necessary to prevent death or great bodily harm to himself or herself or another or to terminate or prevent the commission of a forcible felony.

ILLEGAL CARRY

Title 21 O.S. § 1272: It shall be unlawful for any person to carry upon or about his or her person, or in a purse or other container belonging to the person, any pistol, revolver, shotgun or rifle whether loaded or unloaded or any dagger, bowie knife, dirk knife, sword cane, blackjack, loaded cane, billy, hand chain, metal knuckles, or any other offensive weapon, whether such weapon be concealed or unconcealed, except this section shall not prohibit.

GIVING CHILDREN §1272 WEAPONS

Title 21 O.S. §1273: Makes it a crime for any person within this state to sell or give to any child (meaning person under 18) any of the arms or weapons designated in Section 1272 of title 21

PARENT PERMITTING CHILD TO POSSESS §1272 WEAPONS

Title 21 O.S. § 1273(B): It shall be unlawful for any parent or guardian to intentionally, knowingly, or recklessly permit his or her child to possess any of the arms or weapons designated in Section 1272 of this title, including any firearm, if such parent is aware of a substantial risk that the child will use the weapon to commit a criminal offense or if the child has either been adjudicated a delinquent or has been convicted as an adult for any criminal offense that contains as an element the threat or use of physical force against the person of another.

CARRYING DEADLY WEAPONS WITH INTENT TO INJURE ANOTHER

Title 21 O.S. § 1278: Any person in this state who carries or wears any deadly weapons or dangerous instrument whatsoever with the intent or for the avowed purpose of unlawfully injuring another person, upon conviction, shall be guilty of a felony punishable by a fine not exceeding Five Thousand Dollars ($5,000.00), by imprisonment in the custody of the Department of Corrections for a period not exceeding two (2) years, or by both such fine and imprisonment. The mere possession of such a weapon or dangerous instrument, without more, however, shall not be sufficient to establish intent as required by this section.

CARRYING WEAPONS WITHOUT A LICENSE

Title 21 O. S. § 1289.6: A person shall be permitted to carry loaded and unloaded shotguns, rifles and pistols, open and not concealed and without a handgun license as authorized by the Oklahoma Self-Defense Act pursuant to the following conditions:

1. When hunting animals or fowl;

2. During competition in or practicing in a safety or hunter safety class, target shooting, skeet, trap or other recognized sporting events;

3. During participation in or in preparation for a military function of the state military forces to be defined as the Oklahoma Army or Air National Guard, Federal Military Reserve and active military forces;

4. During participation in or in preparation for a recognized police function of either a municipal, county or state government as functioning police officials;

5. During a practice for or a performance for entertainment purposes;

6. For lawful self-defense and self-protection or any other legitimate purpose in or on property that is owned, leased, rented, or otherwise legally controlled by the person; or

7. For any legitimate purpose not in violation of the Oklahoma Firearms Act of 1971 or any legislative enactment regarding the use, ownership and control of firearms.

CARRYING FIREARMS UNDER THE INFLUENCE

Title 21 O.S. § 1289.9 : It shall be unlawful for any person to carry or use shotguns, rifles or pistols in any circumstances while under the influence of beer, intoxicating liquors or any hallucinogenic, or any unlawful or unprescribed drug, and it shall be unlawful for any person to carry or use shotguns, rifles or pistols when under the influence of any drug prescribed by a licensed physician if the aftereffects of such consumption affect mental, emotional or physical processes to a degree that would result in abnormal behavior. Any person convicted of a violation of the provisions of this section shall be punished as provided in Section 1289.15 of this title.

TRANSFERRING FIREARM TO AN INCOMPETENT

Title 21 O.S. § 1289.10: It shall be unlawful for any person to knowingly transmit, transfer, sell, lend or furnish any shotgun, rifle or pistol to any person who is under an adjudication of mental incompetency, or to any person who is mentally deficient or of unsound mind. Any person convicted of a violation of the provisions of this section shall be punished as provided in Section 1289.15 of this title.

TRANSFERRING FIREARM TO A FELON

Title 21 O.S. § 1289.12: It shall be unlawful for any person within this state to knowingly sell, trade, give, transmit or otherwise cause the transfer of rifles, shotguns or pistols to any convicted felon or an adjudicated delinquent, and it shall be unlawful for any person within this state to knowingly sell, trade, give, transmit or otherwise cause the transfer of any shotgun, rifle or pistol to any individual who is under the influence of alcohol or drugs or is mentally or emotionally unbalanced or disturbed. All persons who engage in selling, trading or otherwise transferring firearms will display this section prominently in full view at or near the point of normal firearms sale, trade or transfer. Any person convicted of violating the provisions of this section shall be punished as provided in Section 1289.15 of this title

MANUFACTURING RESTRICTED BULLETS

Title 21 O. S. § 1289.20: Except for the purpose of public safety or national security, it shall be unlawful to manufacture, cause to be manufactured, import, advertise for sale or sell within this state any restricted bullet as defined in Section 1289.19 of this title.

CHAPTER 4:

USING FORCE UNLAWFUL AND LAWFUL

Title 21 O. S. § 643: To use or to attempt to offer to use force or violence upon or toward the person of another is not unlawful in the following cases:

1. When necessarily committed by a public officer in the performance of any legal duty, or by any other person assisting such officer or acting by such officer's direction;

2. When necessarily committed by any person in arresting one who has committed any felony, and delivering such person to a public officer competent to receive such person in custody;

3. When committed either by the person about to be injured, or by any other person in such person's aid or defense, in preventing or attempting to prevent an offense against such person, or any trespass or other unlawful interference with real or personal property in such person's lawful possession; provided the force or violence used is not more than sufficient to prevent such offense;

4. When committed by a parent or the authorized agent of any parent, or by any guardian, master or teacher, in the exercise of a lawful authority to restrain or correct such person's child, ward, apprentice or scholar, provided restraint or correction has been rendered necessary by the misconduct of such child, ward, apprentice or scholar, or by such person's refusal to obey the lawful command of such parent or authorized agent or guardian, master or teacher, and the force or violence used is reasonable in manner and moderate in degree;

5. When committed by a carrier of passengers, or the authorized agents or servants of such carrier, or by any person assisting them at their request, in expelling from any carriage, railroad car, vessel or other vehicle, any passenger who refuses to obey a lawful and reasonable regulation prescribed for the conduct of passengers, if such vehicle has first been stopped

and the force and violence used is not more than is sufficient to expel the offending passenger, with a reasonable regard to such passenger's personal safety; and

6. When committed by any person in preventing a person who is impaired by reason of mental retardation or developmental disability as defined by Section 1430.2 of Title 10 of the Oklahoma Statutes, a mentally ill person, insane person or other person of unsound mind, including persons temporarily or partially deprived of reason, from committing an act dangerous to such person's self or to another, or enforcing such restraint as is necessary for the protection of the person or for restoration to health, during such period only as shall be necessary to obtain legal authority for the restraint or custody of the person.

Title 21 O. S. § 643(3): When committed either by the person about to be injured, or by any other person in such person's aid or defense, in preventing or attempting to prevent an offense against such person, or any trespass or other unlawful interference with real or personal property in such person's lawful possession; provided the force or violence used is not more than sufficient to prevent such offense.

AGGRAVATED ASSAULT AND BATTERY

Title 21 O. S. § 646: A. An assault and battery becomes aggravated when committed under any of the following circumstances:

1. When great bodily injury is inflicted upon the person assaulted; or

2. When committed by a person of robust health or strength upon one who is aged, decrepit, or incapacitated, as defined in Section 641 of this title.

MISDEMEANOR POINTING FIREARM

Title 21 O. S. § 1279: Except for an act of self-defense, it shall be unlawful for any person to point any pistol or any other deadly weapon whether loaded or not, at any other person or persons. Any person violating the provisions of this section shall, upon conviction, be guilty of a misdemeanor punishable as provided in Section 1280 of this title.

FELONY POINTING FIREARM

Title 21 O. S. § 1289.16 : It shall be unlawful for any person to willfully or without lawful cause point a shotgun, rifle or pistol, or any deadly weapon, whether loaded or not, at any person or persons for the purpose of threatening or with the intention of discharging the firearm or with any malice or for any purpose of injuring, either through physical injury or mental or emotional intimidation or for purposes of whimsy, humor or prank, or in anger or otherwise, but not to include the pointing of shotguns, rifles or pistols by law enforcement authorities in the performance of their duties, members of the state military forces in the performance of their duties, members of the federal military reserve and active military components in the performance of their duties, or any federal government law enforcement officer in the performance of any duty, or in the performance of a play on stage, rodeo, television or on film, or in defense of any person, one's home or property. Any person convicted of a violation of the provisions of this section shall be punished as provided in Section 1289.17 of this title.

CASTLE DOCTRINE

Title 21 O. S. § 1289.25: The Legislature hereby recognizes that the citizens of the State of Oklahoma have a right to expect absolute safety within their own homes or places of business.

STAND YOUR GROUND LAW

Title 21 O. S. § 1289.25(D): A person who is not engaged in an unlawful activity and who is attacked in any other place where he or she has a right to be has no duty to retreat and has the right to stand his or her ground and meet force with force, including deadly force, if he or she reasonably believes it is necessary to do so to prevent death or great bodily harm to himself or herself or another or to prevent the commission of a forcible felony.

DISCHARGING WEAPON IN PUBLIC

Title 21 O. S. §1364: Every person who willfully discharges any pistol, rifle, shotgun, airgun or other weapon, or throws any other missile in any public place, or in any place where there is any person to be endangered thereby, although no injury to any person shall ensue, is guilty of a misdemeanor. Any person convicted of a violation of the provisions of this section after having been issued a handgun license pursuant to the provisions of the Oklahoma Self-Defense Act shall have the license suspended for a period of six (6) months and shall be subject to an administrative fine of Fifty Dollars ($50.00), upon a hearing and determination by the Oklahoma State Bureau of Investigation that the person is in violation of the provisions of this section.

CRUELTY TO ANIMALS

Title 21 O. S.§ 1685: Any person who shall willfully or maliciously torture, destroy or kill, or cruelly beat or injure, maim or mutilate any animal in subjugation or captivity, whether wild or tame, and whether belonging to the person or to another, or deprive any such animal of necessary food, drink, shelter, or veterinary care to prevent suffering; or who shall cause, procure or permit any such animal to be so tortured, destroyed or killed, or cruelly beaten or injured, maimed or mutilated, or deprived of necessary food, drink, shelter, or veterinary care to prevent suffering; or who shall willfully set on foot, instigate, engage in, or in any way further any act of cruelty to any animal, or any act tending to produce such cruelty, shall be guilty of a felony and shall be punished by imprisonment in the State Penitentiary not exceeding five (5) years, or by imprisonment in the county jail not exceeding one (1) year, or by a fine not exceeding Five Thousand Dollars ($5,000.00). Any animal so maltreated or abused shall be considered an abused or neglected animal.

CHAPTER 5:

SEXUAL ASSAULT DEFINED

Title 21 O. S. § 142.20: A Sexual Assault Examination Fund shall be established for the purpose of providing to a victim of a sexual assault a forensic medical examination by a qualified licensed health care professional and to provide to the victim medications as directed by said health care professional.

FALSE ARREST CRIMINAL PENALTY

Title 21 O. S. § 535: Every public officer or person pretending to be a public officer, who under the pretense or color of any process or other legal authority, arrests any person, or detains him against his will, or seizes or levies upon any property, or dispossesses anyone of any lands or tenements without due and legal process, is guilty of a misdemeanor.

SEARCH WARRANT ABUSE

Title 21 O. S. § 536: Every peace officer who, in executing a search warrant, willfully exceeds his authority, or exercises it with unnecessary severity, is guilty of a misdemeanor.

FALSE REPORT TO POLICE

Title 21 O. S. § 589: Sub paragraph (A) : It shall be unlawful to willfully, knowingly and without probable cause make a false report to any person of any crime or circumstances indicating the possibility of crime having been committed, including the unlawful taking of personal property, which report causes or encourages the exercise of police action or investigation. Any person convicted of violating the provisions of this subsection shall be guilty of a misdemeanor punishable by imprisonment in the county jail for not more than ninety (90) days or by a fine of not more than Five Hundred Dollars ($500.00), or by both such fine and imprisonment.

FALSE MISSING CHILD REPORT

Title 21 O. S. § 589 Sub paragraph (B): It shall be unlawful to willfully, knowingly, and without probable cause communicate false information concerning a missing child to a law enforcement agency that causes or encourages the activation of an AMBER alert warning system. Any person convicted of violating the provisions of this subsection shall be guilty of a felony punishable by imprisonment in the county jail for not more than one (1) year or by a fine of not less than One Thousand Dollars ($1,000.00), or by both such fine and imprisonment.

KIDNAPPING

Title 21 O. S. § 745: Every person who, without lawful authority, forcibly seizes and confines another, or inveigles or kidnaps another, for the purpose of extorting any money, property or thing of value or advantage from the person so seized, confined, inveigled or kidnapped, or from any other person, or in any manner threatens either by written instrument, word of mouth, message, telegraph, telephone, by placing an ad in a newspaper, or by messenger, demands money or other thing of value, shall be guilty of a felony, and upon conviction shall suffer death or imprisonment in the State Penitentiary, not less than ten (10) years.

ROBBERY DEFINED

Title 21 O. S. § 797: Robbery in the first degree is when, in the course of committing the theft, the defendant:

1. inflicts serious bodily injury upon the person;

2. threatens a person with immediate serious bodily injury;

3. intentionally puts a person in fear of immediate serious bodily injury; or

4. commits or threatens to commit a felony upon the person.

When accomplished in any other manner, it is robbery in the second degree.

SODOMY DEFINED

Title 21 O. S. § 888: Any person who forces another person to engage in the detestable and abominable crime against nature, pursuant to Section 886 of this title, upon conviction, is guilty of a felony punishable by imprisonment in the State Penitentiary for a period of not more than twenty (20) years, except as provided in Section 3 of this act. Any person convicted of a second violation of this section, where the victim of the second offense is a person under sixteen (16) years of age, shall not be eligible for probation, suspended or deferred sentence.

RAPE DEFINED

Title 21 O. S. § 1111: Rape is an act of sexual intercourse involving vaginal or anal penetration accomplished with a male or female who is not the spouse of the perpetrator and who may be of the same or the opposite sex as the perpetrator under any of the following circumstances:

1. Where the victim is under sixteen (16) years of age;

2. Where the victim is incapable through mental illness or any other unsoundness of mind, whether temporary or permanent, of giving legal consent;

3. Where force or violence is used or threatened, accompanied by apparent power of execution to the victim or to another person;

4. Where the victim is intoxicated by a narcotic or anesthetic agent, administered by or with the privity of the accused as a means of forcing the victim to submit;

5. Where the victim is at the time unconscious of the nature of the act and this fact is known to the accused;

6. Where the victim submits to sexual intercourse under the belief that the person committing the act is a spouse, and this

belief is induced by artifice, pretense, or concealment practiced by the accused or by the accused in collusion with the spouse with intent to induce that belief. In all cases of collusion between the accused and the spouse to accomplish such act, both the spouse and the accused, upon conviction, shall be deemed guilty of rape;

7. Where the victim is under the legal custody or supervision of a state agency, a federal agency, a county, a municipality or a political subdivision and engages in sexual intercourse with a state, federal, county, municipal or political subdivision employee or an employee of a contractor of the state, the federal government, a county, a municipality or a political subdivision that exercises authority over the victim;

8. Where the victim is at least sixteen (16) years of age and is less than twenty (20) years of age and is a student, or under the legal custody or supervision of any public or private elementary or secondary school, junior high or high school, or public vocational school, and engages in sexual intercourse with a person who is eighteen (18) years of age or older and is an employee of the same school system; or

9. Where the victim is nineteen (19) years of age or younger and is in the legal custody of a state agency, federal agency or tribal court and engages in sexual intercourse with a foster parent or foster parent applicant

RAPE BY INSTRUMENTATION DEFINED

Title 21 O. S. § 1111.1: Rape by instrumentation is an act within or without the bonds of matrimony in which any inanimate object or any part of the human body, not amounting to sexual intercourse is used in the carnal knowledge of another person without his or her consent and penetration of the anus or vagina occurs to that person.

RAPE FIRST DEGREE DEFINED

Title 21 O. S. § 1114: Rape in the first degree shall include:

1. rape committed by a person over eighteen (18) years of age upon a person under fourteen (14) years of age; or

2. rape committed upon a person incapable through mental illness or any unsoundness of mind of giving legal consent regardless of the age of the person committing the crime; or

3. rape accomplished where the victim is intoxicated by a narcotic or anesthetic agent, administered by or with the privity of the accused as a means of forcing the victim to submit; or

4. rape accomplished where the victim is at the time unconscious of the nature of the act and this fact is known to the accused; or

5. rape accomplished with any person by means of force, violence, or threats of force or violence accompanied by apparent power of execution regardless of the age of the person committing the crime; or

6. rape by instrumentation resulting in bodily harm is rape by instrumentation in the first degree regardless of the age of the person committing the crime; or

7. rape by instrumentation committed upon a person under fourteen (14) years of age.

<u>CASTLE DOCTRINE PRESUMPTION WHEN</u>

Title 21 O. S. § 1289.25(B): A person or an owner, manager or employee of a business is presumed to have held a reasonable fear of imminent peril of death or great bodily harm to himself or herself or another when using defensive force that is intended or likely to cause death or great bodily harm to another if:

1. The person against whom the defensive force was used was in the process of unlawfully and forcefully entering, or had unlawfully and forcibly entered, a dwelling, residence, occupied vehicle, or a place of business, or if that person had removed or was attempting to remove another against the will of that

person from the dwelling, residence, occupied vehicle, or place of business; and

2. The person who uses defensive force knew or had reason to believe that an unlawful and forcible entry or unlawful and forcible act was occurring or had occurred.

STAND YOUR GROUND

Title 21 O. S. § 1289.25 (D): A person who is not engaged in an unlawful activity and who is attacked in any other place where he or she has a right to be has no duty to retreat and has the right to stand his or her ground and meet force with force, including deadly force, if he or she reasonably believes it is necessary to do so to prevent death or great bodily harm to himself or herself or another or to prevent the commission of a forcible felony.

IMMUNITY CASTLE DOCTRINE AND STAND YOUR GROUND

Title 21 O. S. § 1289.25(F): A person who uses force, as permitted pursuant to the provisions of subsections B and D of this section, is justified in using such force and is immune from criminal prosecution and civil action for the use of such force. As used in this subsection, the term "criminal prosecution" includes charging or prosecuting the defendant.

REFUSING TO AID A MAGISTRATE OR POLICE

Title 21 O. S. § 1318: Every person present at any riot, and lawfully commanded to aid the magistrate or officers in arresting any rioter, who neglects or refuses to obey such command, is deemed one of the rioters, and punishable accordingly.

CHAPTER 6:

LAWFUL TO KILL DOGS OR CATS CHASING LIVESTOCK

Title 4 O.S. §41: It shall be lawful for a person to kill any animal of the family canidae or the family felidae found chasing livestock off the premises of the owner of the animal if the person is the owner or occupant of the property on which the animal is chasing the livestock or if the person is authorized to kill such an animal by the owner or occupant of such property.

LIVESTOCK DEFINED

Title 4 O.S. §41(I)(1): "Livestock" means any cattle, bison, hog, sheep, goat, equine, domesticated rabbits, chicken or other poultry and shall include exotic livestock;

EXOTIC LIVESTOCK DEFINED

Title 4 O.S. §41(I)(2): "Exotic livestock" means commercially raised exotic livestock including animals of the families bovidae, cervidae and antilocapridae or birds of the ratite group

DOMESTIC ANIMALS DEFINED

Title 4 O.S. §85.1: As used in this act, "domestic animals" shall include all domestic animals including, but not limited to, cattle, bison, hogs, sheep, goats, equidae, chickens or other poultry and exotic livestock. The term "domestic animals" shall not include dogs and cats.

HUNTING AND TAKING DEFINED

Title 29 O.S. §2-118: "Hunting or taking" is pursuing, killing, capturing, trapping, snaring and netting wildlife, and all lesser acts such as disturbing, harrying, worrying or placing, setting, drawing or using any net, trap or other device used to take wildlife and includes specifically every attempt to take and every assistance to other persons in taking or attempting to take wild animals, except that the definitions of "taking" and "hunting" wildlife shall not include disturbing, harrying or worrying wild game in field trials or performance tests of dogs nor the act of any person in participating as owner, handler, trainer, official or member of an audience observing such trials, whether resident or nonresident, where wild game is not killed.

HUNTING LICENSE REQUIRED

Title 29 O.S. §4-112: Except as otherwise provided for in the Oklahoma Wildlife Conservation Code or the Oklahoma Farmed Cervidae Act, no person may hunt, pursue, trap, harass, catch, kill, take or attempt to take in any manner, use, have in possession, sell, or transport all or any portion of any wildlife except fish, without having first procured a license from the Department of Wildlife Conservation. The Wildlife Conservation Commission shall designate a consecutive Saturday and Sunday in September of each year as free hunting days in which residents of this state may hunt without first procuring a hunting license pursuant to the provisions of this section.

CHAPTER 7:

AID TO POLICE REQUIRED

Title 21 O.S. § 537: Every person who, after having been lawfully commanded to aid any officer in arresting any person or in retaking any person who has escaped from legal custody, or in executing any legal process, willfully neglects or refuses to aid such officer, is guilty of a misdemeanor

AID TO POLICE IN ARREST REQUIRED

Title 21 O.S. §538: Every person who, after having been lawfully commanded by any magistrate to arrest another person, willfully neglects or refuses so to do, is guilty of a misdemeanor

FALSE REPRESENTATION OF AUTHORITY TO ARREST

Title 21 O.S. §584: Every person who maliciously institutes or prosecutes any action or legal proceeding; or makes or procures any arrest, in the name of a person who does not exist, or has not consented that it be instituted or made, is guilty of a misdemeanor

ASSAULT WITH A DANGEROUS WEAPON DEFINED

Title 21 O.S. §645: Every person who, with intent to do bodily harm and without justifiable or excusable cause, commits any assault, battery, or assault and battery upon the person of another with any sharp or dangerous weapon, or who, without such cause, shoots at another, with any kind of firearm, air gun, conductive energy weapon or other means whatever, with intent to injure any person, although without the intent to kill such person or to commit any felony, upon conviction is guilty of a felony punishable by imprisonment in the State Penitentiary not exceeding ten (10) years, or by imprisonment in a county jail not exceeding one (1) year.

SHOOTING WITH INTENT TO KILL DEFINED

Title 21 O.S. §652(A): Every person who intentionally and wrongfully shoots another with or discharges any kind of firearm, with intent to kill any person, including an unborn child as defined in Section 1-730 of Title 63 of the Oklahoma Statutes, shall upon conviction be guilty of a felony punishable by imprisonment in the State Penitentiary not exceeding life.

DRIVE BY SHOOTING DEFINED

Title 21 O.S. §652(B): Every person who uses any vehicle to facilitate the intentional discharge of any kind of firearm, crossbow or other weapon in conscious disregard for the safety of any other person or persons, including an unborn child as defined in Section 1-730 of Title 63 of the Oklahoma Statutes, shall upon conviction be guilty of a felony punishable by imprisonment in the custody of the Department of Corrections for a term not less than two (2) years nor exceeding life.

MURDER 1ST DEGREE DEFINED

Title 21 O.S. §701.7: A person commits murder in the first degree when that person unlawfully and with malice aforethought causes the death of another human being. Malice is that deliberate intention unlawfully to take away the life of a human being, which is manifested by external circumstances capable of proof.

MANSLAUGHTER 1ST DEGREE

Title 21 O.S. §711: Homicide is manslaughter in the first degree in the following cases:

1. When perpetrated without a design to effect death by a person while engaged in the commission of a misdemeanor.

2. When perpetrated without a design to effect death, and in a heat of passion, but in a cruel and unusual manner, or by means of a dangerous weapon; unless it is committed under such circumstances as constitute excusable or justifiable homicide.

3. When perpetrated unnecessarily either while resisting an attempt by the person killed to commit a crime, or after such attempt shall have failed.

JUSTIFIABLE HOMICIDE DEFINED

Title 21 O.S. §733(A): Homicide is also justifiable when committed by any person in any of the following cases:

1. When resisting any attempt to murder such person, or to commit any felony upon him, or upon or in any dwelling house in which such person is;

2. When committed in the lawful defense of such person or of another, when the person using force reasonably believes such force is necessary to prevent death or great bodily harm to himself or herself or another or to terminate or prevent the commission of a forcible felony; or

3. When necessarily committed in attempting, by lawful ways and means, to apprehend any person for any felony committed; or in lawfully suppressing any riot; or in lawfully keeping and preserving the peace.

RECKLESS CONDUCT WITH A FIREARM DEFINED

Title 21 O.S. §1289.11: It shall be unlawful for any person to engage in reckless conduct while having in his or her possession any shotgun, rifle or pistol, such actions consisting of creating a situation of unreasonable risk and probability of death or great bodily harm to another, and demonstrating a conscious disregard for the safety of another person. Any person convicted of violating the provisions of this section shall be punished as provided in Section 1289.15 of this title

SHOOTING AT A BUILDING DEFINED

Title 21 O.S. §1289.17A: It shall be unlawful for any person to willfully or intentionally discharge any firearm or other deadly weapon at or into any dwelling, or at or into any building used for public or business purposes. Any violation of the provisions of this section shall be a felony punishable by imprisonment in the custody of the Department of Corrections for a term not less than two (2) years nor more than twenty (20) years. The provisions of this section shall not apply to any law enforcement officer in the performance of any lawful duty.

CASTLE DOCTRINE APPLIES TO OWNER OF A BUSINESS

Title 21 O. S.§ 1289.25 (B): A person or an owner, manager or employee of a business is presumed to have held a reasonable fear of imminent peril of death or great bodily harm to himself or herself or another when using defensive force that is intended or likely to cause death or great bodily harm to another if:

FORCIBLE ENTRY OF A DWELLING DEFINED

Title 21 O. S. §1289.25 (E): A person who unlawfully and by force enters or attempts to enter the dwelling, residence, occupied vehicle of another person, or a place of business is presumed to be doing so with the intent to commit an unlawful act involving force or violence.

BRANDISHING FIREARM DEFINED

Title 21 O.S. §1362: If any person shall willfully or maliciously disturb, either by day or night, the peace and quiet of any city of the first class, town, village, neighborhood, family or person by loud or unusual noise, or by abusive, violent, obscene or profane language, whether addressed to the party so disturbed or some other person, or by threatening to kill, do bodily harm or injury, destroy property, fight, or by quarreling or challenging to fight, or fighting, or shooting off any firearms, or brandishing the same, or by running any horse at unusual speed along any street, alley, highway or public road, he shall be deemed guilty of a misdemeanor, and, on conviction thereof, shall be fined in any sum not to exceed One Hundred Dollars ($100.00), or by imprisonment in the county jail not to exceed thirty (30) days, or by both such fine and imprisonment, at the discretion of the court or jury trying the same.

ARSON 1ST DEGREE DEFINED

Title 21 O.S. §1401(A): Any person who willfully and maliciously sets fire to or burns, or by the use of any explosive device, accelerant, ignition device, heat-producing device or substance, destroys in whole or in part, or causes to be burned or destroyed, or aids, counsels or procures the burning or destruction of any building or structure or contents thereof, inhabited or occupied by one or more persons, whether the property of that person or another, or who willfully and maliciously sets fire to or burns, or by the use of any explosive device, accelerant, ignition device, heat-producing device or substance causes a person to be burned, or aids, counsels or procures the burning of a person shall, upon conviction, be guilty of arson in the first degree, which is a felony, and shall be punished by a fine not to exceed Twenty-five Thousand Dollars ($25,000.00), or by imprisonment in the custody of the Department of Corrections for not more than thirty-five (35) years, or by both such fine and imprisonment.

BURGLARY 1ST DEGREE DEFINED

Title 21 O.S. §1431: Every person who breaks into and enters the dwelling house of another, in which there is at the time some human being, with intent to commit some crime therein, either:

1. By forcibly bursting or breaking the wall, or an outer door, window, or shutter of a window of such house or the lock or bolts of such door, or the fastening of such window or shutter; or

2. By breaking in any other manner, being armed with a dangerous weapon or being assisted or aided by one or more confederates then actually present; or

3. By unlocking an outer door by means of false keys or by picking the lock thereof, or by lifting a latch or opening a window, is guilty of burglary in the first degree.

BURGLARY 2ND DEGREE DEFINED

Title 21 O.S. §1435: Every person who breaks and enters any building or any part of any building, room, booth, tent, railroad car, automobile, truck, trailer, vessel or other structure or erection, in which any property is kept, or breaks into or forcibly opens, any coin operated or vending machine or device with intent to steal any property therein or to commit any felony, is guilty of burglary in the second degree

TRESSPASS DEFINED

Title 21 O. S. § 1835: Whoever shall willfully or maliciously enter the garden, yard, pasture or field of another after being expressly forbidden to do so or without permission by the owner or lawful occupant thereof when such property is posted shall be deemed guilty of trespass and upon conviction thereof shall be fined in any sum not to exceed Two Hundred Fifty Dollars ($250.00); provided, that this provision shall not apply to registered land surveyors and registered professional engineers for the purpose of land surveying in the performance of their professional services; and, provided further, that anyone who willfully or maliciously enters any such garden, yard, pasture or field, and therein commits or attempts to commit waste, theft, or damage shall be deemed guilty of a misdemeanor and upon conviction thereof shall be fined in any sum not less than Fifty Dollars ($50.00) nor more than Five Hundred Dollars ($500.00), or by confinement in the county jail for not less than thirty (30) days nor more than six (6) months, or both such fine and imprisonment. For purposes of this section, "posted" means exhibiting signs to read as follows: "PROPERTY RESTRICTED"; "POSTED - KEEP OUT"; "KEEP OUT"; "NO TRESPASSING"; or similar signs which are displayed. Property that is fenced or not fenced must have such signs placed conspicuously and at all places where entry to the property is normally expected.

DISCHARGE OF FIREARM AT BUS

Title 21 O.S. §1903(E): It shall be unlawful for any person to discharge any firearm or hurl or place in the path any missile at, into or within any bus, terminal or other transportation facility. Such person shall, upon conviction, be guilty of a felony punishable by a fine not more than Five Thousand Dollars ($5,000.00) or by imprisonment for not more than five (5) years, or both.

CHAPTER 8:

ASSAULT DEFINED

Title 21 O.S. § 644: Assault shall be punishable by imprisonment in a county jail not exceeding thirty (30) days, or by a fine of not more than Five Hundred Dollars ($500.00), or by both such fine and imprisonment.

DEFERRED SENTENCE DEFINED

Title 21 O.S. § 991c: Upon a verdict or plea of guilty or upon a plea of nolo contendere, but before a judgment of guilt, the court may, without entering a judgment of guilt and with the consent of the defendant, defer further proceedings upon the specific conditions prescribed by the court not to exceed a ten-year period. The court shall first consider restitution among the various conditions it may prescribe. The court may also consider ordering the defendant to:

1. Pay court costs;

2. Pay an assessment in lieu of any fine authorized by law for the offense;

3. Pay any other assessment or cost authorized by law;

4. Engage in a term of community service without compensation, according to a schedule consistent with the employment and family responsibilities of the defendant;

5. County jail confinement for a period not to exceed ninety (90) days or the maximum amount of jail time provided for the offense, if it is less than ninety (90) days;

6. Pay an amount as reimbursement for reasonable attorney fees, to be paid into the court fund, if a court-appointed attorney has been provided to defendant;

7. Be supervised in the community for a period not to exceed two (2) years, unless a petition alleging violation of any condition of deferred judgment is filed during the period of supervision. As a condition of any supervision, the defendant shall be required to pay a supervision fee of Forty Dollars ($40.00) per month. The supervision fee shall be waived in whole or part by the supervisory agency when the accused is indigent. No person shall be denied supervision based solely on the inability of the person to pay a fee;

8. Pay into the court fund a monthly amount not exceeding Forty Dollars ($40.00) per month during any period during which the proceedings are deferred when the defendant is not to be supervised in the community. The total amount to be paid into the court fund shall be established by the court and shall

not exceed the amount of the maximum fine authorized by law for the offense;

9. Make other reparations to the community or victim as required and deemed appropriate by the court;

10. Order any conditions which can be imposed for a suspended sentence pursuant to paragraph 1 of subsection A of Section 991a of this title; or

11. Any combination of the above provisions.

However, unless under the supervision of the district attorney, the offender shall be required to pay Forty Dollars ($40.00) per month to the district attorney during the first two (2) years of probation to compensate the district attorney for the costs incurred during the prosecution of the offender and for the additional work of verifying the compliance of the offender with the rules and conditions of his or her probation. The district attorney may waive any part of this requirement in the best interests of justice. The court shall not waive, suspend, defer or dismiss the costs of prosecution in its entirety. However, if the court determines that a reduction in the fine, costs and costs of prosecution is warranted, the court shall equally apply the same percentage reduction to the fine, costs and costs of prosecution owed by the offender.

DISTRICT ATTORNEY'S DIVERSION PROGRAM

Title 21 O.S. § 991f-1.1: Each district attorney shall create within the district attorney's office a Restitution and Diversion Program and assign sufficient staff and resources for the efficient operation of such program. The purpose of the Restitution and Diversion Program is to allow the district attorney the discretion to divert criminal complaints involving property crimes from criminal court and to monitor restitution payments. At the discretion of the district attorney, the program may be administered by the Bogus Check Restitution Program operated by the county.

STALKING DEFINED

Title 21 O.S. § 1173: Any person who willfully, maliciously, and repeatedly follows or harasses another person in a manner that:

1. Would cause a reasonable person or a member of the immediate family of that person as defined in subsection F of this section to feel frightened, intimidated, threatened, harassed, or molested; and

2. Actually causes the person being followed or harassed to feel terrorized, frightened, intimidated, threatened, harassed, or molested,

shall, upon conviction, be guilty of the crime of stalking, which is a misdemeanor punishable by imprisonment in a county jail for not more than one (1) year, or by a fine of not more than One Thousand Dollars ($1,000.00), or by both such fine and imprisonment.

RESTORATION OF RIGHT TO CARRY FIREARM

Title 21 O.S. § 1283 B: Any person who has previously been convicted of a nonviolent felony in any court of this state or of another state or of the United States, and who has received a full and complete pardon from the proper authority and has not been convicted of any other felony offense which has not been pardoned, shall have restored the right to possess any firearm or other weapon prohibited by subsection A of this section, the right to apply for and carry a handgun, concealed or unconcealed, pursuant to the Oklahoma Self-Defense Act and the right to perform the duties of a peace officer, gunsmith, or for firearms repair

OKLAHOMA SELF DEFENSE ACT

Title 21 O.S. § 1290.1: Sections 1 through 25 of this act shall be known and may be cited as the "Oklahoma Self-Defense Act".

REQUIREMENTS OF APPLICATION FOR SDA

Title 21 § 1290.9: The following requirements shall apply to any person making application to the Oklahoma State Bureau of Investigation for a handgun license pursuant to the provisions of the Oklahoma Self-Defense Act. The person must:

1. Be a citizen of the United States;

2. Establish a residency in the State of Oklahoma. For purposes of the Oklahoma Self-Defense Act, the term "residency" shall apply to any person who either possesses a valid Oklahoma driver license or state photo identification card, and physically maintains a residence in this state or to any person, including the spouse of such person, who has permanent military orders within this state and possesses a valid driver license from another state where such person and spouse of such person claim residency;

3. Be at least twenty-one (21) years of age;

4. Complete a firearms safety and training course and demonstrate competence and qualifications with the type of pistol to be carried by the person as provided in Section 1290.14 of this title, and submit proof of training and qualification or an exemption for training and qualification as authorized by Section 1290.14 of this title;

5. Submit the required fee and complete the application process as provided in Section 1290.12 of this title; and

6. Comply in good faith with the provisions of the Oklahoma Self-Defense Act.

SDA PRECLUSIONS

TITLE 21 O. S. § 1290.10: In addition to the requirements stated in Section 1290.9 of this title, the conditions stated in this section shall preclude a person from eligibility for a handgun license pursuant to the provisions of the Oklahoma Self-Defense Act. The occurrence of any one of the following conditions shall deny the person the right to have a handgun license pursuant to the provisions of the Oklahoma Self-Defense Act. Prohibited conditions are:

1. Ineligible to possess a pistol due to any felony conviction or adjudication as a delinquent as provided by Section 1283 of this title, except as provided in subsection B of Section 1283 of this title;

2. Any felony conviction pursuant to any law of another state, a felony conviction pursuant to any provision of the United States Code, or any conviction pursuant to the laws of any foreign country, provided such foreign conviction would constitute a felony offense in this state if the offense had been committed in this state, except as provided in subsection B of Section 1283 of this title;

3. Adjudication as a mentally incompetent person pursuant to the provisions of the Oklahoma Mental Health Law, or an adjudication of incompetency entered in another state pursuant to any provision of law of that state, unless the person has been granted relief from the disqualifying disability pursuant to Section 1290.27 of this title;

4. Any false or misleading statement on the application for a handgun license as provided by paragraph 5 of subsection A of Section 1290.12 of this title;

5. Conviction of any one of the following misdemeanor offenses in this state or in any other state:

a. any assault and battery which caused serious physical injury to the victim, or any second or subsequent assault and battery conviction,

b. any aggravated assault and battery,

c. any stalking pursuant to Section 1173 of this title, or a similar law of another state,

d. a violation relating to the Protection from Domestic Abuse Act or any violation of a victim protection order of another state,

e. any conviction relating to illegal drug use or possession, or

f. an act of domestic abuse as defined by Section 644 of this title or an act of domestic assault and battery or any comparable acts under the laws of another state.

The preclusive period for a misdemeanor conviction related to illegal drug use or possession shall be ten (10) years from the date of completion of a sentence. For purposes of this subsection, "date of completion of a sentence" shall mean the day an offender completes all incarceration, probation, and parole pertaining to such sentence;

6. An attempted suicide or other condition relating to or indicating mental instability or an unsound mind which occurred within the preceding ten-year period from the date of the application for a license to carry a concealed firearm or that occurs during the period of licensure;

7. Currently undergoing treatment for a mental illness, condition, or disorder. For purposes of this paragraph, "currently undergoing treatment for a mental illness, condition, or disorder" means the person has been diagnosed by a licensed physician as being afflicted with a substantial disorder of thought, mood, perception, psychological orientation, or memory that significantly impairs judgment, behavior, capacity to recognize reality, or ability to meet the ordinary demands of life;

8. Significant character defects of the applicant as evidenced by a misdemeanor criminal record indicating habitual criminal activity;

9. Ineligible to possess a pistol due to any provision of law of this state or the United States Code, except as provided in subsection B of Section 1283 of this title;

10. Failure to pay an assessed fine or surrender the handgun license as required by a decision by the administrative hearing

examiner pursuant to authority of the Oklahoma Self-Defense Act;

11. Being subject to an outstanding felony warrant issued in this state or another state or the United States; or

12. Adjudication as a delinquent as provided by Section 1283 of this title, except as provided in subsection B of Section 1283 of this title.

PRECLUSION FOR FALSE STATEMENTS ON APPLICATION

Title 21 O.S. § 1290.10 (4): Any false or misleading statement on the application for a handgun license as provided by paragraph 5 of subsection A of Section 1290.12 of this title

PRECLUSION FOR MISDEMEANORS

Title 21 O.S. § 1290.10 (5(e)): Conviction of any one of the following misdemeanor offenses in this state or in any other state:

e. any conviction relating to illegal drug use or possession.

PRECULUSION FOR MENTAL ILLNESS

Title 21 O.S. § 1290.10 paragraph 7: Currently undergoing treatment for a mental illness, condition, or disorder. For purposes of this paragraph, "currently undergoing treatment for a mental illness, condition, or disorder" means the person has been diagnosed by a licensed physician as being afflicted with a substantial disorder of thought, mood, perception, psychological orientation, or memory that significantly impairs judgment, behavior, capacity to recognize reality, or ability to meet the ordinary demands of life;

PRECLUSION PERIOD

Title 21 O.S. § 1290.11: The following conditions shall preclude a person from being eligible for a handgun license pursuant to the provisions of the Oklahoma Self-Defense Act for a period of time as prescribed in each of the following paragraphs:

1. An arrest for an alleged commission of a felony offense or a felony charge pending in this state, another state or pursuant to the United States Code. The preclusive period shall be until the final determination of the matter;

2. The person is subject to the provisions of a deferred sentence or deferred prosecution in this state or another state or pursuant to federal authority for the commission of a felony offense. The preclusive period shall be three (3) years and shall begin upon the final determination of the matter;

3. Any involuntary commitment for a mental illness, condition, or disorder pursuant to the provisions of Section 5-410 of Title 43A of the Oklahoma Statutes or any involuntary commitment in another state pursuant to any provisions of law of that state. The preclusive period shall be permanent as provided by Title 18 of the United States Code Section 922(g)(4) unless the person has been granted relief from the disqualifying disability pursuant to Section 3 of this act;

4. The person has previously undergone treatment for a mental illness, condition, or disorder which required medication or supervision as defined by paragraph 7 of Section 1290.10 of this title. The preclusive period shall be three (3) years from the last date of treatment or upon presentation of a certified statement from a licensed physician stating that the person is either no longer disabled by any mental or psychiatric illness, condition, or disorder or that the person has been stabilized on medication for ten (10) years or more;

5. Inpatient treatment for substance abuse. The preclusive period shall be three (3) years from the last date of treatment or upon presentation of a certified statement from a licensed physician stating that the person has been free from substance use for twelve (12) months or more preceding the filing of an application for a handgun license;

6. Two or more convictions of public intoxication pursuant to Section 8 of Title 37 of the Oklahoma Statutes, or a similar law

of another state. The preclusive period shall be three (3) years from the date of the completion of the last sentence;

7. Two or more misdemeanor convictions relating to intoxication or driving under the influence of an intoxicating substance or alcohol. The preclusive period shall be three (3) years from the date of the completion of the last sentence or shall require a certified statement from a licensed physician stating that the person is not in need of substance abuse treatment;

8. A court order for a final Victim Protection Order against the applicant, as authorized by the Protection from Domestic Abuse Act, or any court order granting a final victim protection order against the applicant from another state. The preclusive period shall be three (3) years from the date of the entry of the final court order, or sixty (60) days from the date an order was vacated, canceled or withdrawn;

9. An adjudicated delinquent or convicted felon residing in the residence of the applicant which may be a violation of Section 1283 of this title. The preclusive period shall be thirty (30) days from the date the person no longer resides in the same residence as the applicant; or

10. An arrest for an alleged commission of, a charge pending for, or the person is subject to the provisions of a deferred prosecution for any one or more of the following misdemeanor offenses in this state or another state:

a. any assault and battery which caused serious physical injury to the victim or any second or subsequent assault and battery,

b. any aggravated assault and battery,

c. any stalking pursuant to Section 1173 of this title, or a similar law of another state,

d. any violation of the Protection from Domestic Abuse Act or any violation of a victim protection order of another state,

e. any violation relating to illegal drug use or possession, or

f. an act of domestic abuse as defined by Section 644 of this title or an act of domestic assault and battery or any comparable acts under the law of another state.

The preclusive period shall be until the final determination of the matter. The preclusive period for a person subject to the provisions of a deferred sentence for the offenses mentioned in this paragraph shall be three (3) years and shall begin upon the final determination of the matter.

PRECLUSIVE PERIOD FOR DEFERRED SENTENCE

Title 21 O.S. § 1290.11 (2): The person is subject to the provisions of a deferred sentence or deferred prosecution in this state or another state or pursuant to federal authority for the commission of a felony offense. The preclusive period shall be three (3) years and shall begin upon the final determination of the matter;

PROCEDURE FOR APPLYING FOR SDA LICENSE

Title 21 O.S. § 1290.12: Except as provided in paragraph 11 of this subsection, the procedure for applying for a handgun license and processing the application shall be as follows:

1. An eligible person may request an application packet for a handgun license from the Oklahoma State Bureau of Investigation or the county sheriff's office either in person or by mail. The Bureau may provide application packets to each sheriff not exceeding two hundred packets per request. The Bureau shall provide the following information in the application packet:

a. an application form,

b. procedures to follow to process the application form, and

c. a copy of the Oklahoma Self-Defense Act with any modifications thereto;

2. The person shall be required to successfully complete a firearms safety and training course from a firearms instructor

who is approved and registered in this state as provided in Section 1290.14 of this title or from an interactive online firearms safety and training course available electronically via the Internet approved and certified by the Council on Law Enforcement Education and Training, and the person shall be required to demonstrate competency and qualification with a pistol authorized for concealed or unconcealed carry by the Oklahoma Self-Defense Act. The original certificate of successful completion of a firearms safety and training course and an original certificate of successful demonstration of competency and qualification to carry and handle a pistol shall be submitted with the application for a handgun license. No duplicate, copy, facsimile or other reproduction of the certificate of training, certificate of competency and qualification or exemption from training shall be acceptable as proof of training as required by the provisions of the Oklahoma Self-Defense Act. A person exempt from the training requirements as provided in Section 1290.15 of this title must show the required proof of such exemption to the firearms instructor to receive an exemption certificate. The original exemption certificate must be submitted with the application for a handgun license when the person claims an exemption from training and qualification;

3. The application form shall be completed and delivered by the applicant, in person, to the sheriff of the county wherein the applicant resides;

4. The person shall deliver to the sheriff at the time of delivery of the completed application form a fee of One Hundred Dollars ($100.00) for processing the application through the Oklahoma State Bureau of Investigation and processing the required fingerprints through the Federal Bureau of Investigation. The processing fee shall be in the form of:

a. a money order or a cashier's check made payable to the Oklahoma State Bureau of Investigation,

b. by a nationally recognized credit card issued to the applicant. For purposes of this paragraph, "nationally recognized credit card" means any instrument or device, whether known as a credit card, credit plate, charge plate, or by any other name, issued with or without fee by the issuer for the use of the cardholder in obtaining goods, services, or anything else of value on credit which is accepted by over one thousand merchants in the state. The Oklahoma State Bureau of Investigation shall determine which nationally recognized credit cards will be accepted by the Bureau, or

c. by electronic funds transfer.

Any person paying application fees to the Oklahoma State Bureau of Investigation by means of a nationally recognized credit card or by means of an electronic funds transfer shall be required to complete and submit his or her application through the online application process of the Bureau. The processing fee shall not be refundable in the event of a denial of a handgun license or any suspension or revocation subsequent to the issuance of a license. Persons making application for a firearms instructor shall not be required to pay the application fee as provided in this section, but shall be required to pay the costs provided in paragraphs 6 and 8 of this subsection;

5. The completed application form shall be signed by the applicant in person before the sheriff. The signature shall be given voluntarily upon a sworn oath that the person knows the contents of the application and that the information contained in the application is true and correct. Any person making any false or misleading statement on an application for a handgun license shall, upon conviction, be guilty of perjury as defined by Section 491 of this title. Any conviction shall be punished as provided in Section 500 of this title. In addition to a criminal conviction, the person shall be denied the right to have a handgun license pursuant to the provisions of Section 1290.10 of this title and the Oklahoma State Bureau of Investigation shall revoke the handgun license, if issued;

6. Two passport-size photographs of the applicant shall be submitted with the completed application. The cost of the photographs shall be the responsibility of the applicant. The sheriff is authorized to take the photograph of the applicant for purposes of the Oklahoma Self-Defense Act and, if such photographs are taken by the sheriff, the cost of the photographs shall not exceed Ten Dollars ($10.00) for the two photos. All money received by the sheriff from photographing applicants pursuant to the provisions of this paragraph shall be retained by the sheriff and deposited into the Sheriff's Service Fee Account;

7. The sheriff shall witness the signature of the applicant and review or take the photographs of the applicant and shall verify that the person making application for a handgun license is the same person in the photographs submitted and the same person who signed the application form. Proof of a valid Oklahoma driver license with a photograph of the applicant or an Oklahoma state photo identification for the applicant shall be required to be presented by the applicant to the sheriff for verification of the person's identity;

8. Upon verification of the identity of the applicant, the sheriff shall take two complete sets of fingerprints of the applicant. Both sets of fingerprints shall be submitted by the sheriff with the completed application, certificate of training or an exemption certificate, photographs and processing fee to the Oklahoma State Bureau of Investigation within fourteen (14) days of taking the fingerprints. The cost of the fingerprints shall be paid by the applicant and shall not exceed Twenty-five Dollars ($25.00) for the two sets. All fees collected by the sheriff from taking fingerprints pursuant to the provisions of this paragraph shall be retained by the sheriff and deposited into the Sheriff's Service Fee Account;

9. The sheriff shall submit to the Oklahoma State Bureau of Investigation within the fourteen-day period, together with the completed application, including the certificate of training,

certificate of competency and qualification or exemption certificate, photographs, processing fee and legible fingerprints meeting the Oklahoma State Bureau of Investigation's Automated Fingerprint Identification System (AFIS) submission standards, and a report of information deemed pertinent to an investigation of the applicant for a handgun license. The sheriff shall make a preliminary investigation of pertinent information about the applicant and the court clerk shall assist the sheriff in locating pertinent information in court records for this purpose. If no pertinent information is found to exist either for or against the applicant, the sheriff shall so indicate in the report;

10. The Oklahoma State Bureau of Investigation, upon receipt of the application and required information from the sheriff, shall forward one full set of fingerprints of the applicant to the Federal Bureau of Investigation for a national criminal history records search. The cost of processing the fingerprints nationally shall be paid from the processing fee collected by the Oklahoma State Bureau of Investigation;

11. Notwithstanding the provisions of the Oklahoma Self-Defense Act, or any other provisions of law, any person who has been granted a permanent victim's protective order by the court, as provided for in the Protection from Domestic Abuse Act, may be issued a temporary handgun license for a period not to exceed six (6) months. A temporary handgun license may be issued if the person has successfully passed the required weapons course, completed the application process for the handgun license, passed the preliminary investigation of the person by the sheriff and court clerk, and provided the sheriff proof of a certified permanent victim protection order and a valid Oklahoma state photo identification card or driver license. The sheriff shall issue a temporary handgun license on a form approved by the Oklahoma State Bureau of Investigation, at no cost. Any person who has been issued a temporary license shall carry the temporary handgun license and a valid Oklahoma state photo identification on his or her person at all times, and shall be subject to all the requirements of the Oklahoma Self-

Defense Act when carrying a handgun. The person may proceed with the handgun licensing process. In the event the victim's protection order is no longer enforceable, the temporary handgun license shall cease to be valid;

12. The Oklahoma State Bureau of Investigation shall make a reasonable effort to investigate the information submitted by the applicant and the sheriff, to ascertain whether or not the issuance of a handgun license would be in violation of the provisions of the Oklahoma Self-Defense Act. The investigation by the Bureau of an applicant shall include, but shall not be limited to: a statewide criminal history records search, a national criminal history records search, a Federal Bureau of Investigation fingerprint search, and if applicable, an investigation of medical records or other records or information deemed by the Bureau to be relevant to the application.

a. In the course of the investigation by the Bureau, it shall present the name of the applicant along with any known aliases, the address of the applicant and the social security number of the applicant to the Department of Mental Health and Substance Abuse Services. The Department of Mental Health and Substance Abuse Services shall respond within ten (10) days of receiving such information to the Bureau as follows:

(1) with a "Yes" answer, if the records of the Department indicate that the person was involuntarily committed to a mental institution in Oklahoma,

(2) with a "No" answer, if there are no records indicating the name of the person as a person involuntarily committed to a mental institution in Oklahoma, or

(3) with an "Inconclusive" answer if the records of the Department suggest the applicant may be a formerly committed person. In the case of an inconclusive answer, the Bureau shall ask the applicant whether he or she was involuntarily committed. If the applicant states under penalty

of perjury that he or she has not been involuntarily committed, the Bureau shall continue processing the application for a license.

b. In the course of the investigation by the Bureau, it shall check the name of any applicant who is twenty-eight (28) years of age or younger along with any known aliases, the address of the applicant and the social security number of the applicant against the records in the Juvenile Online Tracking System (JOLTS) of the Office of Juvenile Affairs. The Office of Juvenile Affairs shall provide the Bureau direct access to check the applicant against the records available on JOLTS.

(1) If the Bureau finds a record on the JOLTS that indicates the person was adjudicated a delinquent for an offense that would constitute a felony offense if committed by an adult within the last ten (10) years the Bureau shall deny the license,

(2) If the Bureau finds no record on the JOLTS indicating the named person was adjudicated delinquent for an offense that would constitute a felony offense if committed by an adult within the last ten (10) years, or

(3) If the records suggest the applicant may have been adjudicated delinquent for an offense that would constitute a felony offense if committed by an adult but such record is inconclusive, the Bureau shall ask the applicant whether he or she was adjudicated a delinquent for an offense that would constitute a felony offense if committed by an adult within the last ten (10) years. If the applicant states under penalty of perjury that he or she was not adjudicated a delinquent within ten (10) years, the Bureau shall continue processing the application for a license; and

13. If the background check set forth in paragraph 12 of this subsection reveals no records pertaining to the applicant, the Oklahoma State Bureau of Investigation shall either issue a handgun license or deny the application within sixty (60) days of the date of receipt of the applicant's completed application

and the required information from the sheriff. In all other cases, the Oklahoma State Bureau of Investigation shall either issue a handgun license or deny the application within ninety (90) days of the date of the receipt of the applicant's completed application and the required information from the sheriff. The Bureau shall approve an applicant who appears to be in full compliance with the provisions of the Oklahoma Self-Defense Act, if completion of the federal fingerprint search is the only reason for delay of the issuance of the handgun license to that applicant. Upon receipt of the federal fingerprint search information, if the Bureau receives information which precludes the person from having a handgun license, the Bureau shall revoke the handgun license previously issued to the applicant. The Bureau shall deny a license when the applicant fails to properly complete the application form or application process or is determined not to be eligible as specified by the provisions of Section 1290.9, 1290.10 or 1290.11 of this title. The Bureau shall approve an application in all other cases. If an application is denied, the Bureau shall notify the applicant in writing of its decision. The notification shall state the grounds for the denial and inform the applicant of the right to an appeal as may be provided by the provisions of the Administrative Procedures Act. All notices of denial shall be mailed by first-class mail to the address of the applicant listed in the application. Within sixty (60) calendar days from the date of mailing a denial of application to an applicant, the applicant shall notify the Bureau in writing of the intent to appeal the decision of denial or the right of the applicant to appeal shall be deemed waived. Any administrative hearing on a denial which may be provided shall be conducted by a hearing examiner appointed by the Bureau. The decision of the hearing examiner shall be a final decision appealable to a district court in accordance with the Administrative Procedures Act. When an application is approved, the Bureau shall issue the license and shall mail the license by first-class mail to the address of the applicant listed in the application.

COMPLETED APPLICATION FORM

Title 21 O.S. § 1290.12 paragraph 5: The completed application form shall be signed by the applicant in person before the sheriff. The signature shall be given voluntarily upon a sworn oath that the person knows the contents of the application and that the information contained in the application is true and correct. Any person making any false or misleading statement on an application for a handgun license shall, upon conviction, be guilty of perjury as defined by Section 491 of this title. Any conviction shall be punished as provided in Section 500 of this title. In addition to a criminal conviction, the person shall be denied the right to have a handgun license pursuant to the provisions of Section 1290.10 of this title and the Oklahoma State Bureau of Investigation shall revoke the handgun license, if issued;

COMPLETE FIREARMS SAFETY COURSE

Title 21 O.S. § 1290.14: Each applicant for a license to carry a concealed or unconcealed handgun pursuant to the Oklahoma Self-Defense Act must successfully complete a firearms safety and training course in this state conducted by a registered and approved firearms instructor as provided by the provisions of this section or from an interactive online firearms safety and training course available electronically via the Internet approved and certified by the Council on Law Enforcement Education and Training. The applicant must further demonstrate competence and qualification with an authorized pistol of the type or types that the applicant desires to carry as a concealed or unconcealed handgun pursuant to the provisions of the Oklahoma Self-Defense Act, except certain persons may be exempt from such training requirement as provided by the provisions of Section 1290.15 of this title.

OSBI SUSPENSION OF LICENSE

Title 21 O.S. § 1290.17: The Oklahoma State Bureau of Investigation shall have authority pursuant to the provisions of the Oklahoma Self-Defense Act and any other provision of law to suspend or revoke any handgun license issued pursuant to the provisions of the Oklahoma Self-Defense Act. A person whose license has been suspended or revoked or against whom a fine has been assessed shall be entitled to an appeal through a hearing in accordance with the Administrative Procedures Act. Any administrative hearing on suspensions, revocations or fines shall be conducted by a hearing examiner appointed by the Bureau. The hearing examiner's decision shall be a final decision appealable to a district court in accordance with the Administrative Procedures Act. After a handgun license has been issued, the discovery of or the occurrence of any condition which directly affects a person's eligibility for a handgun license as provided by the provisions of Section 1290.9 or 1290.10 of this title shall require a revocation of the license by the Bureau. The discovery of or the occurrence of any condition pursuant to Section 1290.11 of this title, after a license has been issued, shall cause a suspension of the handgun license for a period of time as prescribed for the condition. Any provision of law that requires a revocation of a handgun license upon a conviction shall cause the Bureau to suspend the handgun license upon the discovery of the arrest of the person for such offense until a determination of the criminal case at which time the Bureau shall proceed with the appropriate administrative action. A licensee may voluntarily surrender a license to the Oklahoma State Bureau of Investigation at any time. Such surrender of a handgun license will render the license invalid. Nothing in this section may be interpreted to prevent a subsequent new application for a license. The licensee shall be informed and acknowledge in writing as follows:

1. The licensee understands that the voluntary surrender of the license will not be deemed a suspension or revocation by the Bureau;

2. A voluntary surrender of a license will not be review-able by a hearing examiner or subject to judicial review under the Administrative Procedures Act; and

3. By surrendering the license, the licensee shall forfeit all fees paid to date.

SURRENDER OF LICENSE TO OSBI

Title 21 O.S. § 1290.17 (A): The Oklahoma State Bureau of Investigation shall have authority pursuant to the provisions of the Oklahoma Self-Defense Act and any other provision of law to suspend or revoke any handgun license issued pursuant to the provisions of the Oklahoma Self-Defense Act. A person whose license has been suspended or revoked or against whom a fine has been assessed shall be entitled to an appeal through a hearing in accordance with the Administrative Procedures Act. Any administrative hearing on suspensions, revocations or fines shall be conducted by a hearing examiner appointed by the Bureau. The hearing examiner's decision shall be a final decision appealable to a district court in accordance with the Administrative Procedures Act. After a handgun license has been issued, the discovery of or the occurrence of any condition which directly affects a person's eligibility for a handgun license as provided by the provisions of Section 1290.9 or 1290.10 of this title shall require a revocation of the license by the Bureau. The discovery of or the occurrence of any condition pursuant to Section 1290.11 of this title, after a license has been issued, shall cause a suspension of the handgun license for a period of time as prescribed for the condition. Any provision of law that requires a revocation of a handgun license upon a conviction shall cause the Bureau to suspend the handgun license upon the discovery of the arrest of the person for such offense until a determination of the criminal case at which time the Bureau shall proceed with the appropriate administrative action. A licensee may voluntarily surrender a license to the Oklahoma State Bureau of Investigation at any time. Such surrender of a handgun license will render the license invalid. Nothing in this section may be interpreted to prevent a subsequent new application for a license. The licensee shall be informed and acknowledge in writing as follows:

1. The licensee understands that the voluntary surrender of the license will not be deemed a suspension or revocation by the Bureau;

2. A voluntary surrender of a license will not be review-able by a hearing examiner or subject to judicial review under the Administrative Procedures Act; and

3. By surrendering the license, the licensee shall forfeit all fees paid to date

REINSTATEMENT OF LICENSE

Title 21 O.S. § 1290.17(E): Whenever a handgun license has been suspended in accordance with the provisions of this act or the administrative rules of the Bureau promulgated for purposes of this act, the license shall remain under suspension and shall not be reinstated until:

1. The person whose license has been suspended applies for reinstatement in accordance with the administrative rules of the Bureau. The Bureau shall not charge any fee in conjunction with an application for a license reinstatement. The person whose license has been suspended must demonstrate that the condition or preclusion which was the basis for the suspension has lapsed and is no longer in effect; and

2. Any and all administrative fines assessed against the person have been paid in full.

In the event a handgun license expires during the term of the suspension, the person shall be required to apply for renewal of the license in accordance with Section 1290.5 of this title.

FORM OF APPLICATION

Title 21 O.S. § 1290.18: The application shall be completed upon the sworn oath of the applicant as provided in paragraph 5 of Section 1290.12 of this title. The application form shall be provided by the Oklahoma State Bureau of Investigation and shall contain the following information in addition to any other information deemed relevant by the Bureau:

1. Applicant's full legal name;

2. Applicant's birth name, alias names or nicknames;

3. Maiden name, if applicable;

4. County of residence;

5. Length of residency at the current address;

6. Previous addresses for the preceding three (3) years;

7. Place of birth;

8. Date of birth;

9. Declaration of citizenship and date United States citizenship was acquired, if applicable;

10. Race;

11. Weight;

12. Height;

13. Sex;

14. Color of eyes;

15. Current driver license number;

16. Military service number, if applicable;

17. Law enforcement identification numbers, if applicable;

18. Current occupation;

19. Authorized type or types of pistol for which the applicant qualified as stated on the certificate of training or exemption of

training which shall be stated as either derringer, revolver, semiautomatic pistol, or some combination of derringer, revolver and semiautomatic pistol and the maximum ammunition capacity of the firearm shall be .45 caliber;

20. An acknowledgment that the applicant desires a handgun license as a means of lawful self-defense and self-protection and for no other intent or purpose;

21. A statement that the applicant has never been convicted of any felony offense in this state, another state or pursuant to any federal offense;

22. A statement that the applicant has none of the conditions which would preclude the issuing of a handgun license pursuant to any of the provisions of Sections 1290.10 and 1290.11 of this title and that the applicant further meets all of the eligibility criteria required by Section 1290.9 of this title;

23. An authorization for the Oklahoma State Bureau of Investigation to investigate the applicant and any or all records relating to the applicant for purposes of approving or denying a handgun license pursuant to the provisions of the Oklahoma Self-Defense Act;

24. An acknowledgment that the applicant has been furnished a copy of the Oklahoma Self-Defense Act and is knowledgeable about its provisions;

25. A statement that the applicant is the identical person who completed the firearms training course for which the original training certificate is submitted as part of the application or a statement that the applicant is the identical person who is exempt from firearms training for which the original exemption certificate is submitted as part of the application, whichever is applicable to the applicant;

26. A conspicuous warning that the application is executed upon the sworn oath of the applicant and that any false or misleading answer to any question or the submission of any

false information or documentation by the applicant is punishable by criminal penalty as provided in paragraph 5 of Section 1290.12 of this title;

27. A signed verification that the contents of the application are known to the applicant and are true and correct;

28. Two separate places for the original signature of the applicant;

29. A place for attachment of a passport size photograph of the applicant; and

30. A place for the signature and verification of the identity of the applicant by the sheriff or the sheriff's designee.

Information provided by the person on an application for a handgun license shall be confidential except to law enforcement officers or law enforcement agencies

MENTAL INCOMPETENCY OF LICENSEE

Title 21 O.S. § 1290.27: When a court adjudicates a person mentally incompetent or orders the involuntary commitment of a person due to a mental illness, condition or disorder under the laws of this state by which a person becomes subject to the provisions of Section 922(d)(4) and (g)(4) of Title 18 of the United States Code, the clerk of the court shall forward a certified copy of the order or adjudication to the Federal Bureau of Investigation or its successor agency for the sole purpose of inclusion in the National Instant Criminal Background Check System database and to the Oklahoma State Bureau of Investigation. The clerk of the court shall also notify the person of the prohibitions contained within the provisions of Section 922(d)(4) and (g)(4) of Title 18 of the United States Code, paragraph 3 of Section 1290.10 or paragraph 3 of subsection A of Section 1290.11 of Title 21 of the Oklahoma Statutes.

DRINKING INTOXICANTS IN PUBLIC

Title 37 O.S. § 8: Except as provided in Section 2 of this act, any person who shall, in any public place, or in or upon any passenger coach, streetcar, or in or upon any other vehicle commonly used for the transportation of passengers, or in or about any depot, platform, waiting station or room, drink or otherwise consume any intoxicating liquor unless authorized by the Oklahoma Alcoholic Beverage Control Act, intoxicating substance, or intoxicating compound of any kind, or inhale glue, paint or other intoxicating substance, or if any person shall be drunk or intoxicated in any public or private road, or in any passenger coach, streetcar, or any public place or building, or at any public gathering, from drinking or consuming such intoxicating liquor, intoxicating substance or intoxicating compound or from inhalation of glue, paint or other intoxicating substance, or if any person shall be drunk or intoxicated from any cause and shall disturb the peace of any person, he shall be guilty of a misdemeanor, and upon conviction thereof shall be punished by a fine of not less than Ten Dollars ($10.00), nor more than One Hundred Dollars ($100.00), or by imprisonment for not less than five (5) days nor more than thirty (30) days, or by both such fine and imprisonment.

INVOLUNTARY CONFINEMENT

Title 43A O.S. § 5-410: The following persons may file or request the district attorney to file a petition with the district court, upon which is hereby conferred jurisdiction, to determine whether an individual is a person requiring treatment, and to order the least restrictive appropriate treatment for the person:

1. A treatment advocate as defined in Section 1-109.1 of this title;

2. The father, mother, husband, wife, grandparent, brother, sister, guardian or child, over the age of eighteen (18) years, of an individual alleged to be a person requiring treatment;

3. A licensed mental health professional;

4. A person in charge of any correctional institution;

5. Any peace officer within the county in which the individual alleged to be a person requiring treatment resides or may be found; or

6. The district attorney in whose district the person resides or may be found.

ADMINISTRATIVE PROCEDURE ACT

Title 75 O.S. § 250: This section and sections 250.1 through 323 of this title shall be known and may be cited as the "Administrative Procedures Act"

CHAPTER 9:

UNLAWFUL TO CARRY LISTED WEAPONS

Title 21 O.S. § 1272(A)(1): A. It shall be unlawful for any person to carry upon or about his or her person, or in a purse or other container belonging to the person, any pistol, revolver, shotgun or rifle whether loaded or unloaded or any dagger, bowie knife, dirk knife, sword cane, blackjack, loaded cane, billy, hand chain, metal knuckles, or any other offensive weapon, whether such weapon be concealed or unconcealed, except this section shall not prohibit:

1. The proper use of guns and knives for hunting, fishing, educational or recreational purposes;

UNLAWFUL TO CARRY WEAPONS WHERE BEER IS CONSUMED

Title 21 O.S. § 1272.1(A): A. It shall be unlawful for any person to carry or possess any weapon designated in Section 1272 of this title in any establishment where low-point beer, as defined by Section 163.2 of Title 37 of the Oklahoma Statutes, or alcoholic beverages, as defined by Section 506 of Title 37 of the Oklahoma Statutes, are consumed. This provision shall not apply to a peace officer, as defined in Section 99 of this title, or to private investigators with a firearms authorization when acting in the scope and course of employment, and shall not apply to an owner or proprietor of the establishment having a pistol, rifle, or shotgun on the premises. Provided however, a person possessing a valid handgun license pursuant to the provisions of the Oklahoma Self-Defense Act may carry the concealed or unconcealed handgun into any restaurant or other establishment licensed to dispense low-point beer or alcoholic beverages where the sale of low-point beer or alcoholic beverages does not constitute the primary purpose of the business.

Provided further, nothing in this section shall be interpreted to authorize any peace officer in actual physical possession of a weapon to consume low-point beer or alcoholic beverages, except in the authorized line of duty as an undercover officer.

Nothing in this section shall be interpreted to authorize any private investigator with a firearms authorization in actual physical possession of a weapon to consume low-point beer or alcoholic beverages in any establishment where low-point beer or alcoholic beverages are consumed.

PROHIBITED PLACES SDA

Title 21 O.S. § 1277: A. It shall be unlawful for any person in possession of a valid handgun license issued pursuant to the provisions of the Oklahoma Self-Defense Act to carry any concealed or unconcealed handgun into any of the following places:

1. Any structure, building, or office space which is owned or leased by a city, town, county, state or federal governmental authority for the purpose of conducting business with the public;

2. Any prison, jail, detention facility or any facility used to process, hold or house arrested persons, prisoners or persons alleged delinquent or adjudicated delinquent, except as provided in Section 21 of Title 57 of the Oklahoma Statutes;

3. Any public or private elementary or public or private secondary school, except as provided in subsections C and D of this section;

4. Any sports arena during a professional sporting event;

5. Any place where pari-mutuel wagering is authorized by law; and

6. Any other place specifically prohibited by law.

B. For purposes of paragraphs 1, 2, 3, 4 and 5 of subsection A of this section, the prohibited place does not include and specifically excludes the following property:

1. Any property set aside for the use or parking of any vehicle, whether attended or unattended, by a city, town, county, state or federal governmental authority;

2. Any property set aside for the use or parking of any vehicle, whether attended or unattended, by any entity offering any professional sporting event which is open to the public for admission, or by any entity engaged in pari-mutuel wagering authorized by law;

3. Any property adjacent to a structure, building or office space in which concealed or unconcealed weapons are prohibited by the provisions of this section;

4. Any property designated by a city, town, county or state governmental authority as a park, recreational area, or fairgrounds; provided, nothing in this paragraph shall be construed to authorize any entry by a person in possession of a concealed or unconcealed handgun into any structure, building or office space which is specifically prohibited by the provisions of subsection A of this section; and

5. Any property set aside by a public or private elementary or secondary school for the use or parking of any vehicle, whether attended or unattended; provided, however, said handgun shall be stored and hidden from view in a locked motor vehicle when the motor vehicle is left unattended on school property.

Nothing contained in any provision of this subsection or subsection C of this section shall be construed to authorize or allow any person in control of any place described in paragraph 1, 2, 3, 4 or 5 of subsection A of this section to establish any policy or rule that has the effect of prohibiting any person in lawful possession of a handgun license from possession of a handgun allowable under such license in places described in paragraph 1, 2, 3, 4 or 5 of this subsection.

C. A concealed or unconcealed weapon may be carried onto private school property or in any school bus or vehicle used by any private school for transportation of students or teachers by a person who is licensed pursuant to the Oklahoma Self-Defense Act, provided a policy has been adopted by the governing entity of the private school that authorizes the carrying and possession of a weapon on private school property or in any school bus or vehicle used by a private school. Except for acts of gross negligence or willful or wanton misconduct, a governing entity of a private school that adopts a policy which authorizes the possession of a weapon on private school property, a school bus or vehicle used by the private school shall be immune from liability for any injuries arising from the adoption of the policy. The provisions of this subsection shall not apply to claims pursuant to the Workers' Compensation Code.

D. Notwithstanding paragraph 3 of subsection A of this section, a board of education of a school district may adopt a policy pursuant to Section 5-149.2 of Title 70 of the Oklahoma Statutes to authorize the carrying of a handgun onto school property by school personnel specifically designated by the board of education, provided such personnel either:

1. Possess a valid armed security guard license as provided for in Section 1750.1 et seq. of Title 59 of the Oklahoma Statutes; or

2. Hold a valid reserve peace officer certification as provided for in Section 3311 of Title 70 of the Oklahoma Statutes.

Nothing in this subsection shall be construed to restrict authority granted elsewhere in law to carry firearms.

E. Any person violating the provisions of subsection A of this section shall, upon conviction, be guilty of a misdemeanor punishable by a fine not to exceed Two Hundred Fifty Dollars ($250.00).

F. No person in possession of a valid handgun license issued pursuant to the provisions of the Oklahoma Self-Defense Act shall be authorized to carry the handgun into or upon any college, university or technology center school property, except as provided in this subsection. For purposes of this subsection, the following property shall not be construed as prohibited for persons having a valid handgun license:

1. Any property set aside for the use or parking of any vehicle, whether attended or unattended, provided the handgun is carried or stored as required by law and the handgun is not removed from the vehicle without the prior consent of the college or university president or technology center school administrator while the vehicle is on any college, university or technology center school property;

2. Any property authorized for possession or use of handguns by college, university or technology center school policy; and

3. Any property authorized by the written consent of the college or university president or technology center school administrator, provided the written consent is carried with the handgun and the valid handgun license while on college, university or technology center school property.

The college, university or technology center school may notify the Oklahoma State Bureau of Investigation within ten (10) days of a violation of any provision of this subsection by a licensee. Upon receipt of a written notification of violation, the Bureau shall give a reasonable notice to the licensee and hold a hearing. At the hearing, upon a determination that the licensee has violated any provision of this subsection, the licensee may be subject to an administrative fine of Two Hundred Fifty Dollars ($250.00) and may have the handgun license suspended for three (3) months.

Nothing contained in any provision of this subsection shall be construed to authorize or allow any college, university or technology center school to establish any policy or rule that has the effect of prohibiting any person in lawful possession of a handgun license from possession of a handgun allowable under such license in places described in paragraphs 1, 2 and 3 of this subsection. Nothing contained in any provision of this subsection shall be construed to limit the authority of any college, university or technology center school in this state from taking administrative action against any student for any violation of any provision of this subsection.

G. The provisions of this section shall not apply to any peace officer or to any person authorized by law to carry a pistol in the course of employment. District judges, associate district judges and special district judges, who are in possession of a valid handgun license issued pursuant to the provisions of the Oklahoma Self-Defense Act and whose names appear on a list maintained by the Administrative Director of the Courts, shall be exempt from this section when acting in the course and scope of employment within the courthouses of this state. Private investigators with a firearms authorization shall be exempt from this section when acting in the course and scope of employment.

H. For the purposes of this section, "motor vehicle" means any automobile, truck, minivan or sports utility vehicle.

Title 21 O.S. § 1277(E): Any person violating the provisions of subsection A of this section shall, upon conviction, be guilty of a misdemeanor punishable by a fine not to exceed Two Hundred Fifty Dollars ($250.00)

<u>NO PERSON MAY PROHIBIT THE LEGAL STORING OF FIREARMS</u>

Title 21 O.S. § 1289.7(a): A. No person, property owner, tenant, employer, or business entity shall maintain, establish, or enforce any policy or rule that has the effect of prohibiting any person, except a convicted felon, from transporting and storing firearms or ammunition in a locked motor vehicle, or from transporting and storing firearms or ammunition locked in or locked to a motor vehicle on any property set aside for any motor vehicle.

B. No person, property owner, tenant, employer, or business entity shall be liable in any civil action for occurrences which result from the storing of firearms or ammunition in a locked motor vehicle on any property set aside for any motor vehicle, unless the person, property owner, tenant, employer, or owner of the business entity commits a criminal act involving the use of the firearms or ammunition. The provisions of this subsection shall not apply to claims pursuant to the Workers' Compensation Act.

C. An individual may bring a civil action to enforce this section. If a plaintiff prevails in a civil action related to the personnel manual against a person, property owner, tenant, employer or business for a violation of this section, the court shall award actual damages, enjoin further violations of this section, and award court costs and attorney fees to the prevailing plaintiff.

D. As used in this section, "motor vehicle" means any automobile, truck, minivan, sports utility vehicle, motorcycle, motor scooter, and any other vehicle required to be registered under the Oklahoma Vehicle License and Registration Act

NO PERSON MAY PROHIBIT THE LEGAL STORING OF AMMUNITION ACCORDING TO LAW

Title 21 O.S. § 1289.7a(A): No person, property owner, tenant, employer, or business entity shall maintain, establish, or enforce any policy or rule that has the effect of prohibiting any person, except a convicted felon, from transporting and storing firearms or ammunition in a locked motor vehicle, or from transporting and storing firearms or ammunition locked in or locked to a motor vehicle on any property set aside for any motor vehicle.

UNCONCEALED HANDGUN DEFINED

Title 21 O.S. § 1290(A)(2): "Unconcealed handgun" means a loaded or unloaded pistol carried upon the person in a belt holster or shoulder holster that is wholly or partially visible, or carried upon the person in a scabbard or case designed for carrying firearms that is wholly or partially visible;

CONCEALED AND UNCONCEALED CARRY AUTHORIZED

Title 21 O.S. §1290.4: As provided by Section 1272 of this title, it is unlawful for any person to carry a concealed or unconcealed handgun in this state, except as hereby authorized by the provisions of the Oklahoma Self-Defense Act or as may otherwise be provided by law.

CONCEALED AND UNCONCEALED CARRY WHILE BOW HUNTING AND FISHING, MUST IDENTIFY SELF AS ARMED TO POLICE AUTHORITIES

Title 21 O.S. § 1290.8: A. Except as otherwise prohibited by law, an eligible person shall have authority to carry a concealed or unconcealed handgun in this state when the person has been issued a handgun license from the Oklahoma State Bureau of Investigation pursuant to the provisions of the Oklahoma Self-Defense Act, provided the person is in compliance with the provisions of the Oklahoma Self-Defense

Act, and the license has not expired or been subsequently suspended or revoked. A person in possession of a valid handgun license and in compliance with the provisions of the Oklahoma Self-Defense Act shall be authorized to carry such concealed or unconcealed handgun while bow hunting or fishing.

B. The person shall be required to have possession of his or her valid handgun license and a valid Oklahoma driver license or an Oklahoma State photo identification at all times when in possession of an authorized pistol. The person shall display the handgun license on demand of a law enforcement officer; provided, however, that in the absence of reasonable and articulable suspicion of other criminal activity, an individual carrying an unconcealed or concealed handgun shall not be disarmed or physically restrained unless the individual fails to display a valid handgun license in response to that demand. Any violation of the provisions of this subsection may be punishable as a criminal offense as authorized by Section 1272 of this title or pursuant to any other applicable provision of law. Any second or subsequent violation of the provisions of this subsection shall be grounds for the Bureau to suspend the handgun license for a period of six (6) months, in addition to any other penalty imposed.

Upon the arrest of any person for a violation of the provisions of this subsection, the person may show proof to the court that a valid handgun license and the other required identification has been issued to such person and the person may state any reason why the handgun license or the other required identification was not carried by the person as required by the Oklahoma Self-Defense Act. The court shall dismiss an alleged violation of Section 1272 of this title upon payment of court costs, if proof of a valid handgun license and other required identification is shown to the court within ten (10) days of the arrest of the person. The court shall report a dismissal of a charge to the Bureau for consideration of administrative proceedings against the licensee.

C. It shall be unlawful for any person to fail or refuse to identify the fact that the person is in actual possession of a concealed or unconcealed handgun pursuant to the authority of the Oklahoma Self-Defense Act when the person comes into contact with any law enforcement officer of this state or its political subdivisions or a federal law enforcement officer during the course of any arrest, detainment, or routine traffic stop. Said identification to the law enforcement officer shall be made at the first opportunity. No person shall be required to identify himself or herself as a handgun licensee when no handgun is in the possession of the person or in any vehicle in which the person is driving or is a passenger. Any violation of the provisions of this subsection shall, upon conviction, be a misdemeanor punishable by a fine not exceeding One Hundred Dollars ($100.00).

D. Any law enforcement officer coming in contact with a person whose handgun license is suspended, revoked, or expired, or who is in possession of a handgun license which has not been lawfully issued to that person, shall confiscate the license and return it to the Oklahoma State Bureau of Investigation for appropriate administrative proceedings against the licensee when the license is no longer needed as evidence in any criminal proceeding.

E. Nothing in this section shall be construed to authorize a law enforcement officer to inspect any weapon properly concealed or unconcealed without probable cause that a crime has been committed.

PRECLUSION PERIOD FOR INPATIENT TREATMENT

Title 21 O.S. § 1290.11(A)(5): Inpatient treatment for substance abuse. The preclusive period shall be three (3) years from the last date of treatment or upon presentation of a certified statement from a licensed physician stating that the person has been free from substance use for twelve (12) months or more preceding the filing of an application for a handgun license;

PREMISES OWNER MAY RESTRICT CONCEAL CARRY ON PREMISES

Title 21 O.S. §1290.22: Except as provided in subsection B of this section, nothing contained in any provision of the Oklahoma Self-Defense Act shall be construed to limit, restrict or prohibit in any manner the existing rights of any person, property owner, tenant, employer, place of worship or business entity to control the possession of weapons on any property owned or controlled by the person or business entity.

SIGNS MAY BE POSTED RESTRICTING THE CARRY OF FIREARMS ON PREMISES

Title 21 O.S. § 1290.22(C): A property owner, tenant, employer, place of worship or business entity may prohibit any person from carrying a concealed or unconcealed firearm on the property. If the building or property is open to the public, the property owner, tenant, employer, place of worship or business entity shall post signs on or about the property stating such prohibition.

BUS IS A PROHIBITED VEHICLE FROM BOARDING

Title 21 O.S. § 1903(D): No person, other than an authorized law enforcement officer, shall board a bus with a dangerous or deadly weapon concealed upon or about his person. Upon the discovery of any such item or material, the company may obtain possession and retain custody of such item or material until it is transferred to the custody of law enforcement officers. Any person convicted of violating this subsection shall be guilty of a felony, and shall, upon conviction, be imprisoned for not more than ten (10) years, or fined not more than Ten Thousand Dollars ($10,000.00), or both.

DUI DEFINED

Title 47 O.S. § 11-902: It is unlawful and punishable as provided in this section for any person to drive, operate, or be in actual physical control of a motor vehicle within this state, whether upon public roads, highways, streets, turnpikes, other public places or upon any private road, street, alley or lane which provides access to one or more single or multi-family dwellings, who:

1. Has a blood or breath alcohol concentration, as defined in Section 756 of this title, of eight-hundredths (0.08) or more at the time of a test of such person's blood or breath administered within two (2) hours after the arrest of such person;

2. Is under the influence of alcohol;

3. Has any amount of a Schedule I chemical or controlled substance, as defined in Section 2-204 of Title 63 of the Oklahoma Statutes, or one of its metabolites or analogs in the person's blood, saliva, urine or any other bodily fluid at the time of a test of such person's blood, saliva, urine or any other bodily fluid administered within two (2) hours after the arrest of such person;

4. Is under the influence of any intoxicating substance other than alcohol which may render such person incapable of safely driving or operating a motor vehicle; or

5. Is under the combined influence of alcohol and any other intoxicating substance which may render such person incapable of safely driving or operating a motor vehicle.

CHAPTER 10:
CHILD ENDANGERMENT AND DEFENSE DEFINED

Title 21 O.S. § 852.1: A person who is the parent, guardian, or person having custody or control over a child as defined in Section 1-1-105 of Title 10A of the Oklahoma Statutes, commits child endangerment when the person:

1. Knowingly permits physical or sexual abuse of a child;

2. Knowingly permits a child to be present at a location where a controlled dangerous substance is being manufactured or attempted to be manufactured as defined in Section 2-101 of Title 63 of the Oklahoma Statutes;

3. Knowingly permits a child to be present in a vehicle when the person knows or should have known that the operator of the vehicle is impaired by or is under the influence of alcohol or another intoxicating substance; or

4. Is the driver, operator, or person in physical control of a vehicle in violation of Section 11-902 of Title 47 of the Oklahoma Statutes while transporting or having in the vehicle such child or children.

However, it is an affirmative defense to this paragraph if the person had a reasonable apprehension that any action to stop the physical or sexual abuse or deny permission for the child to be in the vehicle with an intoxicated person would result in substantial bodily harm to the person or the child.

Nothing in this subsection shall prohibit the prosecution of a person pursuant to the provisions of Section 11-902 or 11-904 of Title 47 of the Oklahoma Statutes.

B. The provisions of this section shall not apply to any parent, guardian or other person having custody or control of a child for the sole reason that the parent, guardian or other person in good faith selects and depends upon spiritual means or prayer for the treatment or cure of disease or remedial care for such child. This subsection shall in no way limit or modify the protections afforded said child in Section 852 of this title or Section 1-4-904 of Title 10A of the Oklahoma Statutes.

C. Any person convicted of violating any provision of this section shall be guilty of a felony punishable by imprisonment in the custody of the Department of Corrections for a term of not more than four (4) years, or by a fine not exceeding Five Thousand Dollars ($5,000.00), or by both such fine and imprisonment.

EXCEPTIONS TO PROHIBITIONS OF §1272

Title 21 O.S. §1272A: A. It shall be unlawful for any person to carry upon or about his or her person, or in a purse or other container belonging to the person, any pistol, revolver, shotgun or rifle whether loaded or unloaded or any dagger, bowie knife, dirk knife, sword cane, blackjack, loaded cane, billy, hand chain, metal knuckles, or any other offensive weapon, whether such weapon be concealed or unconcealed, except this section shall not prohibit:

1. The proper use of guns and knives for hunting, fishing, educational or recreational purposes;

2. The carrying or use of weapons in a manner otherwise permitted by statute or authorized by the Oklahoma Self-Defense Act;

3. The carrying, possession and use of any weapon by a peace officer or other person authorized by law to carry a weapon in the performance of official duties and in compliance with the rules of the employing agency;

4. The carrying or use of weapons in a courthouse by a district judge, associate district judge or special district judge within this state, who is in possession of a valid handgun license issued pursuant to the provisions of the Oklahoma Self-Defense Act and whose name appears on a list maintained by the Administrative Director of the Courts; or

5. The carrying and use of firearms and other weapons provided in this subsection when used for the purpose of living history re-enactment. For purposes of this paragraph, "living history re-enactment" means depiction of historical characters, scenes, historical life or events for entertainment, education, or historical documentation through the wearing or use of period, historical, antique or vintage clothing, accessories, firearms, weapons, and other implements of the historical period.

CARRYING OF WEAPONS OTHERWISE LAWFUL

Title 21 O.S. § 1272(A)(2): A. It shall be unlawful for any person to carry upon or about his or her person, or in a purse or other container belonging to the person, any pistol, revolver, shotgun or rifle whether loaded or unloaded or any dagger, bowie knife, dirk knife, sword cane, blackjack, loaded cane, billy, hand chain, metal knuckles, or any other offensive weapon, whether such weapon be concealed or unconcealed, except this section shall not prohibit:

2. The carrying or use of weapons in a manner otherwise permitted by statute or authorized by the Oklahoma Self-Defense Act.

CARRYING OF PROHIBITED WEAPONS LAWFUL FOR POLICE

Title 21 O.S. § 1272.1: A. It shall be unlawful for any person to carry or possess any weapon designated in Section 1272 of this title in any establishment where low-point beer, as defined by Section 163.2 of Title 37 of the Oklahoma Statutes, or alcoholic beverages, as defined by Section 506 of Title 37 of the Oklahoma Statutes, are consumed. This provision shall not apply to a peace officer, as defined in Section 99 of this title, or to private investigators with a firearms authorization when acting in the scope and course of employment, and shall not apply to an owner or proprietor of the establishment having a pistol, rifle, or shotgun on the premises. Provided however, a person possessing a valid handgun license pursuant to the provisions of the Oklahoma Self-Defense Act may carry the concealed or unconcealed handgun into any restaurant or other establishment licensed to dispense low-point beer or alcoholic beverages where the sale of low-point beer or alcoholic beverages does not constitute the primary purpose of the business.

Provided further, nothing in this section shall be interpreted to authorize any peace officer in actual physical possession of a weapon to consume low-point beer or alcoholic beverages, except in the authorized line of duty as an undercover officer.

Nothing in this section shall be interpreted to authorize any private investigator with a firearms authorization in actual physical possession of a weapon to consume low-point beer or alcoholic beverages in any establishment where low-point beer or alcoholic beverages are consumed.

B. Any person violating the provisions of this section shall be punished as provided in Section 1272.2 of this title.

<u>EXCEPTIONS TO PROHIBITED PLACES FOR CARRYING FIREARMS</u>

Title 21 O.S. §1277 F: F. No person in possession of a valid handgun license issued pursuant to the provisions of the Oklahoma Self-Defense Act shall be authorized to carry the handgun into or upon any college, university or technology center school property, except as provided in this subsection. For purposes of this subsection, the following property shall not be construed as prohibited for persons having a valid handgun license:

1. Any property set aside for the use or parking of any vehicle, whether attended or unattended, provided the handgun is carried or stored as required by law and the handgun is not removed from the vehicle without the prior consent of the college or university president or technology center school administrator while the vehicle is on any college, university or technology center school property;

2. Any property authorized for possession or use of handguns by college, university or technology center school policy; and

3. Any property authorized by the written consent of the college or university president or technology center school administrator, provided the written consent is carried with the handgun and the valid handgun license while on college, university or technology center school property.

The college, university or technology center school may notify the Oklahoma State Bureau of Investigation within ten (10) days of a violation of any provision of this subsection by a licensee. Upon receipt of a written notification of violation, the Bureau shall give a reasonable notice to the licensee and hold a hearing. At the hearing, upon a determination that the licensee has violated any provision of this subsection, the licensee may be subject to an administrative fine of Two Hundred Fifty Dollars ($250.00) and may have the handgun license suspended for three (3) months.

Nothing contained in any provision of this subsection shall be construed to authorize or allow any college, university or technology center school to establish any policy or rule that has the effect of prohibiting any person in lawful possession of a handgun license from possession of a handgun allowable under such license in places described in paragraphs 1, 2 and 3 of this subsection. Nothing contained in any provision of this subsection shall be construed to limit the authority of any college, university or technology center school in this state from taking administrative action against any student for any violation of any provision of this subsection.

EXCEPTION FOR CARRYING FIREARM WITHOUT A LICENSE

Title 21 O.S. § 1289.6(A)(1): A. A person shall be permitted to carry loaded and unloaded shotguns, rifles and pistols, open and not concealed and without a handgun license as authorized by the Oklahoma Self-Defense Act pursuant to the following conditions:

1. When hunting animals or fowl;

CARRYING WITHOUT A LICENSE

Title 21 O.S. § 1289.6(A)(2): 2. During competition in or practicing in a safety or hunter safety class, target shooting, skeet, trap or other recognized sporting events;

CARRYING WITHOUT A LICENSE

Title 21 O.S. §1289.6 B: B. A person shall be permitted to carry unloaded shotguns, rifles and pistols, open and not concealed and without a handgun license as authorized by the Oklahoma Self-Defense Act pursuant to the following conditions:

1. When going to or from the person's private residence or vehicle or a vehicle in which the person is riding as a passenger to a place designated or authorized for firearms repairs or reconditioning, or for firearms trade, sale, or barter, or gunsmith, or hunting animals or fowl, or hunter safety course, or target shooting, or skeet or trap shooting or any recognized firearms activity or event and while in such places; or

2. For any legitimate purpose not in violation of the Oklahoma Firearms Act of 1971.

CARRYING WITHOUT A LICENSE

Title 21 O.S. § 1289.6(B)(1): B. A person shall be permitted to carry unloaded shotguns, rifles and pistols, open and not concealed and without a handgun license as authorized by the Oklahoma Self-Defense Act pursuant to the following conditions:

1. When going to or from the person's private residence or vehicle or a vehicle in which the person is riding as a passenger to a place designated or authorized for firearms repairs or reconditioning, or for firearms trade, sale, or barter, or gunsmith, or hunting animals or fowl, or hunter safety course, or target shooting, or skeet or trap shooting or any recognized firearms activity or event and while in such places.

OPEN DISPLAY OF FIREARMS

Title 21 O.S. § 1289.6(C): C. The provisions of this section shall not be construed to prohibit educational or recreational activities, exhibitions, displays or shows involving the use or display of rifles, shotguns or pistols or other weapons if the activity is approved by the property owner and sponsor of the activity

OPEN CARRY IN A VEHICLE

Title 21 O.S. § 1289.7: Any person, except a convicted felon, may transport in a motor vehicle a rifle, shotgun or pistol, open and unloaded, at any time. For purposes of this section "open" means the firearm is transported in plain view, in a case designed for carrying firearms, which case is wholly or partially visible, in a gun rack mounted in the vehicle, in an exterior locked compartment or a trunk of a vehicle.

Any person, except a convicted felon, may transport in a motor vehicle a rifle or shotgun concealed behind a seat of the vehicle or within the interior of the vehicle provided the rifle or shotgun is not clip, magazine or chamber loaded. The authority to transport a clip or magazine loaded rifle or shotgun shall be pursuant to Section 1289.13 of this title.

Any person who is the operator of a vehicle or is a passenger in any vehicle wherein another person who is licensed pursuant to the Oklahoma Self-Defense Act to carry a handgun, concealed or unconcealed, and is carrying a handgun or has the handgun in such vehicle, shall not be deemed in violation of the provisions of this section provided the licensee is in or near the vehicle.

RETIRED STATUS OF PEACE OFFICER

Title 21 O.S. § 1289.8: A. Any fire marshal inspector who is retired, state, county or municipal peace officer of this state who is retired, or any state, county or municipal peace officer classified as a reserve who is retired, or any federal law enforcement officer who is retired may retain their status as a peace officer, retired, in the State of Oklahoma, and as such may carry a concealed pistol pursuant to the provisions of subsection B of this section. A retired state, county or municipal peace officer may in times of great emergency or danger serve to enforce the law, keep the peace or to protect the public in keeping with their availability and ability at the request of the Governor, the sheriff or the mayor of their retirement jurisdiction. If a retired fire marshal is activated for duty, the peace officer powers of the retired fire marshal are limited to the duties granted prior to retirement.

B. The Council on Law Enforcement Education and Training (CLEET) shall issue an identification card to eligible retired federal, state, county, and municipal peace officers which authorizes the retired peace officer to carry a concealed pistol anywhere in the state of Oklahoma. The identification card shall bear the full name of the retired officer, the signature of the retired officer, the date of issuance, and such other information as may be deemed appropriate by CLEET. The card shall not expire, but may be denied, suspended or revoked as provided by the rules promulgated by CLEET or upon the discovery of any preclusion prescribed in Section 1290.10 or 1290.11 of this title. The Council on Law Enforcement

Education and Training shall request the Oklahoma State Bureau of Investigation to conduct a state and national criminal history records search on each retired peace officer authorized to carry a concealed firearm pursuant to the provisions of this section every four (4) years, and unless a preclusion prescribed in Section 1290.10 or 1290.11 of this title is found to exist, no action shall be necessary. When a preclusion is discovered, the Council shall notify the retired peace officer and shall hold a hearing before taking any action to suspend or revoke the authority to carry a concealed pistol.

C. The retired peace officer shall be required to submit the following information to the Council on Law Enforcement Education and Training (CLEET) and any other information requested by CLEET:

1. A statement from the appropriate retirement system verifying the status of the person as a retired peace officer of the jurisdiction or, if the retired peace officer does not participate in a retirement system, a statement from the appropriate law enforcement agency verifying the status of the person as a retired peace officer of that jurisdiction, and the reason why the retired peace officer does not participate in a retirement system; and

2. A notarized statement, signed by the retired peace officer, stating that the officer:

a. has not been convicted of and is currently not subject to any pending criminal prosecution for any felony offense, any drug-related offense, aggravated assault and battery or any offense involving impairment by drugs or alcohol,

b. has not been forced into retirement due to any mental disorder, and

c. has not suffered any injury or any physical or mental impairment which would render the person unsafe to carry a concealed pistol.

D. A retired peace officer, who has made application for the CLEET identification card authorized in subsection B of this section, shall be authorized to carry a concealed firearm as an off-duty peace officer, pursuant to Section 1289.23 of this title, until the authority to carry a concealed firearm as a retired officer is finally approved or denied by CLEET.

E. The Council on Law Enforcement Education and Training shall promulgate rules and procedures necessary to implement the provisions of this section.

F. Any peace officer, retired, who carries any pistol in violation of the provisions of this section shall be deemed to be in violation of Section 1272 of this title and may be prosecuted as provided by law for a violation of that section.

UNLAWFUL TRANSPORTATION OF LOADED FIREARM IN A LANDBORNE VEHICLE

Title 21 O.S. § 1289.13: Except as otherwise provided by the provisions of the Oklahoma Self-Defense Act or another provision of law, it shall be unlawful to transport a loaded pistol, rifle or shotgun in a landborne motor vehicle over a public highway or roadway. However, a rifle or shotgun may be transported clip or magazine loaded and not chamber loaded when transported in an exterior locked compartment of the vehicle or trunk of the vehicle or in the interior compartment of the vehicle notwithstanding the provisions of Section 1289.7 of this title when the person is in possession of a valid handgun license pursuant to the Oklahoma Self-Defense Act.

Any person convicted of a violation of this section shall be punished as provided in Section 1289.15 of this title.

Any person who is the operator of a vehicle or is a passenger in any vehicle wherein another person who is licensed pursuant to the Oklahoma Self-Defense Act to carry a handgun, concealed or unconcealed, and is carrying a handgun or has a handgun or rifle or shotgun in such vehicle shall not be deemed in violation of the provisions of this section provided the licensee is in or near the vehicle.

STORING FIREARMS IN LOCKED VEHICLE ALLOWED

Title 21 O.S. § 1290.22(B): B. No person, property owner, tenant, employer, place of worship or business entity shall be permitted to establish any policy or rule that has the effect of prohibiting any person, except a convicted felon, from transporting and storing firearms in a locked vehicle on any property set aside for any vehicle.

CONTRABAND IN JAILS

Title 57 O.S. § 21: A. Any person who, without authority, brings into or has in his or her possession in any jail or state penal institution or other place where prisoners are located, any gun, knife, bomb or other dangerous instrument, any controlled dangerous substance as defined by Section 2-101 et seq. of Title 63 of the Oklahoma Statutes, any intoxicating beverage or low-point beer as defined by Sections 163.1 and 163.2 of Title 37 of the Oklahoma Statutes, money, or financial documents for a person other than the inmate or a spouse of the inmate, including but not limited to tax returns, shall be guilty of a felony and, upon conviction, shall be punished by imprisonment in the custody of the Department of Corrections for a term of not less than one (1) year nor more than five (5) years, or by a fine of not less than One Hundred Dollars ($100.00) nor more than One Thousand Dollars ($1,000.00), or by both such fine and imprisonment. Provided, the provisions of this subsection shall not prohibit any Department of Corrections employee who has a valid handgun license pursuant to the Oklahoma Self-Defense Act to keep a firearm in a vehicle on any property set aside for the parking of any vehicle, whether occupied or unoccupied, at any state-owned prison facility, provided the employee has provided annual notification to the Department of Corrections of the brand name, model, serial number, and owner identification information of the firearm, and the firearm is secured and stored in a locked metal storage container located in a locked vehicle. The storage container will be secured in the vehicle by a lockable chain or cable or by utilizing hardware provided by the manufacturer.

B. If an inmate is found to be in possession of any item prohibited by this section, upon conviction, such inmate shall be guilty of a felony and shall be punished by imprisonment for a term of not less than five (5) years nor more than twenty (20) years in the custody of the Department of Corrections.

C. If the person found to be in possession of any item prohibited by this section has committed, prior to the commission of an offense in violation of this section, two or more felony offenses, and the possession of contraband in violation of this section is within ten (10) years of the completion of the execution of the sentence for any prior offense, such person, upon conviction, shall be guilty of a felony and shall be punished by imprisonment in the custody of the Department of Corrections for a term of not less than twenty (20) years. Felony offenses relied upon shall not have arisen out of the same transaction or occurrence or series of events closely related in time and location.

D. Any person who, without authority, brings into or has in his or her possession in any jail or state penal institution or other place where prisoners are located, cigarettes, cigars, snuff, chewing tobacco, or any other form of tobacco product shall, upon conviction, be guilty of a misdemeanor punishable by imprisonment in the county jail not to exceed one (1) year, or by a fine not exceeding Five Hundred Dollars ($500.00), or by both such fine and imprisonment.

E. Any person who knowingly, willfully and without authority brings into or has in his or her possession in any secure area of a jail or state penal institution or other secure place where prisoners are located any cellular phone or electronic device capable of sending or receiving any electronic communication shall, upon conviction, be guilty of a felony punishable by imprisonment in the custody of the Department of Corrections for a term not exceeding two (2) years, or by a fine not exceeding Two Thousand Five Hundred Dollars ($2,500.00), or by both such fine and imprisonment.

F. Any electronic communication device which has no identifiable owner and which is seized as a result of a violation of this section may be disposed of or sold by the agency that seized the device.

G. "Electronic communication" means any transfer of signs, signals, writings, images, sounds, data, or intelligence of any nature transmitted in whole or part by a wire, radio, electromagnetic, photo-electronic, or photo-optical system, and includes, but is not limited to, the transfer of that communication through the Internet.

UNLAWFUL TRANSPORTATION OF FIREARMS IN A BOAT/VESSEL

Title 63 O.S. § 4210.3: It shall be unlawful to transport a shotgun, rifle or pistol in or to discharge such weapons from a vessel, except for the purposes of hunting animals or fowl, and in compliance with existing state and federal laws. Anyone violating the provisions of this section, upon conviction, shall be guilty of a misdemeanor and shall be punished by a fine of not less than Fifty Dollars ($50.00) and not more than One Hundred Dollars ($100.00), or by imprisonment in the county jail for not less than ten (10) days and not more than six (6) months, or by both such fine and imprisonment. Any person in possession of a valid handgun license from this state or a reciprocal state authorized by the Oklahoma Self-Defense Act shall not be deemed guilty of transporting a pistol in violation of this section when a handgun is carried concealed or unconcealed upon or about their person in compliance with the provisions of the Oklahoma Self-Defense Act.

CLEET

Title 70 O.S. § 3311: A. There is hereby created a Council on Law Enforcement Education and Training which shall be, and is hereby declared to be, a governmental law enforcement agency of the State of Oklahoma, body politic and corporate, with powers of government and with the authority to exercise the rights, privileges and functions necessary to ensure the professional training and continuing education of law enforcement officers in the State of Oklahoma. These rights, privileges and functions include, but are not limited to, those specified in Sections 3311 through 3311.14 of this title and in the Oklahoma Security Guard and Private Investigator Act and the Oklahoma Bail Enforcement and Licensing Act. The Council shall be composed of thirteen (13) members as follows:

1. The Commissioner of the Department of Public Safety, or designee;

2. The Director of the Oklahoma State Bureau of Narcotics and Dangerous Drugs Control, or designee;

3. The Director of the Oklahoma State Bureau of Investigation, or designee;

4. One member appointed by the Governor who shall be a law enforcement administrator representing a tribal law enforcement agency;

5. One member appointed by the Governor who shall be a chief of police of a municipality with a population over one hundred thousand (100,000), as determined by the latest Federal Decennial Census;

6. One member appointed by the Board of Directors of the Oklahoma Sheriffs' and Peace Officers Association who shall be a sheriff of a county with a population under fifty thousand (50,000), as determined by the latest Federal Decennial Census;

7. One member appointed by the Oklahoma Association of Police Chiefs who shall be a chief of police representing a municipality with a population over ten thousand (10,000), as determined by the latest Federal Decennial Census;

8. One member shall be appointed by the Board of Directors of the Oklahoma Sheriffs' Association who shall be a sheriff of a county with a population of one hundred thousand (100,000) or more, as determined by the latest Federal Decennial Census;

9. One member appointed by the Board of Directors of the Fraternal Order of Police who shall have experience as a training officer;

10. One member appointed by the Chancellor of Higher Education who shall be a representative of East Central University;

11. One member who is the immediate past chair of the Council on Law Enforcement Education and Training;

12. The President Pro Tempore of the Senate shall appoint one member from a list of three or more nominees submitted by a statewide organization representing cities and towns that is exempt from taxation under federal law and designated pursuant to the provisions of the Internal Revenue Code, 26 U.S.C., Section 170(a); and

13. The Speaker of the House of Representatives shall appoint one member from a list of three or more nominees submitted by an organization that assists in the establishment of accreditation standards and training programs for law enforcement agencies throughout the State of Oklahoma.

The Executive Director selected by the Council shall be an ex officio member of the Council and shall act as Secretary. The Council on Law Enforcement Education and Training shall select a chair and vice-chair from among its members. Members of the Council on Law Enforcement Education and Training shall not receive a salary for duties performed as members of the Council, but shall be reimbursed for their actual and necessary expenses incurred in the performance of Council duties pursuant to the provisions of the State Travel Reimbursement Act.

B. The Council on Law Enforcement Education and Training is hereby authorized and directed to:

1. Appoint a larger Advisory Council to discuss problems and hear recommendations concerning necessary research, minimum standards, educational needs, and other matters imperative to upgrading Oklahoma law enforcement to professional status;

2. Promulgate rules with respect to such matters as certification, revocation, suspension, withdrawal and reinstatement of certification, minimum courses of study, testing and test scores, attendance requirements, equipment and facilities, minimum qualifications for instructors, minimum standards for basic and advanced in-service courses, and seminars for Oklahoma police and peace officers;

3. Authorize research, basic and advanced courses, and seminars to assist in program planning directly and through subcommittees;

4. Authorize additional staff and services necessary for program expansion;

5. Recommend legislation necessary to upgrade Oklahoma law enforcement to professional status;

6. Establish policies and regulations concerning the number, geographic and police unit distribution, and admission requirements of those receiving tuition or scholarship aid available through the Council. Such waiver of costs shall be limited to duly appointed members of legally constituted local,

county, and state law enforcement agencies on the basis of educational and financial need;

7. Appoint an Executive Director and an Assistant Director to direct the staff, inform the Council of compliance with the provisions of this section and perform such other duties imposed on the Council by law. An Executive Director appointed by the Council must qualify for the position with a bachelor or higher degree in law enforcement from an accredited college or university, or a bachelor or higher degree in a law-enforcement-related subject area, and a minimum of five (5) years of active law enforcement experience including, but not limited to, responsibility for enforcement, investigation, administration, training, or curriculum implementation.

The Executive Director of the Council on Law Enforcement Education and Training may commission CLEET staff as peace officers for purposes consistent with the duties of CLEET as set out in state law. The powers and duties conferred on the Executive Director or any staff member appointed by the Executive Director as a peace officer shall not limit the powers and duties of other peace officers of this state or any political subdivision thereof. The Executive Director or any staff member appointed by the Executive Director as a peace officer may, upon request, assist any federal, state, county or municipal law enforcement agency;

8. Enter into contracts and agreements for the payment of classroom space, food, and lodging expenses as may be necessary for law enforcement officers attending any official course of instruction approved or conducted by the Council. Such expenses may be paid directly to the contracting agency or business establishment. The food and lodging expenses for each law enforcement officer shall not exceed the authorized rates as provided for in the State Travel Reimbursement Act; provided, however, the Council may provide food and lodging to law enforcement officials attending any official course of instruction approved or conducted by the Council rather than

paying for the provision of such food and lodging by an outside contracting agency or business establishment;

9. a. Certify canine teams, consisting of a dog and a handler working together as a team, trained to detect:

(1) controlled dangerous substances, or

(2) explosives, explosive materials, explosive devices, or materials which could be used to construct an explosive device;

provided, the dog of a certified canine team shall not be certified at any time as both a drug dog and a bomb dog, and any dog of a certified canine team who has been previously certified as either a drug dog or a bomb dog shall not be eligible at any time to be certified in the other category.

b. Upon retiring the dog from the service it was certified to perform, the law enforcement department that handled the dog shall retain possession of the dog. The handler shall have first option of adopting the dog. If that option is not exercised, the law enforcement department shall provide for its adoption. Once adopted the dog shall not be placed back into active service;

10. Enter into a lease, loan or other agreement with the Oklahoma Development Finance Authority or a local public trust for the purpose of facilitating the financing of a new facility for its operations and use and pledge, to the extent authorized by law, all or a portion of its receipts of the assessment penalty herein referenced for the payment of its obligations under such lease, loan or other agreement. It is the intent of the Legislature to increase the assessment penalty to such a level or appropriate sufficient monies to the Council on Law Enforcement Education and Training to make payments on the lease, loan or other agreement for the purpose of retiring the bonds to be issued by the Oklahoma Development Finance Authority or local public trust. Such lease, loan or other agreement and the bonds issued to finance such facilities shall

not constitute an indebtedness of the State of Oklahoma or be backed by the full faith and credit of the State of Oklahoma, and the lease, loan or other agreement and the bonds shall contain a statement to such effect;

11. Accept gifts, bequests, devises, contributions and grants, public or private, of real or personal property;

12. Appoint an advisory committee composed of representatives from security guard and private investigative agencies to advise the Council concerning necessary research, minimum standards for licensure, education, and other matters related to licensure of security guards, security guard agencies, private investigators, and private investigative agencies;

13. Enter into agreements with individuals, educational institutions, agencies, and business and tribal entities for professional services, the use of facilities and supplies, and staff overtime costs incurred as a result of the user's requests to schedule functions after-hours, on weekends, or anytime such requests extend staff beyond its normal capacity, whereby contracting individuals, educational institutions, agencies, and business and tribal entities shall pay a fee to be determined by the Council by rule. All fees collected pursuant to these agreements shall be deposited to the credit of the C.L.E.E.T. Training Center Revolving Fund created pursuant to Section 3311.6 of this title. The Council is authorized to promulgate emergency rules to effectuate the provisions of this paragraph;

14. Promulgate rules to establish a state firearms requalification standard for active peace officers and meet any requirements imposed on the Council by the federal Law Enforcement Officers Safety Act of 2004;

15. Set minimal criteria relating to qualifications for chief of police administrative training pursuant to Section 34-102 of Title 11 of the Oklahoma Statutes, assist in developing a course of training for a Police Chief Administrative School, and approve all police chief administrative training offered in this state;

16. Appoint a Curriculum Review Board to be composed of six (6) members as follows:

a. one member shall be selected by the Chancellor for Higher Education, who possesses a background of creation and review of curriculum and experience teaching criminal justice or law enforcement courses, who shall serve an initial term of one (1) year,

b. one member shall represent a municipal jurisdiction with a population of fifty thousand (50,000) or more and who shall be a management-level CLEET-certified training officer, who shall serve an initial term of two (2) years,

c. one member shall represent a county jurisdiction with a population of fifty thousand (50,000) or more and who shall be a management-level CLEET-certified training officer, who shall serve an initial term of three (3) years,

d. one member shall represent a municipal jurisdiction with a population of less than fifty thousand (50,000) and who shall be a CLEET-certified training officer, who shall serve an initial term of two (2) years,

e. one member shall represent a county jurisdiction with a population of less than fifty thousand (50,000) and who shall be a CLEET-certified training officer, who shall serve an initial term of one (1) year, and

f. one member selected by the Oklahoma Department of Career and Technology Education from the Curriculum Material and Instructional Material Center, who shall serve an initial term of three (3) years.

After the initial terms of office, all members shall be appointed to serve three-year terms. Any member may be reappointed to serve consecutive terms. Members shall serve without compensation, but may be reimbursed for travel expenses pursuant to the State Travel Reimbursement Act. The Board shall review and establish curriculum for all CLEET academies and training courses pursuant to procedures established by the Council on Law Enforcement Education and Training;

17. Conduct review and verification of any records relating to the statutory duties of CLEET;

18. Receive requested reports including investigative reports, court documents, statements, or other applicable information from local, county and state agencies and other agencies for use in actions where a certification or license issued by CLEET may be subject to disciplinary or other actions provided by law;

19. Summarily suspend a certification of a peace officer, without prior notice but otherwise subject to administrative proceedings, if CLEET finds that the actions of the certified peace officer may present a danger to the peace officer, the public, a family or household member, or involve a crime against a minor. A certified copy of the information or indictment charging such a crime shall be considered clear and convincing evidence of the charge; and

20. Approve law enforcement agencies and police departments in accordance with the following:

a. this section applies only to an entity authorized by statute or by the Constitution to create a law enforcement agency or police department and commission, appoint, or employ officers that first creates or reactivates an inactive law enforcement agency or police department and first begins to commission, appoint, or employ officers on or after November 1, 2011,

b. the entity shall submit to CLEET, a minimum of sixty (60) days prior to creation of the law enforcement agency or police department, information regarding:

(1) the need for the law enforcement agency or police department in the community,

(2) the funding sources for the law enforcement agency or police department, and proof that no more than fifty percent (50%) of the funding of the entity will be derived from ticket revenue or fines,

(3) the physical resources available to officers,

(4) the physical facilities that the law enforcement agency or police department will operate, including descriptions of the evidence room, dispatch area, restroom facilities, and public area,

(5) law enforcement policies of the law enforcement agency or police department, including published policies on:

(a) use of force,

(b) vehicle pursuit,

(c) mental health,

(d) professional conduct of officers,

(e) domestic abuse,

(f) response to missing persons,

(g) supervision of part-time officers, and

(h) impartial policing,

(6) the administrative structure of the law enforcement agency or police department,

(7) liability insurance, and

(8) any other information CLEET requires by rule,

c. within sixty (60) days of receiving an entity's request, CLEET will forward to the entity by certified mail, return receipt requested, a letter of authorization or denial to create a law enforcement agency or police department and commission, appoint, or employ officers, signed by the Executive Director of CLEET, and

d. in cases of denial, the entity may appeal the decision of the Executive Director to the full CLEET Council. The Executive Director shall ensure that the final report is provided to all members of the Council. The Council shall review and make recommendations concerning the report at the first meeting of the Council to occur after all members of the Council have received the report. The Council may, by majority vote:

(1) order additional information be provided,

(2) order confirmation of the opinion of the Executive Director, or

(3) order authorization of the entity.

C. 1. Payment of any fee provided for in this section may be made by a nationally recognized credit or debit card issued to the applicant. The Council may publicly post and collect a fee for the acceptance of the nationally recognized credit or debit card not to exceed five percent (5%) of the amount of the payment. For purposes of this subsection, "nationally recognized credit card" means any instrument or device, whether known as a credit card, credit plate, charge plate, or by any other name, issued with or without fee by an issuer for the use of the cardholder in obtaining goods, services, or anything else of value and which is accepted by over one thousand merchants in this state. "Debit card" means an identification card or device issued to a person by a business organization which permits such person to obtain access to or activate a consumer banking electronic facility. The Council shall determine which nationally recognized credit or debit cards will be accepted as payment for fees.

2. Payment for any fee provided for in this title may be made by a business check. The Council may:

a. add an amount equal to the amount of the service charge incurred, not to exceed three percent (3%) of the amount of the check as a service charge for the acceptance and verification of the check, or

b. add an amount of no more than Five Dollars ($5.00) as a service charge for the acceptance and verification of a check. For purposes of this subsection, "business check" shall not mean a money order, cashier's check, or bank certified check.

D. Failure of the Legislature to appropriate necessary funds to provide for expenses and operations of the Council on Law Enforcement Education and Training shall not invalidate other provisions of this section relating to the creation and duties of the Council.

E. 1. No person shall be eligible for employment as a peace officer or reserve peace officer until the employing law enforcement agency has conducted a background investigation of such person consisting of the following:

a. a fingerprint search submitted to the Oklahoma State Bureau of Investigation with a return report to the submitting agency that such person has no felony record,

b. a fingerprint search submitted to the Federal Bureau of Investigation with a return report to the submitting agency that such person has no felony record,

c. such person has undergone psychological evaluation by a psychologist licensed by the State of Oklahoma and has been evaluated to be suitable to serve as a peace officer in the State of Oklahoma,

d. the employing agency has verified that such person has a high school diploma or a GED equivalency certificate as recognized by state law,

e. such person is not participating in a deferred sentence agreement for a felony, a crime involving moral turpitude or a crime of domestic violence, and does not have any criminal charges pending in any court in this state, another state, in tribal court or pursuant to the United States Code,

f. such person is not currently subject to an order of the Council revoking, suspending, or accepting a voluntary surrender of peace officer certification,

g. such person is not currently undergoing treatment for a mental illness, condition or disorder. For purposes of this subsection, "currently undergoing treatment for mental illness, condition or disorder" means the person has been diagnosed by a licensed physician, psychologist, or licensed mental health professional as being afflicted with a substantial disorder of thought, mood, perception, psychological orientation or memory that significantly impairs judgment, behavior, capacity to recognize reality, or ability to meet the ordinary demands of life and such condition continues to exist,

h. such person is twenty-one (21) years of age. Provided, this requirement shall not affect those persons who are already employed as a police or peace officer prior to November 1, 1985, and

i. such person has provided proof of United States citizenship or resident alien status, pursuant to an employment eligibility verification form from the United States Citizenship and Immigration Services.

2. To aid the evaluating psychologist in interpreting the test results, including automated scoring and interpretations, the employing agency shall provide the psychologist a statement confirming the identity of the individual taking the test as the person who is employed or seeking employment as a peace officer of the agency and attesting that it administered the psychological instrument in accordance with standards within the test document. The psychologist shall report to the employing agency the evaluation of the assessment instrument and may include any additional recommendations to assist the

employing agency in determining whether to certify to the Council on Law Enforcement Education and Training that the person being evaluated is suitable to serve as a peace officer in the State of Oklahoma. No additional procedures or requirements shall be imposed for performance of the psychological evaluation. The psychological instrument utilized shall be evaluated by a psychologist licensed by the State of Oklahoma, and the employing agency shall certify to the Council that the evaluation was conducted in accordance with this provision and that the employee or applicant is suitable to serve as a peace officer in the State of Oklahoma.

a. Any person found not to be suitable for employment or certification by the Council shall not be employed, retained in employment as a peace officer, or certified by the Council for at least one (1) year, at which time the employee or applicant may be reevaluated by a psychologist licensed by the State of Oklahoma. This section shall also be applicable to all reserve peace officers in the State of Oklahoma.

b. Any person who is certified by CLEET and has undergone the psychological evaluation required by this subparagraph and has been found to be suitable as a peace officer shall not be required to be reevaluated for any subsequent employment as a peace officer following retirement or any break in service as a peace officer, unless such break in service exceeds five (5) years or the Council determines that a peace officer may present a danger to himself or herself, the public, or a family or household member.

c. All persons seeking certification shall have their name, gender, date of birth, and address of such person submitted to the Department of Mental Health and Substance Abuse Services by the Council. The Department of Mental Health and Substance Abuse Services shall respond to the Council within ten (10) days whether the computerized records of the Department indicate the applicant has ever been involuntarily committed to an Oklahoma state mental institution. In the event that the Department of Mental Health and Substance Abuse Services reports to the Council that the applicant has been involuntarily committed, the Council shall immediately inform the employing agency.

All basic police courses shall include a minimum of four (4) hours of education and training in recognizing and managing a person appearing to require mental health treatment or services. The training shall include training in crime and drug prevention, crisis intervention, youth and family intervention techniques, recognizing, investigating and preventing abuse and exploitation of elderly persons, mental health issues, and criminal jurisdiction on Sovereign Indian Land.

Subject to the availability of funding, for full-time salaried police or peace officers a basic police course academy shall consist of a minimum of six hundred (600) hours.

For reserve deputies a basic reserve academy shall consist of a minimum of two hundred forty (240) hours.

Beginning January 1, 2014, any reserve peace officer who has completed the two-hundred-forty-hour reserve peace officer certification program, and who has been in active service in that capacity for the past two (2) consecutive years, shall be eligible to attend a three-hundred-sixty-hour basic full-time training academy to become certified as a full-time police or peace officer.

3. Every person who has not been certified as a police or peace officer and is duly appointed or elected as a police or peace officer shall hold such position on a temporary basis only, and shall, within six (6) months from the date of appointment or taking office, qualify as required in this subsection or forfeit such position. In computing the time for qualification, all service shall be cumulative from date of first appointment or taking office as a police or peace officer with any department in this state.

a. The Council may extend the time requirement specified in this paragraph for good cause as determined by the Council.

b. A duty is hereby imposed upon the employing agency to withhold payment of the compensation or wage of such unqualified officer.

c. If the police or peace officer fails to forfeit the position or the employing agency fails to require the officer to forfeit the position, the district attorney shall file the proper action to cause the forfeiting of such position. The district court of the county where the officer is employed shall have jurisdiction to hear the case.

4. The Council may certify officers who have completed a course of study in another state deemed by the Council to meet standards for Oklahoma peace officers providing the officer's certification in the other state has not been revoked or voluntarily surrendered and is not currently under suspension.

5. For purposes of this section, a police or peace officer is defined as a full-time duly appointed or elected officer who is paid for working more than twenty-five (25) hours per week and whose duties are to preserve the public peace, protect life and property, prevent crime, serve warrants, transport prisoners, and enforce laws and ordinances of this state, or any political subdivision thereof; provided, elected sheriffs and their deputies and elected, appointed, or acting chiefs of police shall meet the requirements of this subsection within the first six (6) months after assuming the duties of the office to which they are elected or appointed or for which they are an acting chief; provided further, that this section shall not apply to persons designated by the Director of the Department of Corrections as peace officers pursuant to Section 510 of Title 57 of the Oklahoma Statutes.

F. No person shall be certified as a police or peace officer by the Council or be employed by the state, a county, a city, or any political subdivision thereof, who is currently subject to an order of the Council revoking, suspending, or accepting a voluntary surrender of peace officer certification or who has been convicted of a felony, a crime involving moral turpitude, or a crime of domestic violence, unless a full pardon has been granted by the proper agency; however, any person who has been trained and certified by the Council on Law Enforcement Education and Training and is actively employed as a full-time peace officer as of November 1, 1985, shall not be subject to the provisions of this subsection for convictions occurring prior to November 1, 1985.

G. 1. The Council is hereby authorized to provide to any employing agency the following information regarding a person who is or has applied for employment as a police or peace officer of such employing agency:

a. Oklahoma State Bureau of Investigation and Federal Bureau of Investigation reports,

b. administration of the psychological tests provided for herein,

c. performance in the course of study or other basis of certification,

d. previous certifications issued, and

e. any administrative or judicial determination denying certification.

2. An employing agency shall not be liable in any action arising out of the release of contents of personnel information relevant to the qualifications or ability of a person to perform the duties of a police or peace officer when such information is released pursuant to written authorization for release of information signed by such person and is provided to another employing agency which has employed or has received an application for employment from such person.

3. As used in this subsection, "employing agency" means a political subdivision or law enforcement agency which either

has employed or received an employment application from a person who, if employed, would be subject to this section.

H. 1. A law enforcement agency employing police or peace officers in this state shall report the hiring, resignation, or termination for any reason of a police or peace officer to the Council within ten (10) days. Failure to comply with the provisions of this subsection may disqualify a law enforcement agency from participating in training programs sponsored by the Council. Every law enforcement agency employing police or peace officers in this state shall submit to CLEET on or before October 1 of each calendar year a complete list of all commissioned employees with a current mailing address and phone number for each such employee. In addition to the above, CLEET may impose an administrative fine for violations of this section.

2. A tribal law enforcement agency that has peace officers commissioned by an Oklahoma law enforcement agency pursuant to a cross-deputization agreement with the State of Oklahoma or any political subdivision of the State of Oklahoma pursuant to the provisions of Section 1221 of Title 74 of the Oklahoma Statutes shall report the commissioning, resignation, or termination of commission for any reason of a cross-deputized tribal police or peace officer to CLEET within ten (10) days of the commissioning, resignation, or termination. Failure to comply with the provisions of this subsection may disqualify a tribal law enforcement agency from participating in training programs sponsored by the Council.

I. It is unlawful for any person to willfully make any statement in an application to CLEET knowing the statement is false or intentionally commit fraud in any application to the Council for attendance in any CLEET-conducted or CLEET-approved peace officer academy or Collegiate Officer Program or for the purpose of obtaining peace officer certification or reinstatement. It is unlawful for any person to willfully submit false or fraudulent documents relating to continuing education rosters, transcripts or certificates, or any canine license application. Any person convicted of a violation of this subsection shall be guilty of a felony punishable by imprisonment in the Department of Corrections for a term of not less than two (2) years nor more than five (5) years, or by a fine not exceeding Two Thousand Dollars ($2,000.00), or by both such fine and imprisonment. In addition to the above, CLEET may impose an administrative fine.

J. 1. A police or peace officer shall be subject to disciplinary action to include a denial, suspension, revocation or acceptance of voluntary surrender of peace officer certification upon a showing of clear and convincing evidence for the following:

a. conviction of a felony or a crime of domestic violence,

b. conviction of a misdemeanor involving moral turpitude; provided, if the conviction is a single isolated incident that occurred more than five (5) years ago and the Council is satisfied that the person has been sufficiently rehabilitated, the Council may, in its discretion, certify such person providing that all other statutory requirements have been met,

c. a verdict of guilt or entry of a plea of guilty or nolo contendere or an "Alford" plea or any plea other than a not guilty plea for a felony offense, a crime of moral turpitude, or a crime of domestic violence,

d. falsification or a willful misrepresentation of information in an employment application or application to the Council on Law Enforcement Education and Training, records of evidence, or in testimony under oath,

e. revocation or voluntary surrender of police or peace officer certification in another state for a violation of any law or rule or in settlement of any disciplinary action in such state,

f. involuntary commitment of a reserve or peace officer in a mental institution or licensed private mental health facility for any mental illness, condition or disorder that is diagnosed by a licensed physician, psychologist or a licensed mental health professional as a substantial disorder of thought, mood, perception, psychological orientation, or memory that significantly impairs judgment, behavior, capacity to recognize reality, or ability to meet the ordinary demands of life. Provided, the peace officer certification may be reinstated upon the Council receiving notification of a psychological evaluation conducted by a licensed physician, psychologist or licensed mental health professional which attests and states by affidavit that the officer and the evaluation test data of the officer have been examined and that, in the professional opinion of the physician, psychologist or licensed mental health professional, the officer is psychologically suitable to return to duty as a peace officer. Notwithstanding any other provision of state law pertaining to confidentiality of hospital or other medical records, and as allowable under federal law, CLEET may subpoena or request a court to subpoena records necessary to assure compliance with these provisions. Any confidential information received by CLEET for such purpose shall retain its confidential character while in the possession of CLEET,

g. abuse of office,

h. entry of a final order of protection against applicant or officer, or

i. any violation of the Oklahoma Private Security Licensing Act.

2. Disciplinary proceedings shall be commenced by filing a complaint with the Council on a form approved by the Council. Any employing agency or other person having information may submit such information to the Council for consideration as provided in this subsection.

3. Upon the filing of the complaint, a preliminary investigation shall be conducted to determine whether:

a. there is reason to believe the person has violated any provision of this subsection or any other provision of law or rule, or

b. there is reason to believe the person has been convicted of a felony, a crime involving moral turpitude or a domestic violence offense or is currently participating in a deferred sentence for such offenses.

4. When the investigation of a complaint does not find the person has violated any of the provisions of this subsection, or finds that the person is sufficiently rehabilitated as provided in subparagraph b or f of paragraph 1 of this subsection, no disciplinary action shall be required and the person shall remain certified as a police or peace officer. When the investigation of a complaint finds that the person has violated any of the provisions of this subsection, the matter shall be referred for disciplinary proceedings. The disciplinary proceedings shall be in accordance with Articles I and II of the Administrative Procedures Act.

5. The Council shall revoke the certification of any person upon determining that such person has been convicted of a felony or a crime involving moral turpitude or a domestic violence offense or has entered a plea of guilty, or nolo contendere or an "Alford" plea or any plea other than a not guilty plea for a felony offense, a crime of moral turpitude or a crime of domestic violence or is the respondent in a final Victims Protective Order; provided, that if the conviction has been reversed, vacated or otherwise invalidated by an appellate court, such conviction shall not be the basis for revocation of certification; provided further, that any person who has been trained and certified by the Council on Law Enforcement Education and Training and is actively employed as a full-time peace officer as of November 1, 1985, shall not be subject to the provisions of this subsection for convictions occurring prior to November 1, 1985. The sole issue to be determined at the hearing shall be whether the person has been convicted of a

felony, a crime involving moral turpitude or a domestic violence offense.

6. The Council shall revoke the certification of any person upon determining that such person has received a deferred sentence for a felony, a crime involving moral turpitude or a domestic violence offense.

7. The Council may suspend the certification of any person upon a determination that such person has been involuntarily committed to a mental institution or mental health facility for a mental illness, condition or disorder as provided in subparagraph f of paragraph 1 of this subsection.

8. Every law enforcement agency in this state shall, within thirty (30) days of a final order of termination or resignation while under investigation of a CLEET-certified peace officer, report such order or resignation in writing to the Executive Director of the Council. Any report, upon receipt by the Council, shall be considered as personnel records and shall be afforded confidential protection pursuant to Sections 24A.7 and 24A.8 of Title 51 of the Oklahoma Statutes. Any medical or other confidential records obtained by subpoena pursuant to this subsection shall not be made a part of such report. The Executive Director shall ensure that the report is provided to all members of the Council. The Council shall review and make recommendations concerning the report at the first meeting of the Council to occur after all members of the Council have received the report. The Council may, by a majority vote, order the suspension, for a given period of time, or revocation of the CLEET certification of the peace officer in question if there are grounds for such actions pursuant to this section and the peace officer in question has been provided with notice and an opportunity for a hearing pursuant to the Administrative Procedures Act. Suspension or revocation of CLEET certification pursuant to this paragraph shall be reported to the district attorney for the jurisdiction in which the peace officer was employed, to the liability insurance company of the law

enforcement agency that employed the peace officer, the chief elected official of the governing body of the law enforcement agency and the chief law enforcement officer of the law enforcement agency.

9. For all other violations of this subsection, the hearing examiner shall take into consideration the severity of the violation, any mitigating circumstances offered by the person subject to disciplinary action, and any other evidence relevant to the person's character to determine the appropriate disciplinary action.

10. a. A police or peace officer may voluntarily surrender and relinquish the peace officer certification to CLEET. Pursuant to such surrender or relinquishment, the person surrendering the certification shall be prohibited from applying to CLEET for reinstatement within five (5) years of the date of the surrender or relinquishment, unless otherwise provided by law for reinstatement.

b. No person who has had a police or peace officer certification from another state revoked or voluntarily surrendered and has not been reinstated by that state shall be considered for certification by CLEET.

c. Any person seeking reinstatement of police or peace officer certification which has been suspended, revoked, or voluntarily surrendered may apply for reinstatement pursuant to promulgated CLEET rules governing reinstatement. Except as provided in this subsection, any person whose certification has been revoked, suspended or voluntarily surrendered for any reason, including failure to comply with mandatory education and training requirements, shall pay a reinstatement fee of One Hundred Fifty Dollars ($150.00) to be deposited to the credit of the Peace Officer Revolving Fund created pursuant to Section 3311.7 of this title.

11. A duty is hereby imposed upon the district attorney who, on behalf of the State of Oklahoma, prosecutes a person holding

police or peace officer or reserve peace officer certification for a felony, a crime involving moral turpitude, or a crime of domestic violence in which a plea of guilty, nolo contendere, or an "Alford" plea or any other plea other than a not guilty plea or other finding of guilt is entered by, against or on behalf of a certified police or peace officer to report such plea, agreement, or other finding of guilt to the Council on Law Enforcement Education and Training within ten (10) days of such plea agreement or the finding of guilt.

12. Any person or agency required or authorized to submit information pursuant to this section to the Council shall be immune from liability arising from the submission of the information as long as the information was submitted in good faith and without malice.

13. Any peace officer employed by a law enforcement agency in this state which has internal discipline policies and procedures on file with CLEET shall be exempt from the disciplinary proceedings and actions provided for in this subsection; provided, however, such exemption shall not apply if the peace officer has been convicted of a felony crime, a crime of moral turpitude, or a crime of domestic violence.

14. As used in this subsection:

a. "law enforcement agency" means any department or agency of the state, a county, a municipality, or political subdivision thereof, with the duties to maintain public order, make arrests, and enforce the criminal laws of this state or municipal ordinances, which employs CLEET-certified personnel,

b. "final order of termination" means a final notice of dismissal from employment provided after all grievance, arbitration, and court actions have been completed, and

c. "resignation while under investigation" means the resignation from employment of a peace officer who is under investigation for any felony violation of law, a crime of moral turpitude, a crime of domestic violence, or the resignation from employment of a peace officer as part of an arbitration or plea agreement.

K. 1. Every canine team in the state trained to detect controlled dangerous substances shall be certified, by test, in the detection of such controlled dangerous substances and shall be recertified annually so long as the canine is used for such detection purposes. The certification test and annual recertification test provisions of this subsection shall not be applicable to canines that are owned by a law enforcement agency and that are certified and annually recertified in the detection of controlled dangerous substances by the United States Customs Service. No employee of CLEET may be involved in the training or testing of a canine team.

2. The Council shall appoint a Drug Dog Advisory Council to make recommendations concerning minimum standards, educational needs, and other matters imperative to the certification of canines and canine teams trained to detect controlled dangerous substances. The Council shall promulgate rules based upon the recommendations of the Advisory Council. Members of the Advisory Council shall include, but need not be limited to, a commissioned officer with practical knowledge of such canines and canine teams from each of the following:

a. the Oklahoma State Bureau of Narcotics and Dangerous Drugs Control,

b. the Department of Public Safety,

c. a police department,

d. a sheriff's office, and

e. a university or college campus police department.

3. The fee for the certification test shall be Two Hundred Dollars ($200.00) and the annual recertification test fee shall be

One Hundred Dollars ($100.00) per canine team. A retest fee of Fifty Dollars ($50.00) will be charged if the team fails the test. No such fee shall be charged to any local, state or federal government agency. The fees provided for in this paragraph shall be deposited to the credit of the CLEET Fund created pursuant to Section 1313.2 of Title 20 of the Oklahoma Statutes.

L. 1. Every canine team in the state trained to detect explosives, explosive materials, explosive devices, and materials which could be used to construct an explosive device shall be certified, by test, in the detection of such explosives and materials and shall be recertified annually so long as the canine is used for such detection purposes. The certification test and annual recertification test provisions of this subsection shall not be applicable to canines that are owned by a law enforcement agency if such canines are certified and annually recertified in the detection of explosives and materials by the United States Department of Defense. No employee of CLEET may be involved in the training or testing of a canine team.

2. The Council shall appoint a Bomb Dog Advisory Council to make recommendations concerning minimum standards, educational needs, and other matters imperative to the certification of canines and canine teams trained to detect explosives, explosive materials, explosive devices and materials which could be used to construct an explosive device. The Council shall promulgate rules based upon the recommendations of the Advisory Council. Members of the Advisory Council shall include, but need not be limited to, a commissioned officer with practical knowledge of such canines and canine teams from each of the following:

a. the Department of Public Safety,

b. a police department,

c. a sheriff's office, and

d. a university or college campus police department.

3. The fee for the certification test shall be Two Hundred Dollars ($200.00) and the annual recertification test fee shall be One Hundred Dollars ($100.00) per canine team. A retest fee of Fifty Dollars ($50.00) will be charged if the team fails the test. No such fee shall be charged to any local, state or federal government agency. The fees provided for in this paragraph shall be deposited to the credit of the CLEET Fund created pursuant to Section 1313.2 of Title 20 of the Oklahoma Statutes.

M. All tribal police officers of any Indian tribe or nation who have been commissioned by an Oklahoma law enforcement agency pursuant to a cross-deputization agreement with the State of Oklahoma or any political subdivision of the State of Oklahoma pursuant to the provisions of Section 1221 of Title 74 of the Oklahoma Statutes shall be eligible for peace officer certification under the same terms and conditions required of members of the law enforcement agencies of the State of Oklahoma and its political subdivisions. CLEET shall issue peace officer certification to tribal police officers who, as of July 1, 2003, are commissioned by an Oklahoma law enforcement agency pursuant to a cross-deputization agreement with the State of Oklahoma or any political subdivision of the State of Oklahoma pursuant to the provisions of Section 1221 of Title 74 of the Oklahoma Statutes and have met the training and qualification requirements of this section.

N. If an employing law enforcement agency in this state has paid the salary of a person while that person is completing in this state a basic police course approved by the Council and if within one (1) year after certification that person resigns and is hired by another law enforcement agency in this state, the second agency or the person receiving the training shall reimburse the original employing agency for the salary paid to the person while completing the basic police course by the original employing agency. CLEET shall not be a party to any court action based on this provision.

O. The Council on Law Enforcement Education and Training, in its discretion, may waive all or part of any moneys due to the Council, if deemed uncollectable by the Council.

P. Peace officers, reserve peace officers, tribal peace officers, agencies, bail enforcers, security guards and private investigators shall maintain with the Council current mailing addresses and shall notify the Council, in writing, of any change of address or name. Notification of change of name shall require certified copies of any marriage license or other court document which reflects the change of name. Notice of change of address or telephone number must be made within ten (10) days of the effected change. Notices shall not be accepted over the phone. In any proceeding in which the Council is required to serve notice or an order on an individual or an agency, the Council may send a letter to the mailing address on file with the Council. If the letter is returned and a notation of the U.S. Postal Service indicates "unclaimed", or "moved", or "refused" or any other nondelivery markings and the records of the Council indicate that no change of address as required by this subsection has been received by the Council, the notice and any subsequent notices or orders shall be deemed by the Court as having been legally served for all purposes.

Q. All CLEET records of Bail Enforcers may be released only in compliance with this section and the Oklahoma Bail Enforcement and Licensing Act. All records in CLEET possession concerning other persons or entities shall be released only in compliance with this section and the Oklahoma Open Records Act.

CHAPTER 11:

EXPUNGEMENT

Title 22 O.S. § 18: A. Persons authorized to file a motion for expungement, as provided herein, must be within one of the following categories:

1. The person has been acquitted;

2. The conviction was reversed with instructions to dismiss by an appellate court of competent jurisdiction, or an appellate court of competent jurisdiction reversed the conviction and the district attorney subsequently dismissed the charge;

3. The factual innocence of the person was established by the use of deoxyribonucleic acid (DNA) evidence subsequent to conviction, including a person who has been released from prison at the time innocence was established;

4. The person has received a full pardon on the basis of a written finding by the Governor of actual innocence for the crime for which the claimant was sentenced;

5. The person was arrested and no charges of any type, including charges for an offense different than that for which the person was originally arrested, are filed and the statute of limitations has expired or the prosecuting agency has declined to file charges;

6. The person was under eighteen (18) years of age at the time the offense was committed and the person has received a full pardon for the offense;

7. The person was charged with one or more misdemeanor or felony crimes, all charges have been dismissed, the person has never been convicted of a felony, no misdemeanor or felony charges are pending against the person, and the statute of limitations for refiling the charge or charges has expired or the prosecuting agency confirms that the charge or charges will not

be refiled; provided, however, this category shall not apply to charges that have been dismissed following the completion of a deferred judgment or delayed sentence;

8. The person was charged with a misdemeanor, the charge was dismissed following the successful completion of a deferred judgment or delayed sentence, the person has never been convicted of a misdemeanor or felony, no misdemeanor or felony charges are pending against the person, and at least one (1) year has passed since the charge was dismissed;

9. The person was charged with a nonviolent felony offense, not listed in Section 571 of Title 57 of the Oklahoma Statutes, the charge was dismissed following the successful completion of a deferred judgment or delayed sentence, the person has never been convicted of a misdemeanor or felony, no misdemeanor or felony charges are pending against the person, and at least ten (10) years have passed since the charge was dismissed;

10. The person was convicted of a misdemeanor offense, the person has not been convicted of a felony, no felony or misdemeanor charges are pending against the person, and at least ten (10) years have passed since the end of the last misdemeanor sentence;

11. The person was convicted of a nonviolent felony offense, not listed in Section 571 of Title 57 of the Oklahoma Statutes, the person has received a full pardon for the offense, the person has not been convicted of any other felony, the person has not been convicted of a separate misdemeanor in the last fifteen (15) years, no felony or misdemeanor charges are pending against the person, and at least ten (10) years have passed since the felony conviction; or

12. The person has been charged or arrested or is the subject of an arrest warrant for a crime that was committed by another person who has appropriated or used the person's name or

other identification without the person's consent or authorization.

B. For purposes of this act, "expungement" shall mean the sealing of criminal records.

C. For purposes of seeking an expungement under the provisions of paragraph 10 or 11 of subsection A of this section, offenses arising out of the same transaction or occurrence shall be treated as one conviction and offense.

D. Records expunged pursuant to paragraphs 8, 9, 10, 11 and 12 of subsection A of this section shall be sealed to the public but not to law enforcement agencies for law enforcement purposes. Records expunged pursuant to paragraphs 8, 9, 10 and 11 of subsection A of this section shall be admissible in any subsequent criminal prosecution to prove the existence of a prior conviction or prior deferred judgment without the necessity of a court order requesting the unsealing of the records. Records expunged pursuant to paragraph 4, 6 or 11 of subsection A of this section may also include the sealing of Pardon and Parole Board records related to an application for a pardon. Such records shall be sealed to the public but not to the Pardon and Parole Board.

Title 22 O.S. § 19: A. Any person qualified under Section 18 of this title may petition the district court of the district in which the arrest information pertaining to the person is located for the sealing of all or any part of the record, except basic identification information.

B. Upon the filing of a petition or entering of a court order, the court shall set a date for a hearing and shall provide thirty (30) days of notice of the hearing to the district attorney, the arresting agency, the Oklahoma State Bureau of Investigation, and any other person or agency whom the court has reason to believe may have relevant information related to the sealing of such record.

C. Upon a finding that the harm to privacy of the person in interest or dangers of unwarranted adverse consequences outweigh the public interest in retaining the records, the court may order such records, or any part thereof except basic identification information, to be sealed. If the court finds that neither sealing of the records nor maintaining of the records unsealed by the agency would serve the ends of justice, the court may enter an appropriate order limiting access to such records.

Any order entered under this subsection shall specify those agencies to which such order shall apply. Any order entered pursuant to this subsection may be appealed by the petitioner, the district attorney, the arresting agency, or the Oklahoma State Bureau of Investigation to the Oklahoma Supreme Court in accordance with the rules of the Oklahoma Supreme Court. In all such appeals, the Oklahoma State Bureau of Investigation is a necessary party and must be given notice of the appellate proceedings.

D. Upon the entry of an order to seal the records, or any part thereof, the subject official actions shall be deemed never to have occurred, and the person in interest and all criminal justice agencies may properly reply, upon any inquiry in the matter, that no such action ever occurred and that no such record exists with respect to such person.

E. Inspection of the records included in the order may thereafter be permitted by the court only upon petition by the person in interest who is the subject of such records, the Attorney General, or by the district attorney and only to those persons and for such purposes named in such petition.

F. Employers, educational institutions, state and local government agencies, officials, and employees shall not, in any application or interview or otherwise, require an applicant to disclose any information contained in sealed records. An applicant need not, in answer to any question concerning arrest and criminal records provide information that has been sealed, including any reference to or information concerning such sealed information and may state that no such action has ever occurred. Such an application may not be denied solely because of the refusal of the applicant to disclose arrest and criminal records information that has been sealed.

G. All arrest and criminal records information existing prior to the effective date of this section, except basic identification information, is also subject to sealing in accordance with subsection C of this section.

H. Nothing in this section shall be construed to authorize the physical destruction of any criminal justice records.

I. For the purposes of this section, sealed materials which are recorded in the same document as unsealed material may be recorded in a separate document, and sealed, then obliterated in the original document.

J. For the purposes of this section, district court index reference of sealed material shall be destroyed, removed or obliterated.

K. Any record ordered to be sealed pursuant to this section, if not unsealed within ten (10) years of the expungement order, may be obliterated or destroyed at the end of the ten-year period.

L. Subsequent to records being sealed as provided herein, the district attorney, the arresting agency, the Oklahoma State Bureau of Investigation, or other interested person or agency may petition the court for an order unsealing said records. Upon filing of a petition the court shall set a date for hearing, which hearing may be closed at the discretion of the court, and shall provide thirty (30) days of notice to all interested parties. If, upon hearing, the court determines there has been a change of conditions or that there is a compelling reason to unseal the records, the court may order all or a portion of the records unsealed.

M. Nothing herein shall prohibit the introduction of evidence regarding actions sealed pursuant to the provisions of this section at any hearing or trial for purposes of impeaching the credibility of a witness or as evidence of character testimony pursuant to Section 2608 of Title 12 of the Oklahoma Statutes.

N. If a person qualifies for an expungement under the provisions of paragraph 3 of subsection A of Section 18 of this title and said petition for expungement is granted by the court, the court shall order the reimbursement of all filing fees and court costs incurred by the petitioner as a result of filing the expungement request.

EXPUNGEMENT

Title 22 O.S. §§ 19a: Notwithstanding any provision of Section 18 or 19 of Title 22 of the Oklahoma Statutes, when a charge is dismissed because the court finds that the defendant has been arrested or charged as a result of the defendant's name or other identification having been appropriated or used without the defendant's consent or authorization by another person, the court dismissing the charge may, upon motion of the district attorney or the defendant or upon the court's own motion, enter an order for expungement of law enforcement and court records relating to the charge. The order shall contain a statement that the dismissal and expungement are ordered pursuant to this section. An order entered pursuant to this section shall be subject to the provisions of subsections D through M of Section 19 of Title 22 of the Oklahoma Statutes.

VIOLENT CRIMES DEFINED

Title 57 O. S. § 571: As used in the Oklahoma Statutes, unless another definition is specified:

1. "Capacity" means the actual available bed space as certified by the State Board of Corrections subject to applicable federal and state laws and the rules and regulations promulgated under such laws;

2. "Violent crime" means any of the following felony offenses and any attempts to commit or conspiracy or solicitation to commit the following crimes:

a. assault, battery, or assault and battery with a dangerous or deadly weapon;

b. shooting with intent to kill, assault, battery, or assault and battery with a deadly weapon or by other means likely to produce death or great bodily harm, as provided for in Section 652 of the Oklahoma Statutes;

c. aggravated assault and battery on a police officer, sheriff, highway patrolman, or any other officer of the law;

d. poisoning with intent to kill;

e. shooting with intent to kill;

f. assault with intent to kill;

g. assault with intent to commit a felony;

h. assaults while masked or disguised;

i. murder in the first degree;

j. murder in the second degree;

k. manslaughter in the first degree;

l. manslaughter in the second degree;

m. kidnapping;

n. burglary in the first degree;

o. burglary with explosives;

p. kidnapping for extortion;

q. maiming;

r. robbery;

s. robbery in the first degree;

t. robbery in the second degree;

u. armed robbery;

v. robbery by two (2) or more persons;

w. robbery with dangerous weapon or imitation firearm;

x. child abuse;

y. wiring any equipment, vehicle or structure with explosives;

z. forcible sodomy;

aa. rape in the first degree;

bb. rape in the second degree;

cc. rape by instrumentation;

dd. lewd or indecent proposition or lewd or indecent act with a child;

ee. use of a firearm or offensive weapon to commit or attempt to commit a felony;

ff. pointing firearms;

gg. rioting;

hh. inciting to riot;

ii. arson in the first degree;

jj. injuring or burning public buildings;

kk. sabotage;

ll. criminal syndicalism;

mm. extortion;

nn. obtaining signature by extortion;

oo. seizure of a bus, discharging firearm or hurling missile at bus;

pp. mistreatment of a mental patient;

qq. using a vehicle to facilitate the discharge of a weapon pursuant to Section 652 of Title 21 of the Oklahoma Statutes;

rr. bombing offenses as defined in Section 1767.1 of Title 21 of the Oklahoma Statutes;

ss. child pornography or aggravated child pornography as defined in Section 1021.2, 1021.3, 1024.1 or 1040.12a of Title 21 of the Oklahoma Statutes;

tt. child prostitution as defined in Section 1030 of Title 21 of the Oklahoma Statutes;

uu. abuse of a vulnerable adult as defined in Section 10-103 of Title 43A of the Oklahoma Statutes who is a resident of a nursing facility;

vv. aggravated trafficking as provided for in subsection C of Section 2-415 of Title 63 of the Oklahoma Statutes;

ww. aggravated assault and battery upon any person defending another person from a

xx. human trafficking as provided for in Section 748 of Title 21 of the Oklahoma Statutes; or

yy. terrorism crimes as provided in Sections 1268 et seq. of Title 21 of the Oklahoma Statutes.

Such offenses shall constitute exceptions to nonviolent offenses pursuant to Article VI, Section 10 of the Oklahoma Constitution.

CHAPTER 12:

WRONGFUL DEATH CIVIL STATUTE

Title 12 O.S. §1053: A. When the death of one is caused by the wrongful act or omission of another, the personal representative of the former may maintain an action therefor against the latter, or his or her personal representative if he or she is also deceased, if the former might have maintained an action, had he or she lived, against the latter, or his or her representative, for an injury for the same act or omission. The action must be commenced within two (2) years.

B. The damages recoverable in actions for wrongful death as provided in this section shall include the following: Medical and burial expenses, which shall be distributed to the person or governmental agency as defined in Section 5051.1 of Title 63 of the Oklahoma Statutes who paid these expenses, or to the decedent's estate if paid by the estate.

The loss of consortium and the grief of the surviving spouse, which shall be distributed to the surviving spouse.

The mental pain and anguish suffered by the decedent, which shall be distributed to the surviving spouse and children, if any, or next of kin in the same proportion as personal property of the decedent.

The pecuniary loss to the survivors based upon properly admissible evidence with regard thereto including, but not limited to, the age, occupation, earning capacity, health habits, and probable duration of the decedent's life, which must inure to the exclusive benefit of the surviving spouse and children, if any, or next of kin, and shall be distributed to them according to their pecuniary loss.

The grief and loss of companionship of the children and parents of the decedent, which shall be distributed to them according to their grief and loss of companionship.

C. In proper cases, as provided by Section 9.1 of Title 23 of the Oklahoma Statutes, punitive or exemplary damages may also be recovered against the person proximately causing the wrongful death or the person's representative if such person is deceased. Such damages, if recovered, shall be distributed to the surviving spouse and children, if any, or next of kin in the same proportion as personal property of the decedent.

D. Where the recovery is to be distributed according to a person's pecuniary loss or loss of companionship, the judge shall determine the proper division.

E. The above-mentioned distributions shall be made after the payment of legal expenses and costs of the action.

F. 1. The provisions of this section shall also be available for the death of an unborn child as defined in Section 1-730 of Title 63 of the Oklahoma Statutes.

2. The provisions of this subsection shall not apply to:

a. acts which cause the death of an unborn child if those acts were committed during a legal abortion to which the pregnant woman consented, or

b. acts which are committed pursuant to the usual and customary standards of medical practice during diagnostic testing or therapeutic treatment.

3. Under no circumstances shall the mother of the unborn child be found liable for causing the death of the unborn child unless the mother has committed a crime that caused the death of the unborn child.

DUTY OF PARENT TO PREVENT CHILD'S POSSESSION OF §1272 WEAPONS

Title 21 O. S. § 1273 B

http://www.oscn.net/applications/oscn/DeliverDocument.asp?citeid=69743: B. It shall be unlawful for any parent or guardian to intentionally, knowingly, or recklessly permit his or her child to possess any of the arms or weapons designated in Section 1272 of this title, including any firearm, if such parent is aware of a substantial risk that the child will use the weapon to commit a criminal offense or if the child has either been adjudicated a delinquent or has been convicted as an adult for any criminal offense that contains as an element the threat or use of physical force against the person of another.

FELONY ENHANCEMENT FOR USE/POSSESSION OF CERTAIN WEAPONS

Title 21 O.S. § 1287: A. Any person who, while committing or attempting to commit a felony, possesses a pistol, shotgun or rifle or any other offensive weapon in such commission or attempt, whether the pistol, shotgun or rifle is loaded or not, or who possesses a blank or imitation pistol, altered air or toy pistol, shotgun or rifle capable of raising in the mind of one threatened with such device a fear that it is a real pistol, shotgun or rifle, or who possesses an air gun or carbon dioxide or other gas-filled weapon, electronic dart gun, conductive energy weapon, knife, dagger, dirk, switchblade knife, blackjack, ax, loaded cane, billy, hand chain or metal knuckles, in addition to the penalty provided by statute for the felony committed or attempted, upon conviction shall be guilty of a felony for possessing such weapon or device, which shall be a separate offense from the felony committed or attempted and shall be punishable by imprisonment in the custody of the Department of Corrections for a period of not less than two (2) years nor for more than ten (10) years for the first offense, and for a period of not less than ten (10) years nor more than thirty (30) years for any second or subsequent offense.

B. Any person convicted of violating the provisions of this section after having been issued a handgun license pursuant to the provisions of the Oklahoma Self-Defense Act shall have the license permanently revoked and shall be liable for an administrative fine of One Thousand Dollars ($1,000.00) upon a hearing and determination by the Oklahoma State Bureau of Investigation that the person is in violation of the provisions of this section.

C. As used in this section, "altered toy pistol" shall mean any toy weapon which has been altered from its original manufactured state to resemble a real weapon.

D. As used in this section, "altered air pistol" shall mean any air pistol manufactured to propel projectiles by air pressure which has been altered from its original manufactured state.

NO LICENSE REQUIRED TO USE WEAPONS

Title 21 O.S. § 1289.6 (6): 6. For lawful self-defense and self-protection or any other legitimate purpose in or on property that is owned, leased, rented, or otherwise legally controlled by the person

PREEMPTION

Title 21 O.S. § 1289.24 A (1): A. 1. The State Legislature hereby occupies and preempts the entire field of legislation in this state touching in any way firearms, knives, components, ammunition, and supplies to the complete exclusion of any order, ordinance, or regulation by any municipality or other political subdivision of this state. Any existing or future orders, ordinances, or regulations in this field, except as provided for in paragraph 2 of this subsection and subsection C of this section, are null and void.

IMMUNITY

Title 21 O. S. §1289.25(F): F. A person who uses force, as permitted pursuant to the provisions of subsections B and D of this section, is justified in using such force and is immune from criminal prosecution and civil action for the use of such force. As used in this subsection, the term "criminal prosecution" includes charging or prosecuting the defendant.

ATTORNEY FEES AND COSTS FOR DEFENDING IMMUNITY

Title 21 O. S. § 1289.25 H: H. The court shall award reasonable attorney fees, court costs, compensation for loss of income, and all expenses incurred by the defendant in defense of any civil action brought by a plaintiff if the court finds that the defendant is immune from prosecution as provided in subsection F of this section.

ARREST BY MERCHANT FOR THEFT

Title 22 O. S. § 1343: Any merchant, his agent or employee, who has reasonable grounds or probable cause to believe that a person has committed or is committing a wrongful taking of merchandise or money from a mercantile establishment, may detain such person in a reasonable manner for a reasonable length of time for all or any of the following purposes:

(a) Conducting an investigation, including reasonable interrogation of the detained person, as to whether there has been a wrongful taking of such merchandise or money;

(b) Informing the police or other law enforcement officials of the facts relevant to such detention;

(c) Performing a reasonable search of the detained person and his belongings when it appears that the merchandise or money may otherwise be lost; and

(d) Recovering the merchandise or money believed to have been taken wrongfully. Any such reasonable detention shall not constitute an unlawful arrest or detention, nor shall it render the merchant, his agent or employee criminally or civilly liable to the person so detained.

DETENTION BY MERCHANT FOR CONCEALING

Title 22 O. S. § 1344: Any person concealing unpurchased merchandise of any mercantile establishment, either on the premises or outside the premises of such establishment, shall be presumed to have so concealed such merchandise with the intention of committing a wrongful taking of such merchandise within the meaning of Section 1341 of this title, and such concealment or the finding of such unpurchased merchandise concealed upon the person or among the belongings of such person shall be conclusive evidence of reasonable grounds and probable cause for the detention in a reasonable manner and for a reasonable length of time, of such person by a merchant, his agent or employee, and any such reasonable detention shall not be deemed to be unlawful, nor render such merchant, his agent or employee criminally or civilly liable.

CIVIL LIABILITY OF PARENTS

Title 23 O. S. §10: A. The state or any county, city, town, municipal corporation or school district, or any person, corporation or organization, shall be entitled to recover damages in a court of competent jurisdiction from a parent or parents of any child under the age of eighteen (18) years when the child is living with the parent or parents at the time of the act, and commits any criminal or delinquent act resulting in bodily injury to any person or damage to or larceny of any property, real, personal or mixed, belonging to the state or a county, city, town, municipal corporation, school district, person, corporation or organization. The amount of damages awarded pursuant to this subsection shall not exceed Two Thousand Five Hundred Dollars ($2,500.00).

B. Any victim, or the victim's representative in the event of the victim's death, shall be entitled to recover damages in a court of competent jurisdiction from any person convicted of a violation of subsection B of Section 1273 of Title 21 of the Oklahoma Statutes or as otherwise allowed by law.

CIVIL LIABILITY OF PARENT TO A GOVERNMENTAL AGENCY

Title 23 O. S. § 10 A

CHAPTER 13:

A. The state or any county, city, town, municipal corporation or school district, or any person, corporation or organization, shall be entitled to recover damages in a court of competent jurisdiction from a parent or parents of any child under the age of eighteen (18) years when the child is living with the parent or parents at the time of the act, and commits any criminal or delinquent act resulting in bodily injury to any person or damage to or larceny of any property, real, personal or mixed, belonging to the state or a county, city, town, municipal corporation, school district, person, corporation or organization. The amount of damages awarded pursuant to this subsection shall not exceed Two Thousand Five Hundred Dollars ($2,500.00).

CIVIL NEGLIGENCE DEFINED

Title 25 O. S. § 6: Slight negligence consists in the want of great care and diligence; ordinary negligence in the want of ordinary care and diligence; and gross negligence in the want of slight care and diligence.

SECURITY GUARD INVESTIGATOR ACT

Title 59 O.S. § 1750.1: This act shall be known and may be cited as the "Oklahoma Security Guard and Private Investigator Act".

BAIL ENFORCERS

Title 59 O.S. § 1750.14: A. Except as provided in subsection C or D of this section, any person who is not a resident of this state who intends to apprehend in this state, or attempts to apprehend, a defendant who has failed to appear before any court of this state or another state or any federal court as required by law and has forfeited bail or for purposes of apprehending a defendant prior to breach of an undertaking or bail contract, shall be required to have a client contract with a bail enforcer licensed in this state or to be licensed bail enforcer in this state prior to such apprehension or to be accompanied at the time of the apprehension by a peace officer.

B. Any person who violates the provisions of this section shall be guilty of a violation of the Bail Enforcement and Licensing Act and shall be punished as provided in Section 3 of this act.

C. The provisions of this section shall not apply to law enforcement officers of any jurisdiction.

D. The provisions of this section shall not apply to licensed bondsmen in this state appointed by an insurer doing business in this state with regard to a defendant on a bond posted by that insurer, provided the appointed bondsman has been continuously licensed in this state for a period of five (5) years or more beginning on the effective date of this act.

CHAPTER 14:

POSSESSION OF FIREARM BY FELON

Title 21 O.S. § 1283 A: A. Except as provided in subsection B of this section, it shall be unlawful for any person convicted of any felony in any court of this state or of another state or of the United States to have in his or her possession or under his or her immediate control, or in any vehicle which the person is operating, or in which the person is riding as a passenger, or at the residence where the convicted person resides, any pistol, imitation or homemade pistol, altered air or toy pistol, machine gun, sawed-off shotgun or rifle, or any other dangerous or deadly firearm.

POSSESSION OF FIREARM BY DELINQUENT

Title 21 O.S. § 1283 D: D. It shall be unlawful for any person previously adjudicated as a delinquent child or a youthful offender for the commission of an offense, which would have constituted a felony offense if committed by an adult, to have in the possession of the person or under the immediate control of the person, or have in any vehicle which he or she is driving or in which the person is riding as a passenger, or at the residence of the person, any pistol, imitation or homemade pistol, altered air or toy pistol, machine gun, sawed-off shotgun or rifle, or any other dangerous or deadly firearm within ten (10) years after such adjudication; provided, that nothing in this subsection shall be construed to prohibit the placement of the person in a home with a full-time duly appointed peace officer who is certified by the Council on Law Enforcement Education and Training (CLEET) pursuant to the provisions of Section 3311 of Title 70 of the Oklahoma Statutes.

PROHIBITED MEANS OF KILLING OR CAPTURING GAME

Title 29 O.S. § 5-201: A. Except as otherwise provided for in this section, no person may utilize at any time, for the purpose of killing or capturing any game mammal, game bird, nongame bird or exotic wildlife, the following means:

1. Any trap, net, snare, cage, pitfall, baited hook or similar device;

2. Any drug, poison, narcotic, explosive or similar substance;

3. Any swivel or punt gun of greater calibre than ten (10) gauge;

4. Any device which generates electricity; or

5. Any device which noticeably suppresses noise from a firearm, commonly known as a suppressor.

B. Except as otherwise provided for in this section, no person shall hunt wildlife or exotic wildlife by computer-assisted remote control hunting.

C. Except as otherwise provided for in this section, no person shall engage in any activity that provides, sells, offers for sale, assists in, or provides facilities for computer-assisted remote control hunting of wildlife or exotic wildlife.

D. The following persons shall be exempt from the prohibition in subsection A of this section:

1. The Director, departmental employees and authorized agents when capturing wildlife for propagation or management purposes;

2. Any person, group or governmental agency the Director may by written permit authorize, where any species of nongame birds are causing a nuisance or undue economic loss, as may be determined by the Director. Such permit shall state the method of control and specific procedures and conditions as may be deemed appropriate by the Director;

3. Any person possessing a scientific purposes license under Section 4-118 of this title;

4. Employees of the Oklahoma Department of Agriculture, Food, and Forestry Wildlife Services Division and the United States Department of Agriculture Wildlife Services while engaged in wildlife management activities for the protection of agriculture, property, human health and safety and natural resources; or

5. Any person using nonlethal, nonchemical capture or restraint of animals on licensed commercial hunt areas for management, viewing or photographic purposes.

E. 1. The following persons shall be exempt from the prohibition specified in paragraph 5 of subsection A of this section:

a. any person hunting on property owned by the person, and

b. any guest or other person hunting on property with the permission of the owner of the property.

2. Nothing in this subsection shall be construed to exempt any person from the requirements and provisions of the National Firearms Act and regulations and tax requirements for lawful use of a weapon as described in paragraph 5 of subsection A of this section.

F. A person shall be exempt from the prohibition in subsection B of this section if the person is permanently physically disabled so that the person is physically incapable of using a firearm, crossbow, or conventional bow as certified in writing by a physician licensed to practice medicine. A person who has received certification as provided for in this paragraph shall have in their possession written evidence of the certification while in the field hunting.

G. A person shall be exempt from the prohibition in subsection C of this section if the person is engaged in providing facilities for, assisting in, selling, or offering for sale a computer-assisted remote control hunting activity for a person who is physically disabled as described in subsection F of this section. The physically disabled person shall be physically present where the hunting activity is occurring and be in control and operating the computer-assisted remote control means to take wildlife or exotic wildlife.

H. 1. Any person convicted of violating the provisions of subsection A of this section shall be punished by a fine of not less than One Hundred Dollars ($100.00) nor more than Five Hundred Dollars ($500.00).

2. Any person convicted of violating the provisions of subsection B or C of this section shall be punished by a fine of not less than Two Hundred Fifty Dollars ($250.00) nor more than Five Hundred Dollars ($500.00) or by imprisonment in the county jail not exceeding one (1) year, or by both the fine and imprisonment. In addition, the court may order that the

hunting or fishing license and privileges of any person convicted of violating the provisions of subsection B or C of this section be revoked for a period of not less than one (1) year but not exceeding five (5) years. The cost of reinstating a hunting or fishing license revoked pursuant to this subsection for residents shall be Two Hundred Dollars ($200.00) for each license and for nonresidents shall be Five Hundred Dollars ($500.00) for each license. The reinstatement fee shall be in addition to any other fees required for the hunting or fishing license.

3. Any person convicted of a wildlife offense which involves a species of wildlife listed in Section 5-411 of this title, involves a species of wildlife referenced in Section 5-412 of this title or involves the unlawful possession, taking or killing of the wildlife from an unlawful hunt, chase, trap, capture, shooting, killing or slaughter while using a suppressed firearm during the commission of the wildlife offense, in addition to any other penalty otherwise provided for in law, shall be punished by a fine of not less than Five Hundred Dollars ($500.00) nor more than One Thousand Dollars ($1,000.00) or by imprisonment in the county jail not exceeding one (1) year, or by both the fine and imprisonment. In addition, the court may order that the hunting or fishing license and privileges of the person be revoked for a period of not less than one (1) year but not exceeding five (5) years.

THE AUTHOR

ROBERT R. ROBLES

Robert R Robles, trial lawyer and Senior Oklahoma US Law Shield program attorney, obtained his B.A. degree from the University of Houston in 1978 and his J.D. degree from the University of Oklahoma in 1980. Although born and raised in Houston, Texas, he remained in Oklahoma after law school, was admitted to the practice of law in 1981 and has practiced law in Oklahoma City, as a sole practitioner for over 35 years.

A dedicated trial attorney, Robert litigates in the areas of: death penalty defense, murder defense, criminal defense; plaintiff's claims for personal injury, wrongful death, tort law, civil, and criminal appeals. He is an avid student of forensics, ballistics, engineering/metallurgy and applies his skills to federal and Oklahoma firearm laws.

A life-long hunter and gun enthusiast, Robert has competed in nationally sanctioned bench rest competitions; club sanctioned pistol, military rifle, skeet and trap competitions. He is a member of the NRA, Oklahoma City Gun Club and the Okie Shooters Bench Rest Club. He is passionate about the U.S. Constitution and the right of citizens to keep and bear arms.

Robert is an experienced lecturer on the topic of gun rights and speaks at many of the seminars and workshops sponsored by US Law Shield. He answers thousands of questions posed by US Law Shield members. He resides in Oklahoma City with this wife Connie and his dog Jack.